SIGNS OF THE TIMES

THE END OF THE WORLD AND
THE COMING GOLDEN AGE

ROBERT FITZGERALD

1st WORLD
PUBLISHING

SIGNS OF THE TIMES

ROBERT FITZGERALD

© Robert FitzGerald 2005

Published by 1stWorld Publishing
1100 North 4th St. Suite 131, Fairfield, Iowa 52556
tel: 641-209-5000 • fax: 641-209-3001
web: www.1stworldpublishing.com

First Edition

LCCN: 2005904951
SoftCover ISBN: 1-59540-908-4
HardCover ISBN: 1-59540-931-9
eBook ISBN: 1-59540-932-7

This material has been written and published solely for educational purposes. The author and the publisher shall have neither liability or responsibility to any person or entity with respect to any loss, damage or injury caused or alleged to be caused directly or indirectly by the information contained in this book.

The characters and events described in this text are intended to entertain and teach rather than present an exact factual history of real people or events.

ACKNOWLEDGEMENTS

First and foremost I would like to thank Maharishi Mahesh Yogi and his TM as well as his TM Sidhi meditation techniques for opening my deeper creative and intellectual potential. I began this project at the same time that I began the TM Sidhi technique, and from the first it seemed that this work unfolded before me in a very natural and exciting way even though I knew very little.

I would also like to thank Susan Sayler, astrologer, for the making of this book. I began this project in partnership with her until uncontrollable circumstances pulled her life in another direction. She supplied the astrological knowledge as well as much of the insight and the genius in creating the astrological structure for this model of history contained in the first section.

TABLE OF CONTENTS

PART 1

PART 2

PART 3

PART 1

A HISTORY OF THE AGES

Humanity is on the threshold of a golden age of truly mythical proportions. We are also in a period of increasingly destructive energies, very possibly on the verge of extinction. How we got here is no accident and where we go from here is up to us. This is a common scenario that reverberates through the prophecy of all religions. It is especially central to the teachings of Christianity with shades of the Millennium of Christ and of the end-times of the Apocalypse. And according to history it is very real.

There is an astrological structure to history that is surprisingly accurate. The history of how we got here has been orchestrated by astrology, and how we get to the next level requires an understanding of astrology that is dangerously missing today. The promise of the golden age, as it turns out, is the promise of the Age of Aquarius, and that promise is potentially very beautiful. Enlightened masters from around the world tell us that this promise is beyond our ability to even image. But using the qualities of Aquarius we can try to get a handle on what lies ahead of us.

First let's imagine a world where humanity is finally unified into a single harmonious collective, a world culture of separate and independent nations and religious beliefs united in profound friendship and deep understanding of each other, where global communication, mass media and mass education support the unity of humanity beyond what they promise today. The world culture of this future will support utopian ideals at all levels. Equality, altruism, progressiveness, and brotherhood will infuse the hearts of people everywhere. The present fears and prejudice against peoples of different color will dissolve as we finally release our hurts and fears. This equality will also include women as we come to understand more deeply the connection between men and women, both spiritually and mythologically. Just as the political shift from matriarchy to patriarchy created profound changes in social structure and power around the globe some four thousand years ago, this new vision will create similar changes where the patriarchy will quickly evolve into a more balanced and equitable social system of gender equality.

All branches of knowledge will flourish. This will include both modern scientific systems of knowledge and tried and true spiritual systems, as well as the occult. Science will flourish as never before, but it will no longer be the dry, rational science we are familiar with today. It will become a science concerned not only with facts and a rational understanding of our physical world, but also with the search for higher consciousness. In this drive science will take on elements of what today we might call metaphysics. In our beautiful future we will transcend physics and delve into a higher level of knowledge. Science will discover many as yet unknown laws of nature that will answer and support the crazy ideas of metaphysics as we know them today. This science will give understanding and power to the greater fulfillment of Aquarian hopes, dreams, and wishes. Through the deeper understanding of higher states of consciousness individual genius will flourish in all people, all races, and in both men and women.

Let's imagine a world without poverty, sickness, anger or violence, without greed, prejudice, self-righteousness, or any of the emotional, mental, and physical ailments that afflict us today. In this world love and compassion reign supreme unaffected by fear or other emotions such as anger or hatred. We may all be married to our perfect soul partners in relationships that will feed our sense of completion and happiness.

Let's imagine a world where the impossible becomes easily possible, where miracles are a birthright and an everyday occurrence. The impossible in this new world will include such achievements as immortality where science and the achievement of higher states of consciousness allow human physiology to regenerate itself at a level where we will be able to maintain a state of eternal youth. We will be able to levitate at will as well as perform other impossible feats. All possibilities will open up to us. In this vision let us imagine that we become as gods and goddesses, not in the Greek image of gods and goddesses bickering and fighting with one another, but in a golden age image of heaven brought down to earth where peace and harmony are easy and natural. All our desires are met easily and we become vehicles of the manifold expressions of love and harmony.

These are all qualities of the Age of Aquarius. It will be the New Age. In India and the Orient this New Age will be called the Age of Enlightenment. In Christianity it will be known as the Millennium of Christ, a golden age of incredible potential. It is the Age of Aquarius, and it is coming soon. But we are not there yet. History indicates that the Age of Aquarius will be here in 2160. The year 2000 wasn't the new millennium. What still lies ahead of us is a period of potential apocalyptic destruction.

The great Twentieth Century has drawn to a close. Over the last few decades so too has the utopian promise of the revolutionary science that created that century. Now we seem to be heading back into the worst of times. Over the last three decades violence, depression, and suicide have risen to epidemic levels. There are 30,000 suicides each year in the US with ten to twenty times that many people attempting suicide. This is higher than the murder rate with three successful suicides for every two murders commit-ted. Violent crimes in America have increased per capita four to five times over the level reported to police in the early 60's. By 1995 America had become the most violent civilized nation in history with 10 million violent crimes committed per year. Not very utopian.

We are killing ourselves. Toxic pollution of the environment is spreading. Widespread pollution of the earth's available drinking water is now the major cause of death worldwide. We are also ruining our useable farmland with questionable farming practices. Chemical fertilizers and pesticides used in agriculture wash off into our streams, lakes, and oceans. Severe evaporation of water due to our present irrigation practices is leaving available farmland increasingly salty. More and more land becomes unusable each year at the same time that the world's population is increasing.

Genetic engineering of our food is already showing promise as a major cause of future food shortages. Evidence suggests the possibility that genetically altered food actually decreases food production rather than increasing production as promised by the companies that create genetically altered seed. There is also evidence of human allergic reactions, some severe, to ingesting genetically altered foods. These are foods , sources of nutrition that we rely on for survival.

Genetically engineered pathogens as biological weapons could lead to far more severe consequences than genetic food engineering including the potential annihilation of all life on earth.

In addition there have been massive shifts in weather patterns over the last few decades. El Nino and La Nina type weather has recently become the worst in memory. In the US, along the East Coast and across the Midwest and the South, the hurricane and tornado seasons are becoming increasingly more intense and destructive. Flooding around the world is also noticeably more destructive. The ocean itself is in serious trouble. It has recently become far more violent with a higher than normal average wave height. A toxic Red Tide that occurs annually along the coasts of the US is now spreading up the East Coast, and is even expanding on the West Coast. In 1972 there were 16 coastal areas that were annually affected. By 1995 there were an unprecedented 36 coastal areas affected. The ocean has been over-fished and is highly polluted. Recently scientists have found that there are approximately 150 dead zones in the world's oceans where nothing lives. One of these dead zones covers over 5500 square miles of ocean every summer off the southern coast of the US from Texas to Florida, a dead zone caused by the collected runoff of chemical fertilizers across the Midwest into the Mississippi River and from there into the Caribbean.

Scientists also acknowledge that we are now in a time of greatly increased earthquake and volcano activity. There are approximately 100 times more earthquakes today than there were prior to 1970. A super volcano with a caldera 53 miles long and 28 miles wide encloses much of Yellowstone National Park. Recently it has become active with ground temperatures up to 200 degrees in some areas. Large parts of the park have been permanently closed to visitors. The floor of Yellowstone Lake has risen 100 feet and the surface temperature of this cold alpine lake now reaches 88 degrees. All fish in the lake have died. Some estimate that there is a 30% chance of this volcano erupting in the very near future.

Deforestation around the world is at an all time high. Scientists are now recognizing global warming as a fact. During the winter of 2004 Alaska reported record warm temperatures. The Polar ice cap is melting creating tremendous problems for animal life in that region. This warming is linked to the immanent breakdown of the North Atlantic Current. This current supplies warm temperatures to the northern temperate climates. It is on the verge of shutting down. This current is pushed by the salt or mineral content of the ocean. As it reaches the north seas the minerals absorb the colder temperatures and sink to the bottom of the ocean. This current then follows the ocean bottom back down to the southern part of South America and from there over to the Indian Ocean. It picks up the warm temperatures of this climate and rises. At the surface it reverses itself and flows back to South America and north back to the Caribbean and from there to the north seas. It regulates weather temperatures around the world. As increasing amounts of fresh water dilute the salt content of the northern oceans the current can no longer sink thus short circuiting this essential cycle. Global warming at this point can then easily lead to a new ice age in only a few decades.

The ozone holes over the Polar Regions are still increasing in size while the overall ozone layer surrounding the earth is thinning out leading to an increase in potentially destructive ultraviolet light reaching the earth's surface.

Species extinctions are proceeding at a rate that has only been equaled in the past just prior to the commencement of each of the Big Five Extinctions of almost all life on earth. Archaeologist Richard Leakey Jr. warns that we are on the verge of a sixth big extinction. We seem to be in deep trouble. What exactly is happening and what can we do to survive in these times?

According to a study of history it appears as if we are now in the Biblical end-times. I say this because history follows an astrological structure. Astrological ages are real. It is past time that we recognized the true astrological nature of the times that we are now in and begin to act according to appropriate astrological directives.

There is a story in the New Testament. One day Christ was confronted by a delegation of Sadducees and Pharisees. When they demanded proof of his divinity, that he was the savior; "He answered them, "When it is evening, you say, 'It will be fair weather; for the sky is red.' And in the morning, 'It will be stormy today, for the sky is red and threatening.' You know how to interpret the appearance of the sky, but you cannot interpret the signs of the times.'" Matt. 16:2,3

The Chinese I Ching, hexagram 3, "Chun", states in a similar manner; "Whoever hunts deer without the forester only loses his way in the forest. The superior man understands the signs of the time."

Christ challenged the established Biblical authorities of his day to look past their limited view of the world they lived in, to see a larger picture. The Old Testament is mainly concerned with prophecy, but the established priesthood supposedly could not read the signs of the times in order to see what Christians claim was standing right in front of them. We live in a vastly different world today yet that challenge still stands. Our scientists can not only tell the nature of the weather from various signs, but we can now tell a lot about the nature of our universe from black holes and quasars down to subatomic particle interaction. Quantum mechanics has proven to be a tremendous predictive tool at the subatomic level. Yet we still know next to nothing about the signs of the times. Like the man who hunts deer in the forest we are in danger of losing our way.

The question, then, is what are the signs of the times? The answer is, astrology. Astrology is an ancient discipline that deals specifically with time, astrological ages, the signs of those ages and what they mean for humanity. And, according to history, those signs are accurate.

Are we on the threshold of a glorious New Age? Yes! Are we now in a period of potential world destruction? Yes! According to history as well as astrology we are in the period of time known as the Biblical End-Times, the Final Days, the end of the world, with the Four Horsemen of the Apocalypse and Armageddon. The Biblical Millenium of Christ, the New Age, the Age of Enlightenment, is still a century and a half away. As we sped past the year 2000 and into what we think of as the Millenium we now have to ask will history go on as before or will there be some kind of quantum leap forward involved?

Science predicts a utopian technological world. The reality of the technological promise, focusing as it does on devastating weaponry, more than likely promises a very possible post-devastation nightmare. At the same time religions around the world promise a world of intense spiritual joy and prosperity. A change is happening and everyone at some level feels it. But which of these scenarios will the change follow? Much of the choice may be ours to make.

It seems that we stand at a powerful moment of choice in history. This moment is characterized by religions all over the globe as a time of ending and of beginning. According to these religions we are all given a choice. We can choose to graduate to a new level of existence and achievement in the next cycle of time, or we can choose to ignore the signs of the times and suffer.

From the Biblical Book of Genesis when God first created heaven and earth he did so using a rather specific structure. On the second day he created a dome or vault amidst the waters to separate the waters of consciousness above from those below. And he called this dome heaven. This term dome has also been translated less accurately as firmament. A dome or vault implies something circular, surrounding the skies above earth.

On the fourth day God put lights in the dome of the heavens to separate day from night, so that they would be signs for set-times, for days and years, so that they could provide light upon the earth. These lights are stars and constellations of stars that separate ages of time from each other and times of plenty from times of hardship. These lights, actually too dim to provide enough light for the eye to see by, do provide the light of astrological understanding upon earth. The night and day referred to here is the moving cycle of ages through the twelve signs of the zodiac that illuminates all life below on earth both emotionally and psychologically. It is the cycle of 24 hours that measures the complete day, twelve hours for the light half of day and twelve for the dark night half. This dome and these lights can thus easily be seen as the zodiac holding the star constellations. It is only after the dome of the zodiac had been filled with lights by God that he then created the two great lights, the sun and moon, to rule the day and the night, and to provide physical light for people on the earth to see by. Together these astrological signs are the signs of the times.

Ancient cultures universally saw time as sacred. They often elevated time to the status of god. In some cultures time was the premier god. Often in these cultures the image of god was portrayed with a zodiac. To them time was conscious as well as powerful. Time ruled vast areas of human endeavor. The Greeks called time Chronos and identified him as Kronos, the father of Zeus and the lord of the twelve (astrological) Titans. They also saw time as the zodiacal river Oceanus, the deep river that circled the earth. Time was also the worm Ouroborous, a great tail-eating serpent sometimes seen with a zodiac on its back, forever eating itself as new ages transplanted older ages. Time was also seen as the god Aion, whence our word eon, meaning a long period of time. Aion was at times pictured as the sun god, illuminating human evolution from age to age.

Our own Biblical reference to this term is in our prophetic writings about the beginning of the world and the impending end of the world. The term "world" in our Biblical translations comes from the Greek Bible, the Septuagint, the Bible in use at the time of Christ. The Greek word used is Aionos, referring to the god Aion, literally meaning "long time". Thus we are not coming to the end the world but of our present cycle of ages. We are about to begin a new cycle and thus a new world.

In Egypt the sun god Ra was the ruler of time, changing shape hourly during his travels around the earth and through the twelve signs. Heh was the god of never-ending time pictured with the ankh, the symbol of life, hanging from his neck. In India both Shiva and Vishnu represent time. Shiva is often called Maha Kala, "Great Time." His feminine counterpart in her destructive form is Kali, black time that devours all life in the cycle of birth, hungry growth, and death. Among the Maya in Pre-Colombian America time was seen as a two-headed serpent as well as an aspect of the sun. Time in the Aztec view was associated with Omoteotl, their supreme deity, the mother/father creator, Lord of Fire and Lord of Time. In China the universe is seen as the Tao, the harmonious play of all opposition. This opposition operates through the inter-play of Yin and Yang energies within the circle of the universe. While Yin, the feminine aspect, was seen to be space, Yang, the masculine principle, was seen as time. Thus time and space played on each other creating the astrological universe.

In our own modern culture, the 17th century view saw God as the "Great Watchmaker." He created the universe around the concept of the twelve hours of time, wound it up and let it go.

All images of time are cyclic with the exception of the West. Time flows in circles, around a zodiac, enlivening, vivifying, and ordering life, and thus history. It flows like a river around and around. It eats its own tail. The head of the serpent, as it eats, shines brightly like the Sun, illuminating the specific time period the world is in. In the West, on the other hand, we have inherited a linear perspective of time. We see time as an arrow flowing from the past into the future. Yet even in the linear time of Christianity there are hints of a cyclical, astrological understanding.

Christ required a circle of twelve disciples for his ministry. When Judas was cast out a replacement was required in order to maintain the sanctity and power of that circle of twelve. In the Old Testament Book of Genesis, in the Garden of Eden, God refers to other gods with him. These other gods are a council of sorts that esoteric Hebrew tradition sees as a body of gods called the Elohim. Hebrew esoteric tradition number these Elohim at twelve. In the Book of Exodus in the Old Testament the Israelites are divided into twelve tribes. When they camp God commands them to array themselves, by tribe, in a large astrologically ordered circle or enclosure around the center where the tabernacle would be built. God dwelt in this central tabernacle.

The number twelve was so sacred that other cultures throughout the world also established their geographical boundaries around the concept of the zodiac. Ancient cultures divided their home-lands into twelve tribal lands radiating out from around a central holy thirteenth piece of land where the twelve tribes gathered for sacred religious ceremonies. The twelve tribes of Israel are the most well known, perhaps the only commonly remembered twelve-tribe group.

God as the lawgiver has to create laws that cannot be escaped from by human will or cunning. These laws carry with them their own rewards and punishments in an intimate way that is deeply connected with our human physiology. This system of laws is the astrological system of the zodiac. We are controlled by our astrological patterns, patterns that may be an integral part of our genetic structure. We are blessed with certain strengths, and challenged with certain lessons that make up our personal horoscope charts. We then are "rewarded or punished" automatically according to the spiritual and psychological play of our actions, thoughts, and emotions. In the Orient this is part of what is called karma.

Time revolving through these signs serves to highlight areas of universal study necessary for our evolution. Now is a time of endings and new beginnings. This is a terrible time of harsh lessons, a final test to see how much we have learned, to see if we qualify to graduate to the next level.

ASTROLOGICAL CYCLES OF TIME

"For everything there is an appointed time, even a time for every affair under the heavens: A time for birth and a time to die; a time to plant and a time to uproot what was planted; a time to kill and a time to heal; a time to break down and a time to build; a time to weep and a time to laugh; a time to throw stones away and a time to bring stones together; a time to embrace and a time to keep away from embracing; a time to seek and a time to give up as lost; a time to keep and a time to throw away; a time to rip apart and a time to sew together; a time to keep quiet and a time to speak; a time to love and a time to hate; a time for war and a time for peace."

Ecclesiastes 3:1-8

Under the dome of the heavens there is a time for everything to manifest in an orderly fashion that supports an evolutionary direction to history. In this section we will explore the historical manifestations of the signs of the times

The astrological constellations lie in a circle around the earth along the belt of the equator. Each age is marked by the wobble of the earth's axis as the North Pole points to each age or constellation in succession. This wobble takes 25,920 years to complete one cycle. In one complete cycle there are twelve ages of 2160 years each. Within each age there is a cycle of twelve smaller time periods that I call eras containing 180 years each. And within each era there is a cycle of twelve periods I call phases of 15 years each. The two smaller cycles give a sense of growth and flow to the larger cycle.

At approximately two-thirds of the way through each age a transition occurs that brings to the fore historical developments that lead up to the following age. In the Scorpio Era of any age, a death and rebirth occur. Scorpio rules death and rebirth. Most of the power inherent in the institutions and beliefs founded in that age die and seeds are planted that point to new ways of seeing which are grounded in the succeeding age. This is usually a violent era. Following Scorpio the sign Sagittarius blossoms behind a dynamically emerging new vision. These are periods of Renaissance. Sagittarius rules vision and exploration. It "sees" the impulse of the next age and makes it come alive. It is a fire sign full of creative impulse.

While Pisces rules great world religions we can trace the development of great world religions back to the religious changes of the 8th to 5th centuries BCE. It was here that the Buddha taught in India, as did Lao Tzu and Confucius in China. It was here that the Hebrew Prophetic Revolution laid the groundwork for our present monotheistic Judeo Christian religion.

ZODIAC

The zodiac is composed of twelve signs. Each sign is one astrological age. We will look at the last five ages since 8,640 BCE. We will then look at the twelve eras of our present Age of Pisces from 0 BCE to 2160 CE. Included in this will be a brief look at parallel trends in previous ages that correspond to the sign involved. We will then look at the twelve phases of the Aquarius Era we just left, from 1800 to 1980.

The entire thrust of this model of history, as it turns out, is a vivid portrayal of time in support of the various religious prophecies regarding an end-time. This model historically reveals that in fact we have entered into the "final days" of that end-time. There is a regularly recurring end-time cycle and we are poised at just such an end-time threshold. While the signs of the zodiac involved seem to dictate this end-time, they also give clues as to what must be done in order to survive the transition to the next cycle, the coming Age of Aquarius, known commonly as the Age of Enlightenment.

AGE OF CANCER:
8640 TO 6480 BCE

As the most domestic sign of the zodiac, Cancer rules motherhood, nurturing, the home, family, and tradition. Establishing a secure and well-defined area of operation is basic to this sign. Cancer rules survival and can be an extremely ruthless sign where it concerns security. Matters that pertain to house building, architecture, construction, real estate, and domestic products and services fall under Cancer rule. Like the crab, the symbol for this sign, Cancer is tenacious and very sensitive, seeking the protection of a hard outer shell or house. Cancer is emotional and moody representing times of introspection and focusing on the needs of the community, especially regarding food and shelter. Cancer is located at the bottom of the zodiac and thus acts as the foundation for the accomplishments of all the other signs above it. Cancer rules all foundations.

Capricorn is the opposite sign to Cancer, 180 degrees across the zodiac wheel. It denotes government, heads of state, discipline, and ambition. It is a practical sign and represents the efficient application of resources. The opposite sign to any astrological sign will play an important part in the history of any age, era, or phase.

According to modern western historical thought our ancestors subsisted for millions of years on the proceeds of hunting and gathering. Yet within only a couple of thousand years, during the Age of Cancer, domesticated plants and animals independently appeared in several parts of the Old and New Worlds. Permanent year around mud-brick and stone dwellings replaced temporary camp dwellings of sticks and branches thus ushering in a period of settled village life. It changed the entire foundations of human life and is referred to as the Neolithic Revolution.

Though many Cancer Ages have come and gone before this one, it is generally accepted that it wasn't until this age that nature was inclined to manifest the full possibilities of the sign Cancer in human culture. Prior to this round of the zodiac humanity was presumably focused more on mere survival in a long, slow, linear rise to civilization. Through the Age of Leo and the dawning of the Age of Cancer after 9000 BCE, we might theorize that humanity had reached a point in its evolution that rendered man and woman more adaptable to the fuller expression of Cancer energies.

Cancer is ruled by the Moon, one of our two luminaries. The Moon was seen as the domain of the Greek Goddess Artemis, the Roman Diana. She was also known as Luna and was seen as the twin sister of Apollo, the Sun God, the Sun ruling the neighboring sign of Leo. She is the Goddess of the hunt, and ruling the subconscious she may be pictured hunting wild subconscious fears and prejudices in the process of domesticating humanity. Cancer is pictured today as the crab safe within its protective outer shell. At one time in the past though Cancer was pictured as the domestic cat. Sitting next to her twin at the bottom of the zodiac, the solar ruled Leo, they were presented as a couple. Leo is pictured as the lion, a wild cat next to the Cancer domestic cat.

The Age of Cancer brought with it the Neolithic Revolution. The older stone tools of the Paleolithic period were hunting tools; axe heads, spear points, and arrowheads. The new stone tools of the Neolithic Revolution were agricultural tools for cutting and grinding grains. The Neolithic Revolution was a revolution in the way humanity lived. The wild cat had given way to the domestic cat.

One of the most common areas of activity attributed to Cancer is that of food domestication, agriculture and animal husbandry. The Neolithic Revolution was specifically a change in stone tools from hunting tools to new agricultural tools. The long period of human prehistory known as the Paleolithic, or old stone tool period, was one of hunting and gathering. The old stone tools were hunting weapons. During the most recent Age of Cancer humanity had evolved enough to respond to the best of Cancer energy in a powerful way. All of a sudden a completely new stone technology was created indicating a new agricultural perspective towards living.

Agriculture was "invented" and implemented on a large scale around the globe. At one time it was thought that the agricultural revolution was limited to the Near East with subsequent agricultural activity, at later dates, diffusing out to the rest of the world. Cancer is not a sign concerned with sharing information outside its home boundaries. Cancer is a "stay at home" sign. Diffusion is a process ruled by Gemini, the next age after Cancer.

It is now thought that there was three large agricultural matrices spread around the world that developed independently during the Age of Cancer. The Near East matrix included the traditional area of food domestication in the Near East from Israel to Iran and Iraq. It also included eastern Europe and southern Europe around the Mediterranean, and along the Nile River in Africa to areas in Equatorial Africa.

An Oriental matrix ran from the Rajasthan desert of northern India east through Southeast Asia, up to Central China, and down through New Guinea. Both of these areas were experimenting with food domestication from the very beginning of the age. The Oriental matrix may have begun a few centuries earlier, perhaps as early as 9000 BCE.

The third matrix existed in the Americas. It ran from Chile and the western slopes of the Andes in South America up through Central America into the southern portions of Mexico.

Cancer rules agriculture. The Age of Cancer, dated at 8640 to 6480 BCE, lies perfectly within the dates traditionally given for the Neolithic Revolution, 9000 to 6000 BCE. That the world went through a revolutionary change from hunter-gatherer to farmer and herder at precisely this time, encompassing the entire Age of Cancer, seems more than mere coincidence. It is a powerful indication that astrology works.

The goat was domesticated as the major source of meat at Jericho and sheep were domesticated at Cayonu Tepesi in Anatolia. Rye was grown in Syria in the eighth millennium BCE, and bread wheat, a hybrid of a previously domesticated grain, was grown in Crete and Turkey in the seventh millennium BCE. From Jarmo in the Kurdish hills in Iraq there have been found a beautiful collection of bowls, mortars, and pestles used in the preparation of grain dating to 6500 BCE. In the Aegean and the Balkans wheat, barley, lentils, vetch, and peas were domesticated around 7000 BCE. Goats were domesticated around this same time in Russia near the Jaxartes River in the Kazakh region. Cereal grains and charcoal, indicating the clearing of brush for agriculture, have been found in the Rajasthan desert of India dating to the seventh millennium BCE. In New Guinea ground was cleared for planting by using polished adzes near 9000 BCE, and they kept a domesticated pig and fed him cultivated fodder, possibly yams or sugar cane by 8000 BCE. By 7000 BCE they had already invented and discarded a drainage system in a catchment for agricultural runoff. In Japan, the Jomon culture had domesticated dogs and possibly even pigs by the end of the eighth millennium BCE. In Vietnam, the Bac-san may have domesticated the dog, the water buffalo, and rice between 8000 and 6000 BCE. The Hoabinhian culture in Thailand may have domesticated peas, beans, gourds, peppers, cucumbers, and almonds as early as 8500 BCE. They also invented sickles to harvest their food, adzes to clear their land, and had domesticated a wide variety of animal species between 8500 and 6000 BCE.

In Taiwan and Southeast China archaeological evidence indicates the clearing of land for planting as early as 8000 BCE. In our own western hemisphere evidence for agriculture is seen at Guitanera Cave in the Peruvian Andes, 8500 feet above sea level. Possibly as early as 8500 BCE and certainly by 6500 BCE they were cultivating chili peppers, lima beans, and kidney beans. By 6500 BCE there were settlements on the arid Humboldt Coast of Peru and northern Chili. Remains of bottle gourds, which require lots of water and human cultivation, indicate that the inhabitants either irrigated them with water from nearby valley bottoms, or grew them in the valleys, using the gourds not only for food but also for dishes, pots, fishing floats, and rattles.

In Mexico agricultural occupation began in southern Tarnaulipas around 7500 BCE, the Tehuacan Valley around 7200 BCE and in the valley of Oaxaca maybe as early as 8800 BCE. In South and Central America there is evidence for domesticated kidney beans around 8000 BCE, runner beans around 7500 BCE, lima beans around 8500 BCE, maize and pumpkins around 8800 BCE, and potatoes, sweet potatoes, and ulluco at 8000 BCE.

Animal domestication in the Americas show less evidence than Old World remains. There are three examples that do reflect the Cancer domesticating energy very well. Aside from the dog the guinea pig was domesticated around 7500 BCE in Peru and Bolivia, and kept as a household scavenger as well as providing up to 40% of the available meat supply. Between 8000 and 6000 BCE the camelids (llama, alpaca, guanaco, and the vicuna) were domesticated on a wide scale and used not only for meat but also as pack animals and for their skins. In Mexico in the Tehuacan Valley, around 7500 BCE, an attempt was made to domesticate the horse. The attempt either failed or succeeded far too well. By 7000 BCE the horse was extinct in the New World.

Even outside these three matrices the Cancer energy may have been felt and responded to. In the North American Archaic Culture, situated in the Nevada desert region of present day United States, there is evidence that shows a definite change in diet away from a predominately meat diet to a more predominant vegetable diet by 7000 BCE. The inhabitants also began making nets, mats, baskets and cordage from vegetable fiber by this date.

Cancer also rules house building, community, foundations and boundaries. In the desert region of the Near East food domestication accompanied the building of permanent villages of mud-brick houses that were lived in all year long. These villages replaced the older temporary stick huts built to accommodate roving bands of hunters following herds of wild animals. Now everybody began to settle down in new permanent villages, to establish settled foundations out of which civilization would emerge several thousand years later. Settling down established boundaries for a local village society.

Man did build remarkable shelters prior to this age. There are remains of large communal dwellings in Russia dated to 20,000 BCE. These, interestingly enough, were built during the Age of Capricorn, the opposite sign to Cancer. These dwellings were hollowed out of the soil with mammoth ribs used as supports, which were then covered. These dwellings held up to 400 individuals. Following this humanity seemed satisfied to temporarily live in caves or simple twig and branch shelters, always on the move.

Following 8600 BCE all this changed.

Ganj-dareh in the Zagros Mountains in Iran began as an encampment between 8200 and 8000 BCE. Within a few centuries it grew into a community of permanent mud-brick houses, many two stories tall. At Cayonu Tepesi in southern Turkey substantial houses were built with stone foundations at several levels. Slots were incorporated between parallel foundations apparently to allow air circulation and to help carry a load. The village of Jarmo in northeastern Iraq began around 7000 to 6500 BCE. It contained 25 houses each with an open alley or small court on two sides. The houses contained several smaller rooms, and there were clay ovens and bases for storage silos in each house. As imprints on the floors attest to these people wove mats to place on the ground.

Scores of other settlements throughout the Near East, the Aegean, and the Balkans mirror these examples. During the eighth millennium BCE these agricultural villages spread over the entire area from Khurzistan in southern Iran to southern Anatolia, and by 7000 BCE they even found their way to the islands of the eastern Mediterranean.

While the peoples of Mexico began to experiment with agriculture and animal domestication it appears so far that they chose not to settle down in one place. They camped in certain areas for the growing season and then moved on after the crop was harvested. In Peru this created large villages that inhabitants returned to year after year. A very large village found in the Lomas region near Paloma, Peru, dated to 7000 BCE, is thought to be such a village. The structures found there were of stone foundations on which were placed temporary shelters of sticks and shrubs. What is even more important is the village's apparent population density. Nearly 5000 huts have been found in an area over 1900 feet long, and buried inside or next to these huts were possibly as many as 9000 skeletons.

Aside from this Peruvian settlement all other villages discovered so far, both in the New World and in the Old World, contain a relatively small number of houses and cover only a few acres of ground, with one dynamic exception. In the Natufian culture in Palestine there is the "city" of Jericho. Prior to 8350 BCE there existed at Tell-es-Sultan only the remains of seasonal hunting encampments. Following 8350 BCE the town of Jericho was established and grew to cover up to ten acres of land with permanent mud-brick houses. It is estimated that the city could accommodate some 2000 people. More remarkable still is that Jericho was surrounded by a huge stone wall some ten feet thick and 13 feet high. This wall was accentuated with a solid stone tower 30 feet high and 33 feet in diameter. A stairway was carved into this tower containing 22 steps. Outside this wall was a trench 27 feet wide and 9 feet deep carved out of solid rock. What appears to be an aqueduct system runs along the top of the wall and around the tower. There are walls with no openings in them except along the top was an 18 inch deep channel that was found full of silt, implying running water.

The first question archaeologists had asked about Jericho concerned its wall. Why would a wall be needed? Although they theorized that farmers needed to protect themselves from attack from nomads, there is absolutely no evidence of fighting. So what spurred them to build a massive wall in a hot desert climate? One part of the answer may be that Cancer is defensive in nature. Cancer loves surrounding walls that have substance. This quality helped in the cultural change to permanent houses with solid walls in the first place. In Jericho, as large as it was, it seems perhaps that the population responded by enclosing their entire village with a comforting, surrounding wall in addition to the walls of the houses they lived in.

The other question that arises is how were they able to accomplish this feat considering their level of technology. However they accomplished this feat, whatever technology they utilized, one important part of the answer to this question may be astrological. The Capricorn opposite of Cancer rules the efficient use of resources. It rules government and administration. With the domestication of the dog as a hunting companion in the Age of Leo and the knowledge about domestication learned at that level, Capricorn efficiency applied itself to the task of expanding that knowledge in order to benefit the entire tribe. Rather than domesticate more dogs to help in the hunt it was much more efficient to domesticate those animals that were hunted. And if, by the same process, one could domesticate grain (which would allow it to be grown outside of its native habitat) then an even wider and more abundant food supply could be utilized by the entire tribe. The process of planting and then waiting several months to reap what was sown required Capricorn patience. Capricorn rules patience. It allowed the Capricorn efficient control of the food supply.

The process of building individual family caves from semi-permanent materials allowed people to more efficiently utilize the environment. They could live where they wanted. At Jericho that Capricorn energy went even further. We can surmise that in order to feed and house two to three thousand inhabitants a new more centralized social structure was needed. The loose tribal leadership of a hunting-gathering type of lifestyle would no longer prove adequate to a settled agricultural lifestyle, especially at the population density level of Jericho. The leader or leaders needed to be much more centralized with the power to make decisions for everybody without a lot of arguing and with the expectation that their decisions would be followed. In the building of the wall they had to organize the building in as efficient a way as possible. The wall and the tower had to be planned as well as built, the moat outside the wall dug out of stone, and extra food had to be grown in order to feed all the workers required for this project. There also had to be in place an expanded system for settling disputes. Leadership began to change into government, and the increased ability for administration allowed the planning of larger civic projects.

Cancer rules motherhood and all areas of motherly activity. Agriculture is a woman's art. Living a settled domestic life reflects a huge concern for nurturing and the mother. It has been said that the Neolithic Revolution brought with it the domestication of humanity itself, an emotional as well as a physical settling down.

During this age the major, perhaps even entire, focus of historical development fell directly and completely under Cancer areas of rulership. Archaeologists paint a picture of society undergoing revolutionary changes, but changes that are specifically Cancerian in nature.

THE AGE OF GEMINI:
6480 TO 4320 BCE

After Cancer, the following Age of Gemini saw the Near East blossom into a crafts intensive industrial society. Gemini is the sign of the twins indicating such attributes as duality and division, and the process of interaction, a process that requires a minimum of two participants. The glyph for Gemini shows two upright lines, twins, connecting the horizontal line representative of heaven at the top and the same representing earth at the bottom. Here the opposites of Yin and Yang most completely play out their roles within the realm of history and cultural interaction.

Gemini is ruled by Mercury the messenger of the gods, their vehicle of communication with each other. He was responsible for increase (division and multiplicity) in the animal world. He was the god of wealth, trade, and commerce. He was also the god of travelers and of manual skill and oratory. He ruled invention. In his first 24 hours of life, as an infant, he invented the lyre as well as his winged sandals. He invented fire by rubbing two sticks together.

Gemini rules movement, trade, and communication. The settled life of the Age of Cancer opened up to reveal humanity again on the move, not as roving hunters but as traders traveling settlement to settlement trading crafts and passing along ideas. Gemini rules craftsmanship and mechanical abilities. Here we find the Neolithic Revolution winding down and giving way to a flourish of crafts industries. Invention of all sorts flourished. And with the Sagittarius opposite to Gemini, their combined rulership of the intellect on the Gemini lower mental level and the higher Sagittarius level brought about a revolution in thought, language, and religious ideas and symbology. From this age man brought forth the concepts and symbols that would become the basis of modern religious and mythological thought as well as of modern languages and writing.

Gemini's opposite sign is Sagittarius, a sign that denotes the higher mind. If Gemini is the fact finder Sagittarius is the abstract philosophical mind, which conceptualizes in order to give direction, pattern, and meaning to all the disparate ideas and facts of Gemini. Where Gemini is the local environment Sagittarius is the wider global environment with foreign influences. Sagittarius, ruled by Jupiter, stands as the sign of the lawgiver and Gemini, ruled by Mercury, acts as the sign of the messenger dissipating those laws far and wide. Together the two represent education; Gemini the grammar school education of facts and figures, and Sagittarius the college education of theories and philosophy.

Perhaps the most physical trait of Gemini, and because of that it is the most valuable to archaeologists, was the explosion of crafts industries after 6500 BCE. Throughout the Near East there is ample evidence of a rather sudden explosion of crafts industries each with several subspecialties in terms of production. At the large site of Catal Huyuk in Anatolia, dating to about 6500 BCE, there existed a huge bone industry with approximately fifty different types of specialized bone implements created. The stone industry was equally varied. There existed a statue industry and a baking industry dealing in loaves of bread, as well as many other types of craft production. Of all these industries created after 6500 BCE the ceramics industry stands out as the most important for the archaeologist. To be sure clay pots were created before this age; the Jomon culture in Japan created crude clay vessels as early as 11,000 BCE (the Age of Virgo—like Gemini also ruled by Mercury) and there are some crudely made ceramic vessels from the Age of Cancer. Previous to that there have been found large ceramic kilns dated to approximately 23,000 BCE. But by far the excellence of construction and the sheer productive abundance of ceramic ware created right after 6500 BCE and throughout this age are simply overwhelming.

The invention, so to speak, of pottery occurred independently in many different areas and all right at the onset of this age over a territory extending from the Zagros in present day Iran to the eastern Mediterranean. Soon after this explosion of ceramic invention there appeared the first sophisticated and uniform styles. These coalesced as trade increased into two very distinct styles beginning around 5500 BCE in the Samarran culture style and a little later in the beautiful Halafian style.

The earliest pottery from Catal Huyuk and Tell Hassuna in Assyria (northern Iraq) was unpainted straw tempered ware, with small hole tops and with shell impressions or with lugs or bucket-like handles. Almost immediately, over a wide geographical area, painted decoration began to appear in the form of geometric patterns.

Mercury as the messenger of the gods is always pictured with wings on his head and feet. This image indicates the rapidity of Gemini, the quickness of the Gemini mind in picking up new ideas and expanding his inquiry into new areas. No sooner was pottery established as a rough cottage craft then all of a sudden we find at places like Yarim Tepe (near Mosul in northern Iraq) a large number of two stage domed pottery kilns situated in a clearly demarcated industrial area. Investigation of these kilns using a scanning electron microscope reveal kiln temperatures that approached 1100 degrees centigrade. By the end of the Age of Gemini pottery was refined to an extraordinary sensual beauty, noted for its painted decoration, excellence of firing, and variety of forms. It was applied to a buff or a cream slip polychrome glaze. Red, orange, yellow and black paints were used, sometimes highlighted by white spots.

Architecture exhibited new levels of sophistication with multilevel dwellings. At Hacilar enclosed courtyards are found with domestic and shop buildings. Other locations were more complex. The small and compact nuclear family dwelling common in the Age of Cancer was now supplanted by larger meandering residential units housing extended families. This is a powerful indication of the Gemini influence as brothers and sisters were now included in the central family structure. At two sites near Samarra in Iraq were such units, one comprising 14 rooms.

Between 5500 and 5000 BCE the solid door was invented, within the Hassuna culture, which opened and closed on a hinge post. Later in the Halafian period there is evidence of external buttressing for walls as well as the invention of new architectural styles.

This shift to a technological focus of society was not confined to the Near East. Archaeologists have found the emergence of the new craft of ceramics in at least five other areas: Europe, the arctic fringe of Eurasia, in Japan, China, and the Malay Peninsula. There were many cultures, each with its own pottery style in eastern, southern and central Europe during the sixth and fifth millennium BCE. Among them were Danubian, Starecevo, Nilomedian, and Bandkeranuk. By 4800 BCE the Danubian Culture is noted for the artistry and craftsmanship of their ceramics. In Japan there were some earlier attempts at making pottery dating from 11,000 BCE. Now we witness this activity returning in full bloom with pots being both shell and cord incised. In China at 4800 BCE the Chinese were also creating beautifully decorated ceramics. The late Yang Shao pottery from China shows remarkable similarity to Near Eastern Halafian pottery and in fact was made in the same way but developed independently. And the Hoabinhian culture in Vietnam, Cambodia, and Burma had cord-impressed pottery similar to the Jomon culture pottery in earlier Japan.

In addition to ceramics, metallurgy advanced beyond the few hammered trinkets found at Cayonu Tepesi and Ali Kosh to completely supplant, by the end of this age, the lithic or stone technology of the Neolithic Revolution. From 9000 to 7000 BCE the incipient metallurgic activity of the Near East consisted of small decorations, such as small beads, and small tools such as needles hammered directly out of copper ore. No other process was applied to the raw ore. But in this Age of Gemini metallurgy became a proper industrial craft. The ore was smelted in order to extract the pure copper prior to its being worked. Pieces of smelted and hammered copper were found dating from 5500 to 5000 BCE from southern Anatolia through Assyria to the Zagros mountain region of Iran. Further east in Iran the highland settlements of Tell-I-Iblis and Tepe Yahya were important manufacturing settlements for copper and steatite (soapstone) respectively. During the early fifth millennium in several Assyrian sites such as Tepe Yarim there are indications of a copper and lead industry with many kilns that achieved a high enough temperature to cast copper. With pure copper to work from tools became larger.

A number of cast copper axes and other tools have been found that date to before 5000 BCE. There was also a copper industry in Europe; finds in Yugoslavia, Bulgaria, and Romania have been found that document the whole process from the mining of malachite (a copper rich ore) to the smelting and casting of copper axes as well as the manufacture of pins and arm rings that date to the middle of the fifth millennium BCE.

The development of systems and techniques in Gemini occurred in every possible industry. In Catal Huyuk blocks of obsidian were split with great skill to form mirrors for women who in turn used a wide variety of cosmetics. Woolen textiles were used both for clothing and, judging from ceramics and wall paintings, for rugs and wall hangings. In several towns in Assyria and Mesopotamia there are indications found of a semi-precious stone industry, a leather industry, and the crafting of small stone statuettes. In Anatolia industry flourished producing needles, awls, beads, pendants, fishhooks, hairpins, belt buckles, and elaborately carved dagger handles.

In the Yang Shao culture in China we find evidence of steam cooking, jade working, advanced irrigation, fabric making, and skilled basketry, as well as carpentry, calligraphy, and possibly the raising of silkworms. A separate area for the production of ceramics by part time specialists mirrors the existence of similar sites in the Near East. Around 5000 BCE in the Archaic Culture centered in what is now the New England area of the United States, evidence suggests specialized tool making creating spears, hooks, nets and traps for fish, boats, baskets, cloth, and metal objects.

Gemini Age people drew their raw materials from a very wide geographical area and they reached a very high level of quality control in a variety of crafts. The absence of waste materials from dwellings so far explored argue that craft specialization had gone much farther than one is accustomed to expect of a Neolithic community.

Industry during this age was based upon the Gemini quality of division, multiplicity, and diversity. Part-time craftsmen emerged from the Neolithic agricultural world. With the secure foundation for survival that the Age of Cancer provided the stage was now set for the mind to diversify and wander beyond the needs of survival into new fields of human endeavor.

In the Age of Gemini we don't find society crystallizing into a social hierarchy yet. We find, rather, individuals dividing their time between two or more occupations. Everyone may still have been farmer or animal herder, but no longer full time. They occupied themselves and their hands in off hours by making ceramic pots, various stone or bone or leather implements, by baking bread, indeed by anything else their minds could devise to interest them. As craftspeople they became industrious, and thus industrialists, creating valuable items to trade for other items. Yet still as farmers and herders they retained an equality that would not yet allow for much social stratification.

Tell-es-Sawaan (6000-5000BCE) in central Iraq was a typical farming community with simple irrigation. Of the 128 burials dating to about 5500 BCE, all had at least one craft item and most had several, indicating that Gemini specialization into different branches of livelihood was well under way. It is also important to note that there was no special deference given to children in these graves and this indicates that there was as yet no fixed hereditary status or social hierarchy. And though pottery and other crafts were widely distributed geographically there was no centrally administered or organized bureaucracy within government that controlled trade.

Agricultural knowledge in the Age of Cancer appears to have arisen independently in various areas around the world. The process of diffusion, the spread of knowledge from a central area of invention as people began to travel and visit the neighbors beyond the horizon, would have theoretically begun with the Age of Gemini. From about 7200 BCE the Gemini energy would have just begun to be felt within the last third of the Age of Cancer. Beginning at the end of Cancer and into the Age of Gemini the process of diffusion began tying the world together, spreading both agricultural information and industrialized crafts information ever farther afield.

Archaeologists tell us that the single most traded and exchanged item in the ancient world of this time may have been ideas. Gemini is an air sign meaning that it is more concerned with ideas than with material objects. People of this age were more interested in how something was created than in merely having that object. Halafian pottery, dating to around 5000 BCE, is found, beginning from a small central Halafian area, virtually everywhere throughout the entire Near East. It was once thought that these pots were carried and traded far and wide for their own sake. Now it is surmised that the extremely wide range of distribution was due to the exchange of ideas, the passing from village to village the knowledge of Halafian techniques and design. With them went the geometric designs, copied and incorporated into the cosmology of the Near East.

By the height of the age, at about 5000 BCE, huge interlocking trade networks spread across the Near East, around the Mediterranean Basin, and east up into southern Russia. In the New World, in what is now the northeast part of the United States, the Archaic Culture also had established an extensive trading network by 5000 BCE. It spread west as far as the Yellowstone and south to the Caribbean. People loved to travel during this age.

The archaeological record from this age indicates that communication virtually exploded into cultural consciousness. The degree of interaction between communities and the level of common symbolism found on pottery throughout the Near East attests to the fact that communication and social interaction sprouted into new heights of sophistication. Gemini governs language and the abstract symbols used to create language. The meanings of these symbols and the ways in which they are utilized profoundly influence the speakers' worldview. One's worldview is a particularly Sagittarian matter. The propensity to interact that so characterizes Gemini requires a common set of symbols in order to expedite communication.

There are essentially two language families from which almost all other languages have their root: the proto-Indo-European and Chinese. The proto-Indo-European language family includes, to name a few, Balto-Slavic, Germanic, Celtic, English, Italic, Hellenic (Greek), Anatolian, and Indo-Iranian, which is considered by Western philologists to be the root of Sanskrit. The proto-Indo-European language may have been spoken as early as the beginning of the fifth millennium BCE. At about the same time, not much later than 4800 BCE, some archaeologists have found possible evidence that a parent Chinese language was spoken in the north Chinese Yang Shao culture.

There is no question that the shared concepts that would become the backbone of a common denominator of language and writing was developed and disseminated here. Though a fully developed system of writing can only be traced as far back as 3500 BCE in the form of pictographic writing, the conceptual designs that would later be incorporated together to form a true written language are found and used here in the Age of Gemini.

The pattern of decoration on the pottery of Near Eastern culture at this time, especially that which is termed Halafian after 5000 BCE, consisted of geometric patterns like swastikas, triangles, chevrons, stars, Maltese crosses, rosettes, and stipples, including egg and dot, and stylized representations of animals. Much of this symbolism would be incorporated into later religions and mythologies. They would also independently evolve into picto-graphic and, later, phonetic symbols in written languages. Many locations in the Neolithic and post Neolithic Middle East show the remains of thousands of small conical, spherical, and discord objects found in sites such as Jarmo (6500 BCE) and elsewhere. These objects are directly correlated with later Sumerian cuneiform characters known to represent numbers and commodities such as one, sixty, sheep, and oil.

Religion and language seem to have a strong connection to each other. If Gemini is responsible for language, the Sagittarius concern for religion may have supplied the structure for the creation of language. Throughout the Upper Paleolithic art is representa-tional. From 25,000 BCE we have large collections of Venus figurines. Later, from 17,000 to 13,000 BCE, there is the incredibly beautiful cave art. Between 13,000 and 11,000 BCE, during the Age of Virgo, which like Gemini is also ruled by Mercury, cave art devolved into painting dots and hand outlines on cave walls. After 11,000 BCE art moved out into the sun and onto large boulders and again became representational. Here stylized animal and human hunting figures became important. But after 6500 BCE we find, again, a trend away from representational art towards the abstract.

Abstraction coincided with the creation of specific rooms dedicat-ed as religious shrines built into the new Neolithic communities. In the older Age of Cancer there is no evidence of shrine rooms built to serve the family or community. Around 6500 BCE, at the super site of Catal Huyuk we find numerous shrine rooms. On the walls of these shrines are seen an abundance of rather abstract imagery. Plastered cow or bull horns protrude from the walls. There are scenes of women giving birth to cows (bulls?) or rams heads. Female forms are in relief, modeled from plaster while male forms exist in symbolism such as the bull, the ram, or sometimes the stag, leopards, or boars. Female breasts are shown with the lower jaws of boars. There are also abstracted stick figure reproductions of griffin vultures flying over headless humans and erupting volcanoes.

By the end of this age the semi-representational art of Catal Huyuk had become the totally abstract art of Halafian origin. These symbols came to carry complex conceptual meanings acting as foundation for religious ideas and truths. The small conical objects found in Jarmo arithmetically were based on the 360 degrees of the circle, one of the most universal of religious symbols representing totality and unity. The cross would become the symbolic world tree within the circle, the four directions important in religious thought worldwide. In our own religion it was pictured as the tree of life, and of knowledge of good and evil that began humanity on its journey through life. It would later become the cross that Jesus died on as he took humanity's sins with him into the afterworld. The swastika was the cross in movement, twirling in a circle leaving trailing arms behind.

The head of the cow that women gave birth to came to be stylized into a V with a cross bar half way up. Inverted this cows head became the Phoenician A, alpha, the first letter in our alphabet.

Religion seems to have been important from the beginning of this age. Catal Huyuk was an extremely large town compared to other settlements of that time. Archaeologists have found very little in the way of industrial waste compared to other smaller sites where there is ample evidence of industrial innovation, indicating that it was not an industrial or manufacturing town. On the other hand, they have found a disproportionately large number of shrine rooms leading many to theorize that Catal Huyuk was a large regional religious center where both worship and religious learning took place. It may have served as a prehistoric university town. Industrial artifacts were probably imported rather than manufactured there.

The images at Catal Huyuk showing women giving birth to cows and other animal images finally makes explicit what is implicit in the pregnant images of the Venus figurines of 25,000 BCE. Around 17,000 BCE we enter into the womb of Venus in the Late Paleolithic. Deep inside sacred caves, often accessed through long low and narrow entry passages we enter the interior world of awesome animal imagery. Finally after 6500 BCE the pregnant Mother had finally given birth to her pantheon of sacred children. Those sacred animal principles were now breaking forth into our external worldview.

Sagittarius brought to this age a sense of expansion and exploration. It stimulated the Gemini need to interact, to spread over large horizons creating huge trading networks. In this process the religious aspect of Sagittarius combined with the aspect of division that is Gemini to create a broad new understanding of religion in the Near East. In Cancer the deity would have been the Great Mother Goddess who had birthed all life. In individual places she may have been alone or perhaps associated with a consort. In the division of Gemini there would have been a multiplication of Gods and Goddesses into pantheons as different qualities of the Great Mother were divided into separate entities for greater classification.

The vision of Catal Huyuk would have expanded along with the Gemini tendency towards abstraction in their art. Sagittarius directed Gemini to create great pantheons of Gods and Goddesses who were all descended from each other and were thus brothers and sisters to each other, a particularly Gemini trait. Gemini is pictured as the twins.

The geometric symbols created in Gemini had religious meanings. In creating them, or "writing" them down on pottery, the foundations for written languages was created. In their creation a unified language of religion also came into being. This would lead into the Age of Taurus creating an intellectual foundation that would stimulate the creation of true civilization, an urban revolution. Gemini taught humanity to think and interact. Sagittarius taught humanity to conceptualize beyond the boundaries of tradition and of personal experience. It would be this ability to think beyond the horizon that would help create the next Age of Taurus.

THE AGE OF TAURUS:
4320 TO 2160

Following Gemini came the Age of Taurus from 4320 to 2160 BCE. Again the world changed. Taurus is a sign that is represented by the symbol of the bull. The bull symbolizes strength that is different than the battering strength of the Aries ram. Taurus is the quiet and enduring strength of the earth. It is the strength of solidity and permanence. This strength is seen in the accumulation of wealth and the power that wealth brings. The strength of Taurus flourishes through peace, not war, and it grows by staying in one place rather than through constant movement.

Taurus is ruled by Venus the goddess of love and beauty. She was also the mother of Eros, the god of love, and she was the mistress of pleasures. Through her Taurus seeks to beautify her surroundings, both visual and sensual.

The association of Taurus with wealth is paramount and possessions, banking, and financial enterprise constitute the very basis of this sign's rulership. Nearly all of the developments that came during the Age of Taurus were ones that built upon the previous inventions of the Age of Gemini. The Age of Gemini invention of abstract symbols, used to convey intellectual concepts, gave rise to the first known systems of writing in the Age of Taurus, used at this time for the records of ownership and banking administration. The Age of Gemini concern with occupational diversity gave rise to fully and solidly stratified societies in Taurus. Craftsmanship and trade pursued for the sake of diversity in Gemini now solidified into full time occupations with the goal of making money and becoming prosperous. The religious shrines of Gemini now became full-blown temples, built in solid and monumental fashion.

The Age of Taurus is the age of the Urban Revolution where social changes began the process of creating the world's first known true civilizations. Beginning sometime after 4800 BCE the U'baid people in Mesopotamia moved out onto the river plains of the Tigris and the Euphrates rivers. This area was very poor in natural resources. The U'baid culture did something here that was very Taurus. They redesigned their trading villages into market towns complete with a new invention, money, and with newly invented banks to store that money in. These banks soon began to float loans and collect interest. Bartering gave way to the development of a money economy along with business and banking and the use of copper as a universal medium of exchange, the first known coinage. Money was deposited into these early U'baid banks to be applied, much as we do today, towards projects of civic improvement, which would in turn make more money. And these new U'baid towns became rich. A whole new basis for community living was created.

The invention of wealth was an extremely important development, for it released large segments of the population from bondage to the land. It also expanded the choice of where people could settle. The U'baid culture settled in the hostile climate of southern Mesopotamia. This was an area with extremes of summer heat and winter cold, and unpredictable rainfall. Moreover, it was nearly devoid of all natural resources. There was no stone or wood for construction, and also absent were ores for metal production and precious stones for the production of jewelry or statuary. Yet by 3500 BCE the resource poor U'baids were rich with imported goods. They began, due to this accumulated wealth, to create an urban society. The development of business and banking was the foundation for the principle developments of the later Sumerian civilization. The temples became administrative centers where full time priests prepared the temple business accounts and administered the proper distribution of goods.

Written accounts of temple business in these early periods do not present an account of priestly exploitation of toiling masses. On the contrary. Taurus is an earth sign. They show the earth sign propensity towards efficient administration in a society becoming more solid, stable, and orderly, and focused on prosperity as the means of connecting with Goddesses and Gods. Everyone was involved and benefited from this arrangement. This efficiency was essential to creating and maintaining the stable and peaceful Taurus Age society built around the accumulation and distribution of wealth and goods.

It has been noted that the advance of culture in this age was not marked by any advances in inventiveness or technology. There seems to have been little. The archaeological markers for this age were advances or quantum increases in the level of wealth accumulated. The key feature that distinguishes the Sumerian civilization from the earlier U'baid culture is an abundant increase in wealth rather than technological advance.

Sometime after 3500 BCE the Sumerian culture replaced the U'baid. This was a very peaceful Taurus transition. There is no evidence for invasion of any kind. Either the Sumerians were welcomed in and then became the dominant culture or the U'baid culture merely transformed itself to a more complex and wealthier level of living.

Along the Nile in PreDynastic Egypt the advance in culture, as in the Tigris and Euphrates River valley, was noted mainly by increases in wealth. The Gerzean phase of the early Amratian people was marked primarily by great advances in wealth, culminating around 3000 BCE in the formation of Egypt, the first nation state in history.

The invention of a modern family of languages was first solidified into a system of writing during this Age of Taurus as a means of recording the level of accumulated wealth. Although Gemini rules writing, not Taurus, it is interesting to note that archaeological evidence illuminates a possibly important distinction between language and writing, and the subsequent evolution of writing. Modern language structure, in the proto Indo-European language was created during the Age of Gemini. Along with that came the creation of abstract symbols as means of conveying information, a sort of proto-writing. The writing invented in Taurus is more the application of Gemini abstraction into a practical, solid, and readable Taurus economic concern: the keeping of business and banking records. And this was done on permanent clay tablets and cylinders.

The invention of writing, from U'baid sites as well as from contemporary sites in the Balkans in Eastern Europe, was used partly in the form of cylinder seals, which were used to denote possession and ownership of lands and other goods, as well as other business related functions. One of the earliest known objects with writing and pictographs combined seems to be a record of a real estate transaction dating from 3400 BCE from Mesopotamia. These cylinder seals contained pictographs that later evolved into hieroglyphs and cuneiform writing. In the Uruk Phase of Sumerian development, around 3500 BCE, scribes utilized 1500 separate cuneiform signs in order to keep track of land sales, business transactions, and list the commodities traded or stored. It was not until approximately 2700 BCE that writing was regularly employed for non-business purposes.

Egypt soon followed the Sumerian example creating a written language prior to 3000 BCE. It was again used for the Taurus concerns with money and goods. The first pictographs are used in lists of goods and figure totals, surplus grains paid out to various craftsmen, carpenters, weavers, bakers, musicians, etc.

Another sign of civilization, and of the Taurus-Scorpio archetype, is the development of social stratification reflecting the level of social complexity necessary for civilization. During the entire Age of Gemini little evidence of social complexity exists. But just after 4500 BCE there is seen solid evidence of a sudden change towards a more complex social structure. In southern Mesopotamia the U'baid people began to revolutionize town life. A little later the northern plains followed suit. The area was soon dotted with what some see as full-fledged cities built around increasingly massive temples and temple complexes. These temples were rebuilt over the course of the age, always over the older spot, with successive layers growing larger until we find the mountainous ziggurats, or stepped pyramids, of the Sumerians, and then the huge stone pyramids of Egypt.

The traditional date for the birth of true civilization is 3200 BCE in Sumeria where evidence suggest a high enough degree of cultural diversity and social refinement to indicate that an urban revolution was in progress. Findings in older U'baid sites have prompted some archaeologists to suggest that true civilization began as early as 4000 BCE. The tribal chief gave way to a king, or priest-king, separated now from the growing number of peasants. In between king and peasant various classes began to grow each with varying levels of prestige and power within society. Sumerian society formed itself around four main social classes: the nobility, the more common members of the community who held family lands, the artisans, and the indentured peasants. Within this hierarchy the religious functionaries were the nobles and the temple itself was the state.

The Scorpio opposite to Taurus rules taxation, use of other people's resources, and absolute power and control. By 2900 BCE in Sumeria civilization was in full swing. As we near the end of this age rulers were becoming power hungry and despotic with the ever-increasing accumulation of wealth. The merchant class engaged in wholesaling and contracting. Loans were floated and individual profit, as opposed to the collective profit of society, may have been a prime motivation in stimulating the economy. Economic incentives were given to businessmen who felt, on the other end, the bite of taxation. Monopolies were attempted in the artistic trade as well as in bronze weapons and tools.

Religion in this Age of Taurus was extremely practical and Taurean. Goddess, and God, showed their love for and pleasure in humanity through the medium of physical wealth and articles of comfort. The economic activity of this age revolved around the temple. It became the central area of economic focus, of storage and redistribution of all goods and wealth that came into and out of the state. Almost all merchants and other occupations worked through the temple. Sometime after 3000 BCE a temple in Lagash listed a daily ration for bread and beer for some 1200 men and women. The temple ran a cloth shop employing 205 women and their children. Also employed were bakers, millers, brewers, cooks, fishermen, herdsmen, sailors, and scribes among others. Temples even undertook their own land and sea expeditions in order to procure raw materials. Following the Scorpio opposite to Taurus, which rules corporate structure and the pooling of resources towards the end of totalitarian control, these temples became the corporate centers of society. Free enterprise did not really exist. Society in all its complexity merely reflected the strict order of heaven and of the gods of the Age of Taurus. The temple was the center of all physical expressions of the grace of heaven. Even the pharaohs of the Old Kingdom in Egypt were responsible mainly for overseeing the collection and distribution of goods. The Pharaoh was the divine administrator living on earth in order to ensure that goods were given out fairly.

Taurus rules permanence and solidity. Cities in the Near East and in Egypt were built to reflect not only the Goddess' abundance but also heavenly structure. They grew larger and were built according to the perceived permanent hieratic astrological plan of heaven. As the cities grew the cosmic ordering of society also spread. Cities were built with their sides facing the four directions, the temple in the center, with the priest-king presiding at the very center with the power of heaven flowing through his or her person. The highest class of aristocrats and administrators lived in a ring around the temple. At the outer edges lived the peasant farmer class as the symbolic foundation upon which the social pyramid was built. A mathematically and perhaps astrologically structured calendar was created to regulate how we approached each of the four seasons, appeasing the gods and insuring peace and prosperity.

Taurus solidified every aspect of society that could be regulated into a mirror image of what was known of heavenly structure. Cities were built to face the four points of the compass and the calendar was created to celebrate the four points of the year: the vernal and autumnal equinoxes and the summer and winter solstices. The Mayan calendar in Central America dates its own beginning to this age, at around 3100 BCE.

In Sumeria each city created itself as a complete city-state. In Egypt society was expanded into the creation of the first know nation state in a highly stratified civilization. What we know of the Indus civilization in India dating to before 2400 BCE, indicates an already well established and flourishing civilization complete with a prosperous middle class. The society consisted of a hieratic system of division of labor and an already well-ordered caste system. While western archaeologists and historians tend to dispute non-western histories for lack of physical evidence, Indian historians relate that during this age a vast and complex civilization evolved in India based on the Vedas, their core religious teachings. Called by Indians the Vedic civilization, it was created around a very solid structure of universal proportions and truths as revealed in the Vedas. Included was a strict system of social placement still revered in India today as their caste system. They created a science of building known as stapatyaveda, or building according to strict mathematical proportions that correlate both to the earth's energy field and the rising sun, and to the astrology of the person or family intending to live in that building. In the Orient that system became known as feng shui, and in pre-Christian Europe it was known as geomancy. They also created jyotish, or Indian astrology. Jyotish means the science of light and it was developed in order to understand the structure of an individual's personality here on earth and his or her particular path through this life. In true Taurus fashion real success and happiness depended upon living, working and building according to certain solid and permanent laws of heavenly structure.

The Lung Shao culture in China, around 3245 BCE, sheltered specialized craftsmen who made up a special class of people in a well-ordered social hierarchy. The traditional founder of Chinese civilization, Chin Huang Ti, after which they take their name China, is said by Chinese tradition to have lived around 2800 BCE, at the same time that Egypt was coalescing into a civilized nation state. It was he that laid down all the rules and the structure for living within a civilized and prosperous civilization. In Mesoamerica around 2700 BCE, the Purron phase of the Tehuacan Valley in Mexico also showed evidence of a highly stratified society with definite social classes.

In Peru there has recently been uncovered a huge pyramid complex in an ancient city named Caral that lies 125 miles north of Lima, Peru. It covers some 160 acres of the Supe Valley and has been dated to 2627 BCE. It contains 6 large pyramids built around a large central plaza. It was a complex urban civilization that had regular trading connections with the coast and the rainforests deeper inland. More recent findings indicate that this city was part of a civilized complex of up to 20 cities covering the Supe Valley and two adjoining valleys, the Pativilca and Fortaleza valleys. Construction on these cities may have begun as early as 3000 BCE.

Another aspect of Taurus is its love of monumental proportions. This age introduced, as far as we know, the creation of monumental architecture throughout the Near East and Europe, and in the Americas.

At Eridu in Mesopotamia, considered to be the world's first city, there are 16 levels of temple construction spanning 3500 years. At Uruk there were six separate temples to the goddess Inanna including the Limestone temple built around 3500 BCE. This temple was 282 by 108 feet, built of dressed stone with much of the walls and columns decorated with three-color terracotta mosaic. Over the span of this age temple sites remained sacred and temples were rebuilt over the top of the old temple. This resulted in the creation of truly monumental temple pyramids known in Sumerian times as ziggurats. Often on the top level a sizeable shrine would be constructed that towered over the surrounding city. The most impressive of these stepped pyramids was the ziggurat of Ur, a mountain sized pyramid that could be seen many miles away.

In the Early Dynastic period in Mesopotamia, ca. 2800 BCE, a monumental palace was built at Kish. This palace had hundreds of rooms and was larger than the palace of Versailles in France. Towards the end of this age, as history inched towards the Age of Aries, cities in Syria and Mesopotamia surrounded themselves with huge fortification wall, the most massive since the wall of Jericho.

In Egypt pyramid building supposedly began around 2900 BCE and ended around 2700 BCE. In these two centuries several solid stone pyramids were built in an unmatched feat of engineering. According to Western thought the Great Pyramid of Giza is the supreme example of pyramid building known during this time.

The earliest examples of megalithic stone building are seen in Europe as early as 4100 BCE. Megalithic tombs appear from Scandinavia, the British Isles, France and Spain, and from the western Mediterranean to Corsica and Malta. In Malta, dating to 3000 BCE, is the world's oldest known all stone temple constructed of megalithic blocks. Also found there is the world's oldest known colossal stone statue. It is a fragment of a huge seated woman. Other smaller statues found there were sensually round and roly-poly and have been dubbed "fat ladies".

Archaeologists have found in southern Mexico large round sculpted pre-Olmec stone heads that date to 2000 BCE, corresponding to the very end of the Age of Taurus, into the beginning of the Age of Aries. Archaeologists have dubbed these heads "fat boys". Very few have been found hidden in the jungles of Mexico so far but this find indicates the possibility of civilized cultural activity in the dense jungles of Central America extending back into the

Age of Taurus.

The Peruvian site of Caral dating to 2627 BCE contains 6 stepped stone pyramids, with at least one standing some 60 feet high. Some of the smaller pyramids have rooms at the top level, similar to those found on Sumerian ziggurats.

At various sites in the Indus civilization in India, dating back to at least 2400 BCE, archaeologists have found that the earliest levels of building were the most solid and well built. These levels of construction associated with Taurus Age activity showed that cities, when destroyed, were rebuilt along the exact same plans that the earlier level was built on. Later levels built during the Age of Aries reflected a more haphazard approach.

The possible pantheons of gods and goddesses created in the division of Gemini began to organize themselves into a heavenly social structure in Taurus with the cow goddess, and later the bull god, becoming the supreme deity. Taurus is pictured as a bull/cow, the symbol of Taurus. In the Age of Gemini the cow goddess was prominent from the beginning, perhaps because of its placement in an early astrological view. Taurus, the bull/cow, was originally the first sign of the zodiac, perhaps reflecting a matriarchal vision of the universe, not the masculine sign Aries.

At Catal Huyuk in Anatolia scenes of bulls/cows heads, and women giving birth to horned cows or bulls are prominent on the walls of shrines. By the time of the Halafian culture the bull or cow was becoming more important in the Gemini worldview as the flow of time approached the coming Age of Taurus.

In the early U'baid culture, after 4500 BCE, Ninhurgsal, the dairy goddess, became their premier deity. By the time the Sumerians came to rule Mesopotamia, at the cultural height of the age where the masculine energy of Aries came to be first felt, the cow goddess became the bull god. By the height of the Age of Taurus, around 2700 BCE, the mythologist Joseph Campbell has noted that the bull god, the dead and resurrected bull god, was supreme everywhere. In Egypt during the Old Kingdom, the god Osiris was pictured as a bull. Apis was similarly the bull god of heavenly birth. The mother of pharaoh was seen as Hathor, a cow goddess. In India the bull was worshipped extensively as the sacred animal of Indra, the supreme deity of that time. The sacred bull was

Vrishabha, the bearer of the world. The Indian Christ, known as Krishna, is traditionally dated to about 3200 BCE. He was an incarnation of the god Vishnu, the son of god born into a human body. Krishna is often pictured with cows and surrounded by gopis, or milkmaids who met him every night out in the fields. The cow remains, even today, a sacred manifestation of god throughout India.

The Minoan civilization on the island of Crete also held the bull in high esteem. Frescos dating to the very beginning of the Age of Aries, approximately 2000 BCE, show young men and women acrobatically jumping between the horns of charging bulls. These images portray the Aries athletic energy dancing on the sacred back of the Taurus bull. The Minoan sport of bull jumping may be the ancestor of the modern Spanish bullfight.

There is an interesting reference in the Old Testament that also hints at bull worship by early Hebrews relating to the Age of Taurus. We are all familiar with the story of Moses going up to the top of Mt. Sinai to receive the 10 Commandments. While he was on the mountain the Hebrew people cast all their gold (Taurus wealth) into the shape of a calf in order to worship it. This story is presented in a patriarchal light with the worship of the golden calf being a pagan "blasphemous" practice that angered God. This story as we have it today wasn't put into written form until sometime after the 7th century BCE, well into the Age of Aries and well after the arrival of patriarchal culture. The oral tradition upon which the written accounts have been created may easily go farther back in time than previously thought, perhaps even deep into the Age of Taurus to a time when the golden calf might have been seen as an integral aspect of Moses ascent up Mt. Sinai. His ascent was assured by the creation and worship of this calf.

Archaeological evidence from a new civilization called Ebla indicates that Biblical references are at the least 1000 years older, if not more, than traditionally believed. Ebla was a civilization located at the top of the Fertile Crescent in the Near East. It dates to at least 2500 BCE and thrived from about 2400 BCE until approximately 2250 BCE when it was destroyed. Clay tablets from a provincial Eblan library contain Biblical names we associate with a much later time: David, Micah, Jerusalem, Sodom, Gomorrah, Haran, and Ur. This means that king David lived prior to and was already widely known by 2250 BCE. This would place the story of Moses on Mt. Sinai perhaps centuries prior to that, deep within the Age of Taurus and the Taurus reverence for the bull. The casting and worship of the golden calf conceivably could have been, at that time, in the oral tradition of that age, seen as a powerfully sacred process that was undertaken to support the priest Moses as he ascended the Taurean image of the monumental and permanent (pyramidal?) mountain. The original Mt. Sinai may have been a sacred pyramid or ziggurat.

The bull god was often depicted as a dying, dead and reborn god. This is due to the Scorpio South Pole energy. Scorpio rules death and resurrection. Scorpio stimulated and guided Taurus.

The Scorpio opposition to Taurus directed bull worship towards concerns of death and resurrection. The bull god Oriris in Egypt was the savior god of death and resurrection. In this process Scorpio pushed people to take a serious approach towards death. Osiris was killed and dismembered, cut into 13 astrological parts that were scattered all around the world, the 13th part being placed in the center of the other twelve. He was resurrected by his mother/wife Isis. Osiris became the savior to the Egyptians promising eternal life after the death of the body. Every Egyptian could seek the permanence of eternal life through the deep mystery inherent in Scorpio.

If Taurus Age man and woman identified strongly with the body then they spent much time and energy trying to preserve that body for eternity. The practice of preserving the bodies of their pharaohs was begun in the Old Kingdom. They were preserved against decay as well as for beautifying them on their journey to the underworld. Archaeologists tell us that the pyramids were built as tombs for those pharaohs, as immense Taurean permanent houses for their bodies and souls.

The Egyptian Book of the Dead was originally chiseled into the walls of these pyramids and was then known as the Pyramid Texts. These writings were instructions for the soul, guiding the soul in its afterlife journey towards the eternity of heaven. The Egyptian word for tomb means house of eternity.

In Mesopotamia Tammuz was the god of death and resurrection, and the savior of the Sumerian people. The dead and resurrected

Tammuz became the mythological savior model for subsequent gods of death and rebirth such as Attis, the Greek Dionysus, Adonis, and our own Christ.

The Royal Tombs at Ur are a magnificent display of wealth and material splendor. Dating to approximately 2700 BCE they reflect the Taurean need for wealth and comfort, even in death. Some 16 royal tombs have been discovered and in each case, as in Egypt, the entire household was killed in order to accompany their lord on his way to the greater life beyond. One tomb held close to 80 people on their journey through death with their lord.

Although we know little of the religious views of the Europeans during this age, it is interesting that the major building activity throughout Europe at this time were megalithic tombs dating as far back as 4100 BCE. Death and the passage through death must have become important enough to invest time and energy in the building of these massive stone houses of eternity.

In North America the Archaic Culture by 2500 BCE also was concerned with death and rebirth. Sumptuary burial cults flourished which archaeologists have named Old Copper, Red Ocher, and Glacial Kame. These burial cults reveal an abundance of wealth and a relatively high level of social stratification.

The power of Scorpio may have led humanity and history into the Age of Aries in a particularly mythic manner. It has been assumed that the patriarchal takeover of established matriarchal cultures was simply due to the rise of militaristic patriarchal nomadic peoples around 2000 BCE. The rise of masculine patriarchal cultures in what has been called a Mythic Solarization was in fact supported by the energy of the Age of Aries. But before that could happen the Scorpio energy of the Age of Taurus created an environment of social transformation that allowed the Mythic Solarization to occur. This time marked the height of matriarchal culture and civilization. It also marked the Scorpio death of matriarchal culture and the transformation of civilization into a masculine patriarchal mold as Aries began to exert its influence ever more strongly.

As civilization flourished and attracted to itself increasing amounts of wealth and power, the tendency to abuse the system also increased. Wealth, as always, accumulated at the top. Large burial practices that included the death of large numbers of a ruler's household also tended to take away from individuals the choice of how they might choose to live their own lives. The incoming Aries energy rules individualism. The time became ripe for a massive transformation within society. Hero myths from the following Age of Aries speak of the increasing evil that had infiltrated the matriarchal hierarchy both of heaven and of society. Scorpio rules what we might call evil; death and suffering along with a power hungry need for dictatorial control by those in power. This evil may have necessitated the rise of a new type of god, the warrior hero God who would overthrow the ruling Goddess and establish a new order of rule in heaven. The older Taurus Age thought that revered the megalithic solidity and permanency of society as a whole was giving way to a new thought about the importance of an individuals right to live his or her own life. This would lead, both culturally and mythically, quite naturally into the following Age of Aries.

THE AGE OF ARIES:
2160 TO 0 BCE

We now move out of the peaceful Age of Taurus into the violent Age of Aries. Aries is the ram seeking to butt heads with anything in his way. The sign is ruled by the planet Mars, the Roman god of war. Aries rules war. Aries is the sign that rules strength in its most active form. It is active and challenging, seeking to overcome and prove its strength against any and all obstacles in its way. Aries looks for obstacles in order to present itself with a challenge. Like the ram, symbol of Aries, this signs' strength lay in the intensity of its activity. The bull of Taurus is a much larger animal whose strength is manifest in its stability and durability. The ram with its enormous reserves of energy and activity constantly battering down the barriers of the bull eventually emerges the victor. Even the most inconsequential task becomes a contest where he must fight towards victory. Enyo, the goddess of battle, and Eris, the goddess of discord, are said to be his sister and mother, wife and daughter variously. The vulture and the dog, the battlefield scavengers, are his favorite animals.

Activity, the adventure of the conquest is more important to Aries than the fruits of the conquest. The Arian reward is the honor gained in the victory, not in the city that was conquered or the woman won over. For Aries war is the most noble of activities.

Aries is the antithesis of Taurus. Where Taurus is peace-loving and stable, Aries is warlike, active, and reckless. The most basic attribute of Aries is aggression and action, competition, and the quest for independence and self-discovery. Aries rules the personality in general. It is the sign of the child; creative and self-centered, and carries with it the key phrase "I AM".

At one time Taurus was seen as the first sign of the zodiac and Aries as the last. The cycle of the hero's journey through the zodiac began with the solid and physical world around us. Through a complete cycle an individual would strive through various lessons and challenges, reflected in the signs, to come to know his true self. The cycle would be complete with Aries and the individual's battle for final independence. Here he is "born" into heaven and eternity, finally free of all limitations imposed by the solid world we presently inhabit. Aries rules birth. The Aries individual was then a hero, half man and half god, an enlightened warrior.

Sometime during the middle of the Age of Aries the signs of the zodiac were rotated to make Aries the first sign. Many think this change was made in order to reflect the precessional change of time from Taurus to Aries. This may be. But there is possibly a more profound reason for this change. On the one hand the change merely reflects the competitive Arian need to be first. On the other hand Aries would see his age as pivotal in the precessional history of the world. The values of Taurus, solid and money oriented, would be seen as somewhat "evil" in its focus on sensual objects and solid earthly stability, especially with the Scorpio opposite energy coloring Taurus.

At this momentous time, the beginning of a new paradigm, Aries supported a massive mythic solarization around the world that marked the end of the older matriarchal social structure and inaugurated a new patriarchal system of religion and government. Hero mythologies were created in response to this change. The old Babylonian Mother Goddess Tiamat was perceived as increasingly restrictive and deadening to the newer energies of Aries. Marduk, the Babylonian hero god, emerged as the champion of the oppressed. He rose up against Taimat and defeated her bringing in a profound change in the structure of heaven. Taurus Age ideals were overturned by heroes of all cultures. The man-bull of Crete, the Minotaur, was slain by the Aries Greek hero Theseus. The Hebrew hero Samson slew the civilized and wealthy (Taurus) Philistines "hip and thigh", destroying their massive temple in a final act of heroic individual strength. The entire Old Testament depicts a cultural battle between the patriarchal god YHWH and the pagan matriarchal Taurus Age religions of the other peoples living in Canaan, the land promised by God to his chosen people.

Through all of this the pantheon of gods and goddesses changed from a feminine static focus to a more masculine active focus. A mythic solarization took place around the globe from about 2500 to 1500 BCE. Masculine gods replaced older feminine goddesses in sacred pantheons everywhere as a reflection of the universal reaction to the new Aries energy and the collective intuition that something new was in the process of happening to Time and history. To honor this new knowledge Aries was exalted to the position of being the first sign of the zodiac. Taurus was demoted astrologically at the same time that the feminine was demoted in mythologies the world over.

Historically Aries manifested itself as an age of action, for better or worse. In the Age of Aries humanity entered an age of war and empire building. Man invented all manner of physical competition and strove for adventure and independence.

Since the beginning of human history tribal squabbles have always been a part of social interaction. It took Aries to manifest out and out war on a large scale and install the military as the foundation for government. In the last few centuries of the Age of Taurus Egypt and Mesopotamia both displayed a growing trend towards militarism. Prince Narmer led an army to reunite Upper and Lower Egypt around 3200 BCE but this seems to have been an isolated event. The Age of Taurus was remarkably peaceful even with the lure of incredible wealth that these cultures presented to other peoples.

In Egypt, from 2300 BCE, times became markedly more anarchic with the growth of individualism, social revolution, and the invasion of Negroid and Asiatic tribes. The collapse of "civilized" living, which followed the collapse of the Old Kingdom of Taurus Age Egypt, indicated Egypt's perilous dependence on the absolute power and authority of society and the pharaoh. Even when the Middle Kingdom was established at the beginning of this Age of Aries ending the near anarchy of the First Intermediate Period, things would never be the same again. Men began to reflect a new interest in their own individuality in opposition to the needs of society as a whole.

A new form of civilization was being created, that of the empire, and in this new age they come and go with incredible speed. Around 2300 BCE Sargon of Akkad conquered the Sumerians and established the first military empire in history. They were, in turn, conquered by the Gutians who were then overthrown by a resurgent and more militaristic Sumerian Third Dynasty. Warfare was inaugurated as a national pastime. The Sumerian Third Dynasty was soon invaded by yet another warrior culture, the Elamites about 2000 BCE. The Amorites, known as the Old Babylonians, conquered Mesopotamia around 1800 BCE under Hammurabi.

The Hittites overran Mesopotamia about 1600 BCE. The Hittites invented iron weaponry and machinery designed to lay siege to a city further changing the face of armed warfare. The process of smelting iron came too late to save the Hittite armies. It wouldn't be until the rise of the Assyrians that whole armies would be equipped with iron weapons. The Hittites had the best siege equipment around, and their war-horses were bigger, and thus stronger, than those of any other people. They could easily pull large three-man war chariots. Their siege tactics terrified their enemies. One of their kings, Suppilulimas, overran the strongly fortified city of Carchemish in Mitanni in just eight days. The rest of the Mesopotamian world was astonished at this feat. This quickly led to improved city defenses, redesigned gates, and possibly the idea of secret exits built into walls to counter attack a besieging enemy.

The Hyksos were the first to introduce the war chariot as a devastating new weapon when they invaded Egypt about 1800BCE. The Myceneans conquered Crete. The list continues through the Phrygians, the Assyrians, the Scythians, the Chaldeans, and the Persians, everyone in their turn conqueror and conquered. The Age of Aries closed behind Alexander the Great and the first world empire, and finally the rise of the powerful Roman armies.

The Assyrians rose to military ascendancy twice. The second time, around 1000 BCE, they began to use deliberate and calculated terror as a weapon against their enemies. Those who revolted were impaled on stakes or skinned alive among other tortures. They would then publicize these tortures as warnings to others.

Egyptians were becoming warriors and conquerors. During the Middle Kingdom military expeditions penetrated south as far as Cush and possibly to the northeast as far as Syria. The Middle

Kingdom lasted until around 1790 BCE when they were invaded by a collection of peoples known as the Hyksos. Egyptian propaganda from a later period depicted this time as a dark age and a 'shameful and cruel foreign conquest' by the 'hehaukhasut' or princes of foreign countries. The ancient origin of these foreigners is uncertain, as is the manner in which they conquered Egypt as well as the extent of their domination.

The Hyksos used weapons that were new to the Egyptians including the horse-drawn chariot and the compound bow. They had a superior military culture that also included body armor and very sharp rapier-like bronze swords of a type that would come to dominate warfare in the second millennium BCE. With the expulsion of the Hyksos Egypt established the New Kingdom, which was now militaristic and imperialistic. A large professional army was now maintained. The two viziers to the king were now usually generals, their posts primarily military commands. Imperial Egypt became the most powerful state in the Near East.

The Greeks defined the ideal of Aries establishing warring feudalistic city-states who fought for the love and adventure of fighting. Their religion of Olympic gods, goddesses and heroes, all fighting among themselves, honored the glory of war and individual achievement as seen in battle. It was the ultimate Aries Age religion.

As the age closed military empires were becoming successively larger. The Persian Empire in the 6th century BCE extended from the Aegean to the borders of India. Later Philip of Macedon and Alexander the Great defined the possibility of world conquest creating an empire larger than the Persian. The Romans took up this desire and began the process of creating their truly vast empire as the age closed.

In China the Lung Shan culture between 2000 and 1850 BCE was basically a peaceful farming culture with little evidence of warfare. They did build large pounded defensive earth walls around many of their settlements, and there appear frequently in their settlements large amounts of arrowheads, spears, clubs, and daggers. Some human remains suggest scalping and beheading indicating a possible increase in conflicts.

Around 1850 BCE they were invaded and conquered by the

militaristic Shang Dynasty. By the end of their reign they were able to field armies of over 30,000 men led by nobles fighting against neighbors as well as against more warlike barbarians. Their success was also based on the new horse drawn war-chariot supported by infantry. The infantry was armed with bronze metal tipped arrows and laminated bows. Records indicate staggering numbers of casualties on both sides in military campaigns.

In 1122 BCE they were themselves invaded and conquered by the Chou Dynasty who proceeded to create an even larger and more comprehensive militaristic society. Within both of these dynasties loose confederacies of states often arose for short periods of time only to be defeated by other states that had grown militarily stronger or by more powerful confederacies.

Eventually the Chou dissolved between 480 to 221 BCE into what is called the Warring States Period. It was a nightmare of military struggle during which the Chou fragmented into seven major powers and about the same number of minor ones. After a decisive battle in 221 BCE the Ch'in king claimed control of most of the old Chou territory and extended the borders west to Szechwan and south to the Canton delta. After 210 BCE the empire was racked with revolutions and counter-revolutions. The empire was finally restored in 202 BCE with the founding of the Early Han Dynasty.

Across the seas in the New World, in Mexico, the Olmecs had come to power by 1200 BCE peaking around 900 BCE. Not much is known about them but they did leave hints as to their Aries nature. They commonly portrayed themselves with clubs some-times in the act of beating prisoners. They carved many huge heads out of six-foot high boulders. These Olmec Heads are shown wearing helmets indicating the possibility that war and warrior life were important. But then again, these helmets could have been athletic. If they were the Aries energy remains the same. Whether in war or in sports, the Aries ideal is competition, the striving to prove oneself in overcoming an opponent. The Olmec Heads indicate that Aries was, in some fashion, important and honored.

Farther south in Peru a new and large city was discovered in the late 1990's in the Casma valley dated to about 1500 BCE. Covering some 6 square miles Casma contains several pyramids that contain carved scenes of war and violence. The more recently discovered city of Caral just south of Casma, dated to 2600 BCE, shows the earlier civilization as peaceful, with no fortifications or signs of war or violence of any kind.

In the Indus civilization the Indo-European invasions that brought increased violence and war to the Near East also affected India. The Indus civilization was a flourishing and stable Taurus Age civilization by 2400 BCE. After 1700 BCE the Indo-Europeans led a violent invasion into India. Dead bodies were left where they fell in the streets of some sites such as Mohenjo-daro. Many fled south before the overwhelming military might of the invaders.

War and competition were deeply honored. In the Near East writing was applied to story and myth. Religions of abundance became religions of the warrior hero. The gods and goddesses of the older pantheon began to war among themselves. In Mesopotamia the young warrior god Marduk rose up in defiance of the great Mother Goddess Tiamat and defeated her. Everywhere the young god replaced the older goddess in a vast mythic solarization that took place around the world at the beginning of Aries.

The Greek religion of Olympus, with great heroes such as Hercules, survives today as the most complete expression of the warrior path to glory and heaven. Our own Judaic roots also are heavily Aries. The Old Testament is presided over, whether we recognize it or not, by a god of war who leads his army of chosen people into a promised new land to conquer. No matter how many times we read that Jehovah is loving and compassionate the literary images presented to us in the Bible are of a war god who is angry and jealous, who is constantly punishing his people for insubordination, or who is constantly testing them with great hardship to strengthen his army of people and see how they meet adversity in a spiritual context. Jehovah is the ram, the highest shepherd, and we his flock. This is very Aries. Aries is pictured as the ram. Jehovah, who is called I am, I am that I am, is thus very Aries. The Aries key phrase is "I am"; Taurus is "I have."

The heroes of the Old Testament are also presented as violent Arian leaders. Moses challenged the might of the Pharaoh. Sampson slew the Philistines. David slew Goliath. Even Elijah, the prophet of God, was Arian in his demeanor. He personally slaughtered the priests of the Phoenicians with his bare hands.

The written account we have of our religious fathers reflects the time when these stories were first written within the Hebraic tradition, around 700 BCE, late into the Age of Aries. Although spiritual truths do not change, the flavor of those truths do change from age to age. By the time the Old Testament was written down the warlike flavor of the times strongly inspired the early writers to portray the old religious truths in an Arian environment of heroic endeavor. Sampson, Saul, and David are remembered for their victories. The long line of Hebrew prophets is similarly remembered for their belligerent stand against Jewish leaders who embraced the older Taurean paradigm. The prophets are portrayed as warriors of God.

The Old Testament expands this Arian quality of independence to include a whole people; God's Chosen People. From the time of Moses there arises this Arian need for independence, and separation, and the need to become exalted over others. God leads his Chosen in conquest of Canaan. He continually sends heroes in times of need to help the Hebrews defeat powerful enemies. Moses leads his people not out of literal slavery in Egypt, but out of the slavery of wealth and comfort, and the idea of permanent social stations in life that robs one of his or her initiative. This is Taurus, symbolized by the image of Egypt. As they enter into the "promised land" of Canaan they become the warriors that Aries demands of them conquering as they go along. As an independent people, no longer subdued by the needs of the state, they set themselves apart and their god becomes a jealous god.

Balancing and guiding Aries is Libra, the sign of the balance scales. Libra rules relationships, marriage, and law codes, or codes of conduct regulating social interaction. At the beginning of the Age of Aries, with its Libra opposite sign, independent action began to require codes of conduct to regulate Arian activity. As early as 2400 BCE simple law codes were created to outline social and sexual interaction.

Urukagina, a king of Lagash, issued a series of laws around 2400 BCE that reflect a certain degree of organization that illustrates the transition from collections of kingly edicts into the more formal codes that would follow. Ur-Nammu, the founder of the Third Dynasty of Ur in Sumeria, issued a more comprehensive code of laws around 2100 BCE. The Code of Hammurabi around 1750 BCE was a much more complex and sophisticated approach to law.

We find in the Code of Hammurabi a much greater complexity dealing with such matters as marriage and the family, property, inheritance and slander. There are laws dealing with malpractice, shoddy construction, dowry matters, and fixed prices for commodities.

In the Code of Hammurabi apparently trivial offenses such as "gadding about" were punishable by death. In Hammurabi's Code adultery was also punishable by death whereas in earlier Sumerian law adultery didn't even necessarily result in divorce. The later Assyrian code made abortion and unnatural vice death penalties and women were no longer allowed to appear in public without their faces veiled. The apparent shallowness of some of these laws and their severe punishment may indicate a growing concern for maintaining the established rules of conduct of the state versus the growing needs and vices of the individual.

In Egypt the literature of the Middle Kingdom reflects a legal change of sorts as religion was now being seen more as an ethical system of human conduct. Justice became more important in the sight of the sun god than before. The earliest examples of Egyptian ethical philosophy, from the Old Kingdom, were maxims of sage advice similar to the Old Testament book of Proverbs. They were mainly maxims of practical wisdom, but they occasionally exalted such concerns as tolerance, moderation, and justice. In the Middle Kingdom this practical religion changed. A more sophisticated Epicureanism developed. This increase in ethical considerations involved man's actions, with moderation as an ideal; it became a source from which other peoples developed their own codes of morality. Such ideals as justice, benevolence and equality were exalted. Where Mesopotamia became legalistic Egypt became ethical.

Mesopotamian law is where we first come across the ideal of "an eye for an eye and a tooth for a tooth". This ideal is highly Aries in nature. Mesopotamian law was semi-private or individual in its administration of justice. It was incumbent upon the victim himself, or his family, to bring the offender to justice. The court served principally as an umpire in disputes between plaintiff and defendant, not as an agency of the state concerned with maintaining public security, as it would become in the Age of Pisces.

The Hebrew religion was based solidly on a code of laws. God was portrayed as the supreme lawgiver. The legal code of the early Hebrews, the Torah, or the Law of Moses, was built around the divine transmission of the Ten Commandments given to Moses on Mount Sinai. The Torah has some unique features. Many of its provisions show Babylonian influence. Some sections, for example, are worded in a fashion closely similar to the Code of Hammurabi. But with the Hebrews there is a greater humanitarianism evident than in earlier law codes. Special sections provide for the welfare of widows, orphans, and even slaves. The finest example of Jewish law is the Deuteronomic Code. It is based in part on an older "Code of the Covenant" which was created in considerable measure from the laws of the Canaanites and Babylonians.

In classical Greece law was fully developed. The Greek lawgivers Draco and Solon have become names nearly synonymous with the idea of lawmaking and legislature. Courts and trials were now commonplace. Yet even here judges were not full time legalists as much as elders of society sitting in judgment.

Plato notes, in true Aries fashion, that war is an art with significance. In reality war is violent and messy. Libra gave to war certain boundaries and codes of conduct. Armies fight according to rules. Prisoners are taken and not slaughtered if they surrender. Negotiations are entered into either to forestall war or to end one. And even Libran marriages are entered into in order to create military allies out of potential enemies and to enlarge an empire. The lesser tendencies towards brawling and murder on an individual level are sublimated into the socially acceptable institution of the army, where fighting remains under tight control. Society is theoretically protected from internal violence, channeling that tendency outwards through its armies.

In addition to social legal codes Libra rules creative literature. This impulse spurred society to take written language out of the spiritual warehouse and apply it to those aspects of spirituality more closely associated with story. The Old Babylonians took various fragments of the story of Gilgamesh and tied them together in the Epic of Gilgamesh. The hero mythology of ancient Greece served as source material for the literature of Homer, the Iliad and the Odyssey. Mythology may have taken on a greater importance because of the literary aspect. Hero mythology with its element of personal challenge appeals to the heroic desires within each of us.

The power of hero mythology is its ability to touch the listener's, or reader's, heart. That made hero myth the perfect vehicle for literary creativity. Following Homer literature, or the story of individual achievement, expanded in classical Greece to include both drama and comedy performed on the stage.

Hebrew mythology, much of it borrowed from older Babylonian and Sumerian sources, was humanized and written down as history, the story of their evolution, in a highly literary style. The myth of an older time now was presented as literature. Because myth was always seen as truth and not as fable, the story of the Old Testament likewise was presented as truth, and thus as history. We still tend to take it to be literal history today.

Aries brought with it the need to break away from the imprisoning social structure of the megalithic state and strive to achieve freedom on an individual level. The next step for humanity would be transcending beyond even the individual body to seek the ultimate freedom of heaven. This would be the focus of Pisces.

THE AGE OF PISCES:
0 - 2160 CE

Society has been led, step-by-step, through a logical, cosmic pattern of growth. Humanity was taught to settle down, open his and her heart and domesticate his and her life in Cancer. Humanity was then taught to reach out and share ideas in Gemini. As their worldview expanded people were then taught to seek and enjoy the abundance freely given by God as a way of life. And then humanity was taught to challenge themselves, to push themselves to greater levels of achievement, to go beyond, to overcome obstacles in a warlike Aries world. Next came the Age of Pisces where we have been taught to contact the mystical nature of existence beyond this world.

Pisces is the sign of the fish. It is pictured as two fish swimming in opposite directions yet attached at the center. This represents the essential dual nature of reality, opposition connected at the heart. What is real and what is unreal, and how are they connected? Does the solidity and apparent reality of the physical world require the heartfelt existence of the spiritual in order to exist? Pisces rules illusion, while the heart planet Venus is exalted in Pisces.

Pisces is ruled by the planets Jupiter and Neptune. Jupiter is the king of the Gods, the Roman name for Zeus, a Greek name from an Indo-European root word that means transcendent. In addition he is also portrayed as being very physical with a very long list of extramarital affairs to his name. This is symbolic of the dual nature of Pisces, with extreme spirituality existing side-by-side with sexual physical appetite. The co-ruler of Pisces is Neptune, god of the oceans and brother to Jupiter. He had almost as many sexual affairs as Jupiter did yet his transcendent nature is seen in the symbol of the seas he ruled. Astrologically Neptune is the planet of transcendent spirituality.

During the Age of Taurus every individual had a set place in society. Caste systems were put in place to insure an orderly structure within which society could operate. Society flourished under the supreme leader of that society such as the En, or the priest-kings of Sumer, and the Pharaoh in Egypt. With the Age of Aries the focus changed towards that of the average individual, if he was willing to tap into his own heroic nature. The Pharaoh could no longer attain heaven for all of society. Each individual had to do that for him or herself. While the ruler remained important the message now was that every person must fight his or her own battles. War became an important exterior expression of that message and the mythology of the Hero arose to foster that endeavor. Now with the Age of Pisces the outward directed energy of Aries began the process of turning inward. The enemy is no longer portrayed as an opposing warrior or some mythical monster to be slain with superior force of arms. The enemy now is Satan, the Great Cosmic God of Evil, and to achieve victory the struggle is now portrayed as internal and spiritual.

Pisces rules the transcendent aspect of religion, spirituality, prophets and prophecy. It rules large institutions, bureaucracy and dogma. This age has been an age where large world religions have ruled beyond the reach of empires for the most part. The empire, more often than not, became religious theocracy bowing to the direction of the churches they were associated with.

For the Western World for most of the history of this age, the single most important event in this history was the birth and ministry of Jesus of Nazareth, the Christ, and the embodiment of the Piscean savior. His teachings have affected the historical direction of Western Civilization more than any war or empire ever dreamed of. The religious institution of Christianity served to dominate western life for 1500 years and it still affects us strongly today.

Christ came as the answer to Piscean prophecy. During the 8th and 7th century BCE the seeds of the Age of Pisces were sown at that time when a group of men arose in Israel who were collectively known as the prophets. They began telling of the coming of the Messiah, the savior who would lead all of mankind to salvation. The way in which they spoke of the Messiah reflected the Aries military ideal much more than the Pisces. When Christ came and did reveal himself he was too humble and otherworldly for their liking. He was not the Arian conqueror they were expecting. He was far too Piscean in a world still struggling with the legacy of Aries. The Greek ideal of the hero was now being transformed into the Pisces ideal of the saint, something Aries Jewish history was unfamiliar with.

Christianity did not arise all by itself as the only religion turning towards a more Piscean expression. During the first century BCE salvationist religions emerged everywhere and were all brought to Rome as Rome's conquests expanded. They came from Egypt, Phrygia, and from the farthest reaches of Rome's expanding influence. Mithraism soon became the most influential of all these religions. These religions collectively made deep impressions on the minds of Roman citizens. Still their mythologies regarding a savior were only that, remaining in the realm of myth. Christianity took that myth one step further insisting that myth had actually come to life, that God and the physical universe had organized a real historical expression of mythic desire. This idea was not new.

The Hindu religion worships two instances of the same thing happening in past ages. The god Vishnu literally incarnated on earth in the personage of Rama, and later Krishna, at critical times in the past in order to restore spiritual purity and save humanity during periods of transition. Now it was the Christ who came to earth to live out a mythically organized life and show humanity the way to salvation. The reality of his life, as preached by his followers, and followers of those followers, reached increasing numbers of people. In this we can see the Piscean rulership of prophecy and fulfillment of prophecy, as well as of illusion. In Pisces fashion the apparent illusion of prophecy, the myth of the savior, became reality.

The early Church began as a collection of separate localized and independent churches. Eventually it became the official religion of Rome after having survived early attempts by Rome to destroy it. With the eventual collapse of Rome it was the Christian Church that kept Roman institutions such as law and education alive. As various Germanic tribes invaded the empire and even the city of Rome itself, the Church began the religious conquest of Germany and the rest of Europe.

The early Christian Church grew rapidly and soon began to spread out into Germanic Europe. When Rome split into two empires, east and west, the eastern empire became a religious theocracy centered at Constantinople. The western empire was overrun by Germanic tribes and eventually fell. The Church, as the official religion, maintained the structure of Roman life, with the result that the Germanic tribes were remade into a European Christian theocracy.

As the world sank into the depths of the Dark Ages it was Christian monks who kept learning alive. They ran the schools and copied manuscripts while the main branch of the Church, the Papacy and the hierarchy of cardinals and bishops, focused on the law and meted out justice. Agriculture had almost vanished from Europe by this time. Monks were generally the best farmers in Europe keeping the art of farming alive during a period of constant famines. In Pisces fashion the Church virtually controlled every aspect of society from birth to death. Out of this Europe recreated itself as the Holy Roman Empire, a theocracy based directly on Christian faith and theology.

The eastern half of the empire also quickly evolved into a Piscean theocracy, the Byzantine Empire, under the guidance of the Eastern Orthodox Church. When Constantine moved the capital of the Empire to his new city of Constantinople in the east he essentially split Christianity in two. The seat of St. Peter would always remain in Rome. The Imperial decision to move the capital of the empire could not change that and the Church began to split into two separate churches. The empire would soon follow suit, splitting into two separate political entities.

In North Africa Christian religious doctrine created a conflict over the nature of God. Traditional Catholic views held that God had a three-part expression seen as the Trinity of the Father, the Son, and the Holy Ghost. Some other sects, especially in North Africa, took a more transcendental view stating that God was only One, unity, beyond all forms of division and separation. This doctrinal conflict would lead eventually to the creation of a new religion, and the new theocracy of Islam.

The Holy Prophet Mohammed founded this new religion of Islam. Almost from the start this religion was political, tied to the creation of a new, political spiritual view of life. Islam spread quickly out after Mohammed's death and conquered an empire established from the outset as a religious theocracy.

In India deep changes were also at work. With the Age of Pisces the older Hindu pantheon of Aries warrior gods under Indra took a back seat to the new focus on the higher transcendental gods, the Trinity consisting of Brahma, Vishnu, and Shiva. Vishnu is the preservative aspect of the universe. It is Vishnu that incarnates from time to time to help save the world. As he incarnates he becomes another, an offspring of himself, a Son of God, but one in unity. As Christ's teachings were spread in the West, more and more people worshipped this Divine Child in the form of Vishnu in India.

Shiva is the transcendent god of destruction in India. At this time, when the apocalyptic teachings of the Christian Church in the West, based on ideas of the end of the world, had become a major focus of the Christian religion, millions in India began to worship Shiva, the god of destruction, endings and transcending in that same apocalyptic process.

Buddhism, created with the teachings of Buddha around 500 BCE, took a different approach to this same energy. He did away with the ages old accumulation of gods and goddesses thus taking away the outward images of religion. The only reality was inward spirituality, in the transcendent mind. Our minds, properly trained through meditation, are fully capable of experiencing the divine directly. In this he rested on the Virgo opposite to Pisces to a great extent. Virgo rules the mind and mental health, as well as technique and analysis. The ideal was now solely to purify the mind through meditation. It is this process and this process alone that allows for individual salvation during this time of transition.

Buddhism began as a more Aries religion than Christianity. It was focused on the Aries ideal of the individual. Buddhism changed during the first century BCE and the near entry into Pisces with the creation of Mahayana Buddhism. In this school those who become enlightened become bodhisattvas. They do not leave this earth, vowing not to transcend to heaven, or Nirvana, until all other human beings have also found salvation. The power of meditation could easily help others to achieve transcendence. They vowed to remain on this plane of existence in order to teach and help others during this time of endings.

At the same time that Christianity and Islam spread west over Europe and the Americas and into Africa, Buddhism spread east from India to Southeast Asia, China and Japan. The many nations of the earth were being united into the worlds first huge multinational groups.

In the New World relatively little is known of their religious traditions. There is one tradition though that is very Piscean and unites most of the various religions in this hemisphere. This tradition revolves around the myth of the Pale Prophet, the lost white brother. The Pale Prophet is said to have visited peoples throughout the New World. He taught, and then left with the promise that he would return when the end of this time was near. This is very similar to the Christian message. We are awaiting the Second Coming ourselves.

The anthropologist Taylor Hansen has published many of these myths, collected by her father, in a book called *HE WALKED THE AMERICAS*. These stories suggest that Christ, after he was crucified and ascended to heaven in fulfillment of the mythic Piscean parameters of his life here on earth, he then came back in his original body and left eastwards to continue his mission of teaching. The first story places this enigmatic figure in Japan. He is then taken by ship to a south sea island and dropped off. He teaches for a while and then is taken to the next island eastward. In this fashion he eventually reaches Central America. Teaching there for a while he then heads south into South America, then across the northern portion of that continent. From there he takes boat across the Caribbean to the mouth of the Mississippi. He then travels and teaches northwards to Canada, west to the coast and south through California. He returns eventually to Central America where he then leaves by boat east across the Atlantic. It is here that the stories stop.

All the images of the Pale Prophet are the same. He is Caucasian in coloring. He has a beard, which was not common in the New World. He wore a long white robe that was common among those of the Near East. Around the bottom of the robe were embroidered small crosses. And he had the scars of nails in the palms of his hands.

His message was the same in all stories. It was the message of the Buddha and of Christ, love and compassion. He is remembered most profoundly in the Aztec religion as Quetzacoatl, a god born of a virgin mother. He was said to be white. He left and swore that one day he would return. When Cortez and his small band of men conquered the huge Aztec empire he unwittingly did so with the help of Aztec prophecy. He landed at the precise time of the Aztec New Year. Their calendar had 360 days. The extra five days held magical significance. It would have been the time of transcendence and connection with the gods, perhaps a time when Quetzacoatl might return. Cortez was taken to be Quetzacoatl prophetically returning and consequently taken in triumph into the palace.

The Hopi also look for the return of a long lost brother from the east. Just as prophetically Spaniards showed up at the appointed place and at the appointed time. There was supposed to be a certain ritual of exchange that would reveal the lost brother as the real brother. The Spanish did not know this ritual and failed the test. The Hopi retreated back up to the protection of their Mesas and await to this day the prophesied return of their savior.

Unfortunately this spiritual unification carried with it darker Piscean energies. Pisces rules dissolution, escapism, and irrational fears. Pisces is pictured as two opposing fish swimming in opposite directions yet connected at the heart. Pisces thus presents us with two seemingly opposing worlds and we must seek to find their harmonious connection.

All the religions that grew up in this age have been religions of duality, entailing a great cosmic war between good and evil with our personal souls as the battlefields. Thus we have come to see our own religion as the path of good while other religions become the tool of evil. Christians versus pagans, savages and heretics, True Believers versus infidels, Jews versus gentiles, the universe was split into two great warring camps. In the process so was the human supplicant. The soul fought against the desires of the body for spiritual supremacy. Dogmas, prejudices, and hatreds have deeply colored the spiritual quest of this age. The Spanish Inquisition tortured and murdered in the name of spirituality. Women were branded witches and were burned; pogroms were carried out against the Jews; Crusades were sent to free the Holy Land from the Arabs, and "heathens" were butchered in order to spread the word of God in the New World. And more recently Eastern Europeans, Jews, and Gypsies were gassed in Nazi concentration camps in order to purify the world for the new god of science and genetic purity.

It has been these negative aspects of Pisces that has precipitated a split between science and religion over the past few centuries. The violent wars between the Protestant and Catholic Churches in Europe in the 16th and 17th centuries so appalled the new scientific humanistic mind that they distanced themselves from anything religious or emotional, seeing it as irrational. Reason and rational thought became the only sane way to live life. Scientists have thus built a dogmatic prejudice into their system of thought against anything emotional, intuitional or religious. In addition scientific thought came up against the Piscean tendency of the Church during this age to insist on the fantastical reality of many very unreal aspects of Christian myth. Reality versus illusion.

This split between science and religion, created for humanistic reasons, is still the very same split, good versus evil, reason verses voodoo, that has marred the spiritual growth of this age.

It does seem, though, that the two, light and dark, must go hand in hand. If heaven is so beautiful and the things of this earth are now so evil, if reason is so sane and practical, and the emotional-ism of mythic beliefs and "superstition" is so detrimental to a sane society, then Pisces must show us the heart felt connection between the two. Christ and the Buddha both taught, as central to their message, the path of love, compassion, and forgiveness, to turn one's other cheek to whatever enemy arises before us in order to find that center where opposition, the great battle between light and dark, becomes a loving dance. During this age humanity needed to experience both the beauty of spiritual practice and bliss, and the horror of our dark side in order to eventually experience a balance, to find our center. The symbol of Pisces, as we remember, is two fish swimming in opposite directions yet connected at the heart, in the middle.

Pisces rules paranoia and fear. During the fourth century BCE Greek philosophy first separated the mind from the body. This small split would eventually lead to the rise of fear and paranoia within both man and society. The internal focus of Pisces turned the old violence of Aries inward, to the very heart of society. The Third Punic War between Rome and Carthage in North Africa, in the 2nd century BCE, was a new type of war. It marked the beginning of a "new brutalism" in warfare, never seen before. Based on the increasing fear that Carthage might again try to invade Rome and take over her trading networks Rome sought to fight a preemptive war. Rome defeated Carthage, killed all men and boys of fighting age, tore down to the ground all her buildings, plowed salt into her arable farmlands, sold all the women and children into slavery, and had priests put a curse on what had been Carthage to prevent her rise from the ashes ever again.

The first century BCE in Rome was internally brutal. The Roman general Sulla, during his rule, created huge gangs of slaves answerable only to him. These gangs roamed city streets doing his bidding. He created proscription lists that included Roman senators that were essentially hit lists. Anyone whose name was on it could legally be killed by anyone else. The property of that person was then split between the executioner and Sulla. Internal violence on this level against one's own citizenry was unheard of before.

By the time that the Medieval Church was being created St. Jerome was exalted as one of the Church Fathers in part because he embodied the fearful, but pious, schizophrenic split within the Church. He idealized the mental longing for purity in constant battle with the sexual longing of the loins for fleshly connection.

In the Old Testament the idea of Satan was first simply that of the process of opposition. The word means "opposer". One of the earliest uses of Satan in Christian mythology was as a test in the Book of Job, Satan clearly subservient to the will of God. Satan asked God's permission to test the spiritual resolve of Job. By Christian Pisces times Satan had started to become the great Evil battling God for supremacy. Begun with the Zoroastrian religious split between Ahura Mazda, god of light, and Ahriman, god of darkness Christians suddenly began to see Satan everywhere. Heresies were the work of Satan. Women were sexual and a constant temptation to men, thus they were seen as witches and as embodiments of the Devil. Pagans were Devil worshippers. The enemy was everywhere both outside Christian society and within.

If pagan Rome could use violent persecution against Christians then, as St. Augustine reasoned, it was only right and just that Christianity, the Church, use violence itself to keep the faith free of pagan influence. With this line of reasoning St. Augustine brought violence and fear into the fold of accepted Christian expression. Church ideals became dogma and violence was sanctioned as a means of correcting heretical ideas.

By the late Middle Ages this violence came to rest in the Church institution of the Inquisition. Violence and brutality were seen as necessary to force a recalcitrant individual to admit guilt. The goal was to save the soul even if the body was tortured to death. What was different was feared. Jews, gypsies, and women were all favorite targets for a very fearful Church. During the 12th and 13th centuries, following the successful first Crusade, subsequent Crusades descended into brutality attacking Jews and others before ever leaving Europe for the Holy Land. At the beginning of the Fourth Crusade they even stopped to sack the Christian city of Byzantium, releasing their fears and angers in a rampage of rape and murder.

The Renaissance unleashed yet another period of Christian savagery. The late 15th and early 16th century was a period of increasing treachery, fratricide, and violent depravity. Violent pogroms, or ethnic cleansings, against the Jews became common in the early 16th century. In one instance in 1506 the Portuguese sought to evict Jews in order to confiscate their businesses and wealth. When the Jews were too slow to leave 4000 of them were slaughtered in one night. Violent intrigue was everywhere. Murder was tolerated at all levels of society, up to and including the Pope, against anyone perceived to be a threat to power, including family members.

The Protestant Reformation brought with it even more butchery as their own fears of Satan ran rampant. The 16th century was very bloody. Christians slaughtered Christians in the name of the Catholic Christ or the Protestant. Within four years after the Diet of Worms and the formation of the Lutheran Church 250,000 Germans were killed or executed.

Racial prejudice, based on these same Piscean neurotic fears that spurred Christians towards unbridled violence and depravity, gained power and spread during this age. Jewish separation from other peoples in the name of purity, Jews versus gentiles, expanded with Christianity. The great cosmic fight between God and Satan, and between maintaining spiritual cleanliness seen in Judaism, became a fearful source of hatred with Christians. Now it was Christian versus pagan. This split translated itself into white versus black, or color, and allowed the religious foundation for the practice of slavery. White skin translated into purity while black skin was seen as an obvious connection with darkness and animal ignorance. This split is also partly behind the modern bloodshed of terrorism let loose by Islamic fundamentalists against the white Christian West, True Believers versus infidel as well as Christian versus pagan. Both sides portray the other as evil and as Satan.

Pisces rules large institutions. Much of what had been individual or isolated in the past now coalesced into large institutional bureaucracies. The growth of the great religions of this age was due in part to this process of institutionalization. Although the Church had become the official religion of Rome it remained separate. It had created its own bureaucracy to run and regulate Church business. When the empire finally fell to the barbarians it was Roman bureaucracy that kept the empire running smoothly. The Church then stepped in and proceeded to bring the emerging Germanic kingdoms together under Church control. The Church had its own hierarchy with the Pope at its head. This hierarchy became, over the course of a thousand years, a political power of its own overseeing non-religious as well as religious functions in order to insure its own growth.

During the ninth century the Church sought to establish itself as a political Papal Monarchy competing with Charlemagne's rule in Germany over the question of who was the greater authority, the secular rule of the king or the spiritual rule of the Pope. The Church began to raise her own armies to keep rebellious kings in line with Church doctrine. She raised her own money and jealously guarded her own privileges from secular governments. She had become an autonomous institution that transcended national boundaries.

The Eastern Orthodox Church also spread out beyond national boundaries, covering Eastern Europe and Russia. In North Africa and the Near East the Moslem religion became almost from the beginning a religion of conquest. Mohammed's followers quickly brought all of North Africa and the Near East under religious control. In the Orient Buddhism spread outwards from India to eventually encompass Southeast Asia and China. The Christian Church in the West, Islam in North Africa, and Buddhism in the east were the world's first large multi-national institutions. The religions of the Age of Pisces sought to become universal. The means through which they tried to achieve their growth was by becoming large self-sufficient institutions.

At the end of the Late Republic in the first century BCE the Roman Emperor Augustus created reforms that established in Rome a huge bureaucracy. Bureaucracies have little to do with government efficiency. It is a system that promotes job security within a labyrinth of self-serving positions within an administration. The mindless functioning of the bureaucracy in Rome kept the empire alive for centuries after it began to die. Rome was sacked and still she endured. A barbarian sat on the throne and still Rome remained Rome. The date 476 for the fall of Rome is mainly a historian's convenience. The populace of Rome most likely wasn't even aware that Rome had fallen. As German barbarians entered the city their politics were swallowed up in the bureaucracy. And since the 3rd and 4th centuries with the official acceptance of Christianity Roman bureaucracy was mainly staffed by Christian civil servants.

In China a similar administrative change took place. Beginning around 202 BCE the Han Empire began the process of transforming the Chinese government into a huge bureaucracy. For two thousand years Chinese culture remained essentially unchanged even under centuries of foreign domination because of the power of the bureaucracy to absorb foreigners and foreign ideas. During those periods of foreign rule the conquerors, within a century, became more Chinese than the Chinese themselves.

Law also grew into complete legal systems. Prior to the Principate of Rome, begun under Caesar Augustus, the law covered only major areas of contention with rulers or their lieutenants acting as arbiters in a case of law. Throughout most of the Age of Aries retribution was, in most part, left to the families involved to exact. Beginning with Augustus the law rapidly grew to encompass practically every aspect of life, and judgment in a case came to rest with professional jurists. During the first century of this age a class of jurists arose whose writings on points of law, including dissenting views in a case, collectively became the foundation for practically all subsequent legal jurisprudence. The law was now becoming an established and separate profession complete with permanent courts.

To support this change of legal view, from justice to legality, society began to slowly take upon itself the institutionalization of punishment for crimes. Prior to this age prison was just a holding place for offenders prior to trial. By the time of the Renaissance prison had become a punishment in its own right. Pisces rules prisons and imprisonment. Prison systems were expanding as functions of the legal system and of government.

Although Plato in his LAWS speaks of a prison system, no evidence exists of such an organized system. The huge increase in slavery in the last two centuries before the Age of Pisces began to change this picture radically. Slaves needed to be punished at times yet they were required for work; they could not be disfigured. Labor in the Roman mines became a punishment that brought in huge profits for the government. This began the evolution of a state run institution for controlled punishment. Eventually in the later Empire labor as punishment was expanded to include all members of society, not just slaves. When wars of conquest ended convict labor replaced slave labor as the bulk of prisoners sentenced to the mines.

Imprisonment, as a specific punishment was taken up by the Church during the Medieval Eras, and the secular arm of government followed suit after the 16th century. Since that time imprisonment as the punishment of choice has led to the huge state run penal systems we see in every country of the world today.

Health and medicine also grew into a separate bureaucratic institution during this age. During the previous age individual physicians tended the sick in patients homes. In rare instances only did a physician take a sick person into his or her own home for a few days. With the Age of Pisces this changed. In the West Rome began this process of creating hospitals in order to help their armies. They began to house their sick and wounded in buildings with many separate rooms in order to help keep their soldiers healthy and speed up recovery.

King Asoka in India built one of the very first hospitals in response to the Buddhist ideal of compassion. In a similar response to spiritual ideals, the Christian ideal of compassion, the Church took up the Roman initiative in medical care and created their own hospitals. During the early middle ages these were more welfare institutions and poor houses located outside city walls. With the rise of larger cities during the 13th century every city in Christendom and in the Moslem world had at least one hospital dedicated to the care of the poor and disabled. They were now built inside city walls. A new focus on justice and brotherhood grew up during the 19th century that spurred the evolution of the hospital into the much more modern caring medical institution that we are familiar with today.

There also is a parallel in education. As with law and medicine education was a social endeavor prior to Roman times. But with the Romans an institutional change always took place. Where the ancient Hebrews and Greeks, and perhaps Egyptians and Mesopotamians before them were thinkers, the Romans in their need to create social order set about the task of creating large social institutions around the various bodies of knowledge that they deemed important.

The Romans took education, a Mercury ruled Virgo opposite to Pisces concern, and created a very formal system of schooling consisting of a primary school, a grammar school and a rhetoric school (the forerunner of the modern college). As with everything else the Christian Church inherited this institution upon Rome's collapse. Medieval education continued this tradition teaching two sets or levels of knowledge. One was the quadrivium consisting of four subjects, the other the trivium with three subjects. The religious development of Scholasticism, a logical philosophical approach to religious understanding during the Late Medieval period, lead to the establishment of the first universities in the West. The literalism of the Protestant Reformation and the humanism and scientific thought of the Renaissance widened the scope of knowledge and the needs of education. This trend increased with the increase of science and other areas of knowledge growing into the educational system we are familiar with today.

This entire process of Pisces evolution has been directed by the opposing energy of Virgo. Virgo rules purity, chastity, humility, and healing. It rules analysis. It is a mental sign ruled by the planet Mercury, which rules the mind. In Virgo mythic fashion Christ is born of a virgin mother, and he came to us as a healer, full of humility, teaching the path of service.

In the historical process of this age the human interior, the spirit and the ego, became the focus of evolution. In Virgo fashion it needed to be purified. To purify it required a spiritual healing to release all of the collective fears, prejudices, and hatreds of humanity. This lead to the insane violence of this age alongside the rise of transcendental religions of belief and salvation. During this age the mystical aspects of our world religions and spirituality became the focus of our evolution. It has been taught in all religions that through meditation and prayer, through humble service, and through moral purity we open our minds and consciousness to the expansion of Pisces, to contact with heavenly worlds, bliss, and ecstasy. This will help prepare us for the enlightened Age of Aquarius.

As we prepare to enter the next Age of Aquarius in 2160, it will be the lessons we learned from Pisces/Virgo that will act as the foundation for what astrologically may easily be a true Golden Age of Enlightenment.

THE AGE OF AQUARIUS:
2160 TO 4320 CE

The next step in this historical evolution will be the promise of Aquarius after 2160 CE. Aquarius rules science, genius, levitation, immortality, and all possibilities. It rules brotherhood and world communication. It will be an age where humanity will learn to act from the consciousness of the spiritual, a necessary foundation received from Pisces, no longer needing to seek it so desperately.

Aquarius will be an age of great scientific achievement. Secrets of immortality will finally be discovered. Disease will be cured. People will discover laws of physics that allow for "miracles" such as levitation and other paranormal abilities and psychic talents as universal and everyday activities. The planet Mercury is exalted in Aquarius meaning the mental qualities of Mercury will find their greatest expression in this coming age. The spiritual ability of the God mind within each of us to create anything it wants without any technological limits will become a focus in Aquarius. Imagine the genius of the human mind being able to miraculously create with mental power alone. World communication, as an example, would become more telepathic without relying on technology.

The Aquarian rulership of mental genius combined with the attainment of all possibilities indicates the possibility that the miracles of Christ, and more, will become part of our repertoire of natural abilities. The humanist ideal that man can achieve all that he and she desires will become the next focus of evolution. The fabled magical powers of magicians and wizards out of fantasy will reveal laws of nature that we have yet to find that will support what we now call magic and spiritual powers as being very real and possible. The Age of Aquarius can become the spiritual and scientific golden age prophesied in all religions, the Millennium of Christ where bliss, happiness and glory will become the norm. The science of this next age will no longer be limited by its present prejudice against esoteric traditions. What is now considered esoteric, or hidden knowledge, will become a part of mainstream science. Religion will become scientific, redefined in scientific terminology. All in all it promises to be a truly wonderful age.

Leo is the opposite sign to Aquarius. It will direct the unfoldment of Aquarius energy. Leo rules aristocracy, ego, and rulership. It also rules omnipotence, omniscience, and the spirit. It is ruled by the Sun, the solar brilliance of the patriarchal godhead. With the Leo opposite energy humanity, and the religious and spiritual traditions of Aquarius, will proceed from the premise that every man, woman, and child is, within themselves, the son or daughter of God, learning their own abilities to perform miracles. We will feel as if we are gods. We will inherit spiritual aristocracy from the Father, as well as the Mother. We will become omniscient and omnipotent.

Within the context of a strong spiritual matrix learned in the Age of Pisces, Leo will teach people to become the sons and daughters of God. As we each become spiritually strong within we will reach out into society, into science and technology, with greater levels of creativity. We will stimulate higher levels of genius and scientific advances in Aquarius as we strive to achieve all possibilities.

THE SIGNS OF THE TIMES
THE ERAS OF THE AGE OF PISCES

Time is very fluid, flowing easily from moment to moment within a smooth continuous dance. Each block or chunk of time has its own evolution within its lifespan. Ages do not clunk from one age to another with sudden, jarring movement, one long unrelenting age of Aries suddenly and loudly banging into the next long Age of Pisces. There is growth involved. An Age is born, matures and dies through a series of twelve astrological eras that guide the age's lifespan. Each era is 180 years long with twelve eras equaling 2160 years. The sequence of these eras is, for some reason, reversed from the backwards precessional cycle of the ages. They flow in the forward astrological direction from Aries to Taurus around to Pisces.

Before an age is birthed there is a gestation period of growth within the womb of the previous age much like the pregnancy of human beings. This process begins with the Scorpio Era, some 720 years prior to the end of the mother age, the age that gives birth to the new, young age. At this point within the age there is a death of that age as a distinct and separate time period. The seeds are planted within its womb for the next age to begin its own growth. In the following Sagittarius Era of that age, a flowering of energies occurs. Sagittarius is a fire sign and rules vision. There is a vision of the future that grows from within the body of the mother and she begins to glow with new life. It is at this time, Scorpio-Sagittarius, that history begins to spin off in new directions. In our own times, our present Age of Pisces, the Renaissance in Europe carried with it the new Aquarian ideals of humanism and science, trends of history that have remained powerfully with us through the last few centuries leading us to the future in Aquarius.

In the last age the spiritual and religious revolution most powerfully seen in the Age of Pisces, began as early as the 6th and 7th centuries BCE, in the Scorpio and Sagittarius Eras of the Age of Aries. The Hebrew Prophetic Revolution began the process of changing Judaism into a universal mystical religion. Zoroaster in Mesopotamia created Zoroastrianism. Lao Tzu reintroduced Taoism to the Orient and Confucius created an ethical religion in China. Buddha redefined the transcendent nature of the universe in India. And in Hinduism the minor gods led by Indra and Agni, were replaced in importance with the mystical transcendent gods of Shiva, Brahma and Vishnu. These spiritual developments grew to create the spiritual focus of the Age of Pisces.

Even earlier the warfare of the Age of Aries did not arise catastrophically overnight. Centuries before, in the Scorpio and Sagittarius eras of the Age of Taurus Sumerians began creating small armies or police forces, armed with bronze weapons, to protect convoys of state owned wealth and raw materials in a time of increasing individual violence. It would seem that the warrior societies that suddenly rode into Egypt and Mesopotamia with Aries must have grown into their warrior vision over some several centuries, nurturing their vision and maturing until the Age of Aries called them out to battle.

The eras have a powerful influence on history and the collective unconscious. Without going into too much depth we should take a brief look at some of these eras to get a greater understanding of time and of history.

The eras flow in a forward progression, Aries, Taurus, Gemini, Cancer, Leo, Virgo, Libra, Scorpio, Sagittarius, Capricorn, Aquarius, and Pisces. Those eras that are fire signs, Aries, Leo and Sagittarius are host to large numbers of "golden ages" of various cultures. In the Aries Era it was most notably the glory of the newly created Roman Empire. In Leo it was the golden age of Charlemagne in Europe, Alfred the Great in Britain and the Golden Baghdad Caliphate in the Islamic empire. It was also the golden age of the Tang Dynasty in China. In Sagittarius it was the glory of the various Renaissances in Europe, a Renaissance in Persia, a golden age in the Ming Dynasty in China, and the golden resurgence of culture in the Aztec and Inca empires in the New World. These fire signs are times when cultures and nations have a greater tendency to flare up brightly with the fire of creativity.

A Brief Look at the Eras

Aries Era: 0 to 180 CE

This Aries Era within the Age of Pisces, 0 to 180 CE, is mainly an extension of the previous Age of Aries. Aries is the first sign of the zodiac and is the sign of new birth. Aries rules war and fighting. This is a period of new beginnings. Here the great Roman Empire is created with Rome expanding her frontiers to their farthest extent under Trajan. Rome produced her greatest emperors and generals during this time from Caesar Augustus (27 BCE to 4 CE) to Vespasian, Nerva, Trajan, Hadrian, and Marcus Aurelius. Fighting in the Roman army as a career option gained unheard of popularity during this era. The army was flooded with so many applicants that many were turned away. Recruits were forced to seek letters of recommendation and even patrons in order to enlist. Victory arches erected for victorious generals became very popular and many generals actually instigated wars on the frontiers in order to have an arch erected in their honor.

The Libra opposite to Aries rules legal and social codes. Since the beginning of the Age of Aries codes of law have become increasingly important. Now with the Age of Pisces those codes become large institutions. Begun under Augustus the law began to expand to include vast areas of interaction. Three areas of law were created: civil law, common law which included all peoples and their property regardless of nationality or citizenship, and natural law, an extension of Stoicism which saw all men as equal and entitled to certain basic rights. Permanent courts were established staffed by professional jurists. These jurists were allowed certain individual freedoms to comment on cases before the court and their opinions were written down and eventually became the foundation for the creation of the modern legal system in the West.

TAURUS ERA: 180 TO 360 CE

The subsequent Taurus Era witnessed a change in focus towards money and the economy. Taurus rules money, banking, and wealth and Pisces rules dissolution. The emperor Commodus came to the throne in 180 and immediately began to drain the treasury with extravagant gladiatorial fights and huge feasts. The treasury then had to be regularly refilled which was often accomplished by plundering the rich Roman cities in the east and by confiscating the estates of rich individuals and families. Following the reign of Commodus in 193 CE the treasury was so depleted that the throne was actually auctioned off to the highest bidder. It was a short-lived experiment. Soon after, with the rule of Caracalla in 211, citizenship was extended to all peoples of the empire in order to widen the available tax base.

Rome became progressively more bankrupt during the third century. The main focus of Roman administration was trying to deal with their failing economy. In 180 the silver content of the denarius was 68%. By 270 it was down to a mere .02%. Throughout the West money virtually disappeared and with it went banking, business and all commerce. The Scorpio opposite rulership of taxation was also apparent during this time. Taxation was increased to unbearable proportions which itself ruined whole cities. Administrators living in Roman cities were burdened with the responsibility for any uncollected taxes. If they were uncollected they were to be taken out of the pockets of those administrators. As money disappeared taxes were increasingly paid in produce and in goods. Eventually unable to collect taxes at all administrators fled to the Taurean peace and quiet of the country. Most cities in Europe during the third century were virtually abandoned.

Inflation rose rapidly along with greed and corruption. The army became unpopular as a vocation, in stark contrast to the previous era. Conscription was reinstated in order to keep Roman military strength up to minimum levels. Rome turned to paying tribute to Germanic tribes on the frontier rather than relying on the lost fighting ability of her armies. Many peasants turned to selling their children in order to escape the heavy financial burden.

The heavy financial disaster of the third century was finally halted when Diocletion ascended to the throne in 284. He created the Roman caste system, in true Taurus fashion, binding all people to their professions and made those professions hereditary. Sons were required to remain in the professions of their fathers. He also instituted wage and price freezes in order to halt the rampant inflation.

Even with the halt of economic decline under Diocletian heavy taxation continued. The West was an essentially poor area to begin with and Diocletian's efforts could not bring back prosperity. After 305 he abdicated the throne and Constantine took his place. Constantine subsequently moved the seat of the empire to the new city of Constantinople in the economically more prosperous east. At the same time Rome was failing economically the new Christian Church grew and became a cohesive force. The religion went from a collection of individual churches to a unified and centralized religion that by 360 was impervious to any political decisions by the empire.

The Church grew very rich while the empire went bankrupt. As people tried to find security in the economic disaster of the third century they began to donate all of their wealth and belongings to the Church in exchange for a secure life within the bounds and welfare of the growing Church.

GEMINI ERA: 360 TO 540

Gemini is the sign of the twins. It rules the process of division. It rules travel, and movement. One of the most dramatic historical developments we see during this era is the sudden rise in mass movements collectively known as the Barbarian Invasions. Germanic incursions into Roman territory had begun as early as the second century BCE and there had been a steady stream of movement into the empire ever since. But after 360 that stream quite suddenly became a flood that had disastrous results for

Rome. The Huns, coming from the east, conquered the Ostrogoths in 375 forcing, through the ferocity of their fighting, the Visigoths into Roman territory. The Visigoths defeated a Roman army in 378 and rolled into Italy. In 410 under Alaric they plundered Rome before moving into southern Gaul. In 406 the Vandals entered Spain and from there they moved to North Africa in 429. Using Carthage as a naval base the Vandals attacked and plundered Rome in 455.

The Huns, led by Attila, set out for Constantinople in 445 before turning west. In 452 they were halted at the gates of Rome ostensibly by the intercession of Pope Leo I. In 476 Odovacar, chieftain of the Scirians, deposed the Roman emperor Romulus Augustulus and made himself emperor. It is this date that is assigned as the official fall of Rome. After Attila's death the Ostrogoths regained their own freedom from the Huns and under Theodoric they conquered Rome in 489.

At the beginning of the fifth century Roman legions were recalled from Britain to defend the empire against the Germanic tribes. After Roman legions left for Rome, Jutes, Angles, and Saxons subsequently began their own movements from their homelands on the North Sea. In 568, 28 years after this era ended, the Lombards entered Italy, becoming the last of the great Barbarian invaders to plague the empire.

Countering this mass movement of Germanic peoples into Rome, the Church, both from Rome and from Constantinople, sponsored their own movement out into the lands and peoples of the frontier. Missionaries in large numbers were sent out and new churches established. The missionaries sent out into Germanic areas were the only people who could read and write. In Gemini fashion this skill took on paramount importance. Gemini rules language and writing. Missionaries began by copying down local myths and legends. Their ability to read back these legends impressed the locals who then looked upon the missionaries with greater respect. As they copied these myths they took the liberty to also alter them adding in Christian ideas and concepts of morality. Germanic people slowly became dependent upon missionaries for the retelling of their myths and Germanic religions were, in the process, Christianized.

As the barbarians moved into Rome they were themselves

becoming Romanized, and more importantly, Christianized. Missionaries became the administrators of justice and the holders of tradition within Germanic society. They became the new European elite at the same time that Germans were deposing Romans as rulers of the empire.

The second major historical tendency of this era lay in the Mercury ruled Gemini area of division and multiplication. In the previous Taurus Era Constantine moved the capital of the empire to the east, to Constantinople. That move was economically motivated. By 395, with Gemini, the empire was now officially split in two. The western empire centered in Rome was constantly beset by the problem of the Germanic invasions. The eastern empire centered in Constantinople was wealthier than the west and far more able to fend off the Germans. Still with all her wealth she was beset internally by often crippling divisions between power blocks that seriously hampered imperial administration throughout this era.

The Church also split into two separate churches. The Greek Orthodox Church became the official church of the eastern empire while the Catholic Church remained the official church in the west. There was also a further split within the Church between regular clergy comprising monks serving under powerful abbots, and the secular clergy consisting of the Pope, bishops, and the rest of the political hierarchy within the Church.

Ideas further split the Church. The concept of heresy was originally taken to mean simply an incorrect view of proper Christian dogma. In this Gemini Era heresy increased dramatically, with differing views taking on intellectual importance. Powerful factions rose up to contend with the established orthodox view with the result that heresy came to be seen as an outright crime, an offense to God. The Church was split into several different ideologies each with huge followings that arrayed themselves against the accepted orthodox or catholic view. In North Africa and Syria the Monophysite movement rejected the Orthodox Trinitarian idea of a three-part god. They believed in a single unified God, an idea that would support the rise of Islam two centuries later.

While the western world was assailed with forces that divided and fragmented her, the Gupta Dynasty in India entered a golden age based on the Gemini quality of intellectual inquiry. When Christianity came to be the only legal religion within the empire

Christians took the opportunity to turn the tables on those who had persecuted them in the past. Christians began persecuting non-Christians along with Christian heretics with relish. Many of these fled to India where they were readily accepted. Their various religious views were fused into the great tapestry of Hindu religious thought resulting in a golden age.

CANCER ERA: 540 TO 720 CE

Cancer rules security and protection. Some picture Cancer as the enclosing arms of the mother cradling and nurturing her baby. Cancer rules women, nurturing, and community. The sign Cancer is associated with foundations and the beginnings of society. The Neolithic Revolution during the Age of Cancer domesticated man and created the agricultural foundations for the growth of community and eventually civilization.

Prior to 540 CE monasticism was a rather haphazard and individual institution. In 540 St. Benedict created his famous monastic order, which combined discipline and order with agriculture as an economic foundation. Life in the monastery became very much more community oriented than before. In 577 St. Benedict's rule reached Pope Gregory the Great. Because of its agricultural base Gregory pushed this rule as the norm for all future monastic endeavors. This focus was aided by disease bringing into focus the Pisces Age energy underlying this Cancer Era. The dissolution of agriculture, community, home, and nurturing.

In 541 the Great Plague of Justinian spread from Egypt to Constantinople. It killed so many people that it brought European agriculture to a halt. At its height it killed over 5000 people a day in Constantinople. The sudden lack of farmers and agriculture created a devastating famine that, combined with the disease, affected Europe, the Near East, and Asia for the next 60 to 70 years. The disease combined with petty tribal fighting between Germanic tribes dramatically depopulated Europe. The result was that the land reverted back to its wild state. Pisces rules dissolution, and in this Age of Pisces the Cancer focus on agriculture created a condition where agriculture came to a halt. This plague killed so many people and dispirited the rest that Europe quickly sank into what has been called the Dark Ages. The population decline was so severe that a law was enacted that forbade any woman of childbearing age from entering a monastery. As few women ever lived beyond childbearing age during this time this meant all women, regardless of age, were banned from monasteries.

Cancer rules property and boundaries. Monasticism, because it was essentially self-contained in Cancer fashion and did not require a nearby secular settlement for its success, became the dominant form of Christianity at this time. Irish missionaries spread throughout the mainland of Europe spreading the idea of monasticism to a much-depleted Europe. In 597 Pope Gregory the Great responded to the popularity of the Irish monastic system, sending the monk Augustine to take over and thus control monasticism for Rome.

Because of the agricultural focus of Benedict's Rule, and because of the protective walls of these monasteries, in addition to the promise of Christian salvation, monastery life came to be seen as the only way out of a very bleak existence. The monks in these monastic communities led the thrust to re-establish agriculture in Europe. They cleared forests and drained swamps. In 598 the Slavs introduced a new lightweight plow that enabled farmers to open up virgin clay-heavy soil to production. Monasteries were the centers of this activity. They learned about soil conditions and soon became the best and most knowledgeable farmers in all of Europe. Many who had land holdings willed their lands to monasteries in return for a secure and well-ordered life. In this manner the Church became the largest and wealthiest landowner in Europe.

In North Africa the Arabs were organized loosely around the tribal unit. Around 630 the Prophet Mohammed founded the Islamic religion, the foundation for the Saracenic civilization, a theocracy. Following the death of Mohammed this religion became strongly concerned, in Cancer fashion, with acquiring land and creating the caliphate, a political unit designed to oversee a theocratic Islamic political empire. The faithful quickly spread out conquering and acquiring land for their new religion. In less than a century they gained control of half the western civilized world from the border of India to the Straits of Gibraltar. The caliphate kept the new religion under the Saracenic civilization cohesive and successful.

In the New World there is possibly evidence of a similar "dark age" to the one that plagued Europe. The Mayan civilization in the Yucatan in Mexico was approaching the height of their great achievements when, suddenly, around 600 they lost all that they had built. Farther north near Mexico City is Teotihuacan, the impressive site of the pyramids of the Sun and the Moon. Around 600 the population of Teotihuacan suddenly dropped very sharply and by 700 the city was abandoned and deliberately burned. Was a severe plague or series of diseases involved? Was agriculture similarly affected creating famine?

LEO ERA: 720 TO 900 CE

Leo is ruled by the brilliance of the Sun. Leo is a masculine sign and the Sun, which rules Leo, has come to symbolize, in many patriarchal religions, the ultimate God. Leo rules spirit, omniscience, and omnipotence, but there is more. Leo is pictured as the lion, king of the zodiacal jungle. Apollo the Sun God was the god of fine arts, music, and poetry. He was the patron of the "fiery" creative arts. His sign Leo is a fire sign and due to that elemental designation it is a sign that rules golden ages, or acts as a rich period of time for cultural golden ages to flourish. And that is what history reveals most profoundly during this era.

In 751 Pepin established the Carolingian Dynasty and in 800 Charlemagne reestablished Pope Leo III in Rome and was crowned by the Pope in turn. The Pope then bowed down to the king. This simple act had far reaching Leonine consequences. Popes could henceforth anoint kings reserving for themselves the right to confer legitimacy and supernatural authority over kings. In return even Popes bowed down to secular kings in order to insure secular survival in God's society. With this unity between Church and state Europe entered into a golden age known as the Carolingian Revival.

Charlemagne, for whom this golden age is named, brought the best scholars from all over Europe to his capital at Aachen where they were given the freedom, in Leo-Aquarius fashion, to pursue their own studies within their own areas of interest. This learning led to the establishment of higher quality schools and libraries in several monasteries in Western Europe during the ninth century. Under him a more refined written script called Carolingian miniscule was created that led to a standardization of calligraphy and literature in the West that we still use in an altered form today. Art flourished in architecture, as Charlemagne sought to beautify his capital city, and in smaller Christian art treasures where gold and jewels were elaborately used. In much of this art Christ is shown nailed to the cross but not in obvious pain. Rather he is portrayed as majestic and Leonine.

The Catholic Church also entered into a golden age of its own. Soon after Pepin created the Carolingian Dynasty in 751 he gave to the Church St. Peters church, the city of Ravenna and five Adriatic coastal cities. This Donation of Pepin became the Papal States wherein the Church could exercise her own temporal powers. Under Charlemagne the Church's dream of a unified and universal Christian society was realized.

After the death of Charlemagne the Church was able to push its claim of superiority over secular kings to completion under Pope Nicholas I from 856 to 867. In Leonine fashion, Leo ruling aristocracy, will, and dominance, Nicholas merely acted superior, expecting kings to automatically respect his right to rule over them. He established an independent Papal Monarchy that at least temporarily had exclusive rule over its vast domain.

As the Holy Roman Empire created by Charlemagne broke up, Alfred the Great created a golden age of culture in England between 871 and 899. He united England and then undertook a cultural and intellectual regeneration, attracting renowned scholars to his court.

In the Arab Empire of the Moslems, the Abbasid Dynasty over-threw the Omayyid Caliphate in 750 and moved the capital to Baghdad. From there Islamic culture entered a brilliant golden age of learning and artistic endeavor. Baghdad rivaled the splendor of Byzantium both in her architecture, where the Moslem mosque began to take shape, and in her visual arts.

Islamic literary achievements were equally important. They accumulated writings of every sort during this era, including the writings of the Classical Greeks. Their translations would later enter Europe and reintroduce classical thought to the

Christian world.

The Tang Dynasty in China also brought with it a brilliant golden age of cultural achievement. But as we are looking at the Leo Era, these golden ages often mix with yet another Leo quality; the heroic love of fighting. Within the unity of the Tang Dynasty the country began to break up into smaller localized areas ruled by warlords. It has been estimated that under Tang rule there were no fewer than 700 military rebellions finally leading to a feudalistic society under the Tang. Fighting increased because it was now an exciting and enjoyable pastime for men of noble birth. The aristocracy became a warrior aristocracy and lords became warlords.

In Europe Charlemagne was the supreme warlord. He instituted concepts of medieval loyalty and the sworn inquest. Leo rules loyalty, oath, and allegiance. Charlemagne created the hierarchy of vassalage based on allegiance and loyalty, and on reciprocal obligation. Vassals were warriors who swore oaths of allegiance to their chosen lord and in return lords gave lands, or fiefs, to their vassals. Vassals belonged to their lords in some respects, but in Leo fashion those lords belonged to their vassals as well. Lords were expected to earn the right to be lord. They were expected to treat their vassals with deep respect and support, equal to what he expected from them. From this feudal concept the military function was seen as of paramount importance. The warrior aristocracy emerged in the name of "the Knightly Class".

Towards the end of the 8th century the Scandinavian people responded to the Leonine love of fighting mounting expeditions of plunder into Christian Europe and the British Isles. These were not yet movements of people as seen in the 10th century. They were hit and run attacks, the Viking warrior seeking the same excitement in combat that the European warrior sought.

In the Islamic world the same tendency arose almost at the same time that the Abbasid golden age was flourishing. Local governors were already becoming more independent weakening the central government of Baghdad. In the later literature of both civilizations the romantic heroism of this era's greatest warriors would stand as the only tales worth telling. The Song of Roland, written centuries after he died, glorified the Leonine ideals of this era. Charlemagne (Charles the Great), Alfred the Great, Charles "the Hammer" Martel, and Roland remained the premier heroes of Medieval

Europe until the Renaissance. Leo rules legendary figures giving to the heroes of this era power to incite the imagination even centuries later. In North Africa Harun al-Rashid served as the prototype for the Islamic classic *The Tale of a Thousand and One Nights.*

VIRGO ERA: 900 TO 1080 CE

Virgo is the sign of the Virgin, symbolic not only of sexual continence, but also of purity and health, both physical and mental. Mentally Virgo is a sign that signifies a condition of self-analysis and self-improvement. Virgo, like Gemini, is ruled by the planet Mercury. Mercury rules the lower mind and logical thinking processes. The Virgo focus on purity and chastity is thus deeply connected to the mind as well as the body.

Because of the Mercury rulership of this era we find strong similarities to the Gemini Era between 360 and 540. Division and fragmentation, and mass migrations, again tear at the fabric of society.

Based upon the love of fighting society had structured itself, in the previous era, into a feudalistic warrior society. The barbarian Norsemen merely raided the British Isles and Europe throughout the 9th century. But by the end of that century a change has been noted. The Vikings were no longer content to raid for the excitement of battle and glory. Now in the 10th century they began to move, colonizing as they went. They entered Normandy in 911 and eventually went as far as Sicily and the Aegean. In 985 the Danes had conquered England and in 1066 the Norsemen invaded Britain and established a Norman kingdom there. They ventured west to Greenland and in 1002 Leif Erickson, blown off course by a storm, discovered the New World, landing at Newfoundland. In the other direction Viking ships sailed Germany's big rivers migrating all the way to Russia. They established the city of Kiev and subsequently the new Russian nation.

As the Vikings were streaming into Europe and elsewhere, a counter movement of European Christian missionaries entered into the Scandinavian homeland of the Vikings. In addition to the missionary movements into Scandinavia, the need for travel and movement surfaced in the form of the pilgrimage to the Holy Land during the 11th century. Pilgrimages to the Holy Land became common throughout this century. At the same time other peoples from northern and eastern Europe also began their own migrations into the heartland of Christian Europe, among them the Slavs and the Magyars in a scene reminiscent of the Germanic migrations into the empire of Rome in the 5th and 6th centuries. And in Mexico with the Post Classic Period of the Maya, the Toltecs along with other upland tribes from middle Mexico began migrating into the Peten Maya area creating a demoralizing effect and a reversion to Archaism.

The other main parallel between Virgo and Gemini is in the area of social and political division. Virgo rules fragmentation. Following the Treaty of Verdun in 843, which divided Charlemagne's empire among his three grandsons, the central authority of the king began to diminish. As we enter the 10th century, and the Virgo Era, the king could no longer maintain the loyalty of his vassals. They had become essentially their own lords, and the king was now wholly dependent upon their support for his position. The king was so in title only. Feudalism in the 10th century developed into a new way of life because of the small and fragmented nature of society rather than because of the glory of the fight. It had now become an economic necessity.

Europe was now divided up into small sections of land only large enough for one man to rule. He was lord of the manor and feudalism quickly became Manoralism. The manor was self-contained with all the various craftspeople required to sustain the individual manoral society. At the same time trade between towns or population centers ground to a complete halt. Manors became isolated communities. Europe fragmented.

On the national level even after the Holy Roman Empire was reunited by Otto the Great, Europe still remained extremely fragmented. Otto's reign was plagued by almost constant revolt as was the reign of his successor, Otto III. Within the Church the papacy reached its lowest point of internal unity through this era. Religious administrative fragmentation served to make the papacy a mere pawn in European politics. Infighting was rampant within the Church with different factions constantly fighting amongst themselves. The division between the Eastern Orthodox Church centered in Constantinople and the Catholic Church in the West finally became permanent with the Great Schism in 1054.

The Byzantine Empire also experienced the disintegration of Virgo as political control disintegrated into a chronic condition of internal factionalism between the aristocracy and the bureaucracy as well as a struggle between a military faction and an intellectual faction.

The new Russian nation established by Viking settlers began as a loose collection of cities severely hampered by political fragmentation. In China the feudalism of the Tang Dynasty further fragmented into the dominant social organization throughout this era.

In the Arab world political unity also disintegrated. Local officials throughout the empire took to themselves the titles of emir and sultan as they increasingly ruled over a fragmented feudal empire. In 929 the Omayyid Caliphate was reestablished at Cordoba in Spain dividing the Islamic political world against the Abbasid Caliphate. By 1031 the Cordoba Caliphate had disintegrated into small feudal states that would make it easier for Europe to later reconquer Spain. In Egypt the Fatimids further divided the Abbasid Caliphate by setting up their own dynasty. By 1057 the Abbasid Caliphate had disintegrated to the point of surrendering, without a fight, all of their temporal powers to the Sultan of the Seljuk Turks. In the religion of the Faithful constant civil wars and revolts divided religious teachers and their teachings. Religious thought broke down into extremes of mysticism and fanaticism.

Like Gemini, the Mercury rulership of this era gives to it a focus on crafts and working with the hands. Out of the manoral closed society, crafts people in each manor or town became essential to life as they supplied everything needed for survival as well as for comfort. There was no trade during this era. From this self-contained system crafts guilds were created in order to insure a certain minimum level of quality as well as to perpetuate crafts knowledge. The Virgo Era earth quality of administration urged these craftspeople to create a governing system that would allow for the transmission of craft knowledge to young apprentices within the manor. In larger towns and cities these guilds further served to control the local job market. No one was allowed to practice a trade without belonging to a local guild thus protecting local jobs from outsiders moving to a town and competing with the established market.

The intellectual mental quality of Mercury, the ruling planet, directed these guilds towards an educational end. These crafts guilds slowly began to take on the task of collecting and disseminating a wider field of knowledge. Some expanded to become trade schools, and some of these then became our first universities. The oldest university in Europe was established in Salerno, Italy dating from the 11th century. Not quite as fragmented as Europe the Islamic world also developed their own institutes for higher learning at this same time. Their oldest universities date also from the 11th century, in Cairo, Egypt and in Toledo, Spain.

Perhaps the most important endeavors in this era were in the area of medicine and the Virgo concern with health. The most outstanding thinker of this era was an Arab physician known to the West as Avicenna. His *Canon of Medicine* was so well organized and written that it became the standard for European medicine for centuries.

With the rise in medical knowledge the Saracens also began to organize and build modern hospitals for the care of the sick. Thirty-four great hospitals are known to have been built in the major Islamic cities of Persia, Syria, and Egypt. Arab physicians such as Al-Tasrif and Arab alchemists discovered many new drugs as well as the process of contagion. They also discovered the nature of measles and small pox.

LIBRA ERA: 1080 TO 1260 CE

The sign Libra is pictured today as the scales, a device that weighs in the balance pairs of opposites, including relationships and action. Libra is concerned with social codes of conduct including law codes in order to insure social balance and harmony. The scales as the symbol for Libra are of Roman origin. The older Egyptian interpretation saw the Libra symbol as the Sun rising over the horizon. Libra is the seventh sign of the zodiac and the first sign to rise above the horizon as one travels around the circle. Libra indicates the rise of culture and society out of the slow historical elements of the lower half of the zodiac, into an environment of cultural exuberance signified by the signs above the horizon. Libra is ruled by the planet Venus, which also rules Taurus, and Venus imparts a need for beauty and prosperity.

Now that we have entered into the Libra Era we enter into a whole new area of history. The zodiac is naturally divided into two halves, from the first house to the seventh. This axis is marked astrologically by a line that indicates the ascendant, or rising sign, at the beginning of the first house, and the descendent at the beginning of the seventh house. The first six signs of the zodiac, Aries through Virgo, occupy the lower arc of the circle. This lower half of the zodiac wheel astrologers attribute overall to introversion and introspection. There is a tendency here for a slower more inward expression of life that is not conducive to great expressions of cultural liveliness.

With the Libra Era we enter the top half of the wheel of life occupied by the upper six signs, Libra through Pisces. These signs astrologically relate to an overall trend of extroversion and cultural exuberance. History seems to become much fuller.

Towards the end of the 11th century, just as the Libra Era was beginning to emerge, the Libra energy of socializing, of interacting with one's environment, stimulated the revival of trade. Libra rules trade. Merchants and artisans began to set up stalls along the outside walls of their local churches. This began a process of commercial expansion in Europe. Towns grew up around these stalls, followed by cities as merchants grew wealthier. Venice, a satellite of Byzantium, grew in strength during the 12th century because of a growing trade with the east and supported by her strong navy. She was able to break away from Byzantine control and by 1204 she controlled the Cyclades, many Aegean islands and much of the Black Sea coasts. Following her lead Genoa and Pisa both began to create their own maritime trading empires. Located on the north coast of the Black Sea Trebizond rose to become a powerful Greek trading center.

Most trade between Europe and Asia came overland. The Mongols invaded Eastern Europe and Russia between 1200 and 1260. Genghis Khan then set up a very safe and efficient trade route through his empire between Europe and the Orient. He built the best roads since the famous roads of the early Roman Empire in the Aries Era. He established roadhouses and set up a system of speedy communication. He encouraged trade and his soldiers policed the road insuring a peaceful flow of trade. With the increased ease of trade to Europe the first international trade fair was held in Champagne during this time.

By the end of this era merchants in northern Europe had banded together to create the commercial Hanseatic League. Increased trade and merchandise brought people in increasing numbers into the new and expanding cities. In this era Europe changed from a rural society to an urban society. By 1100 Europe was becoming wealthy enough to embark on a building campaign of tremendous proportions. The century from 1150 to 1250 is known as the Age of the Great Cathedrals. They employed the new Gothic architecture built to express a soaring spirit. Libra rules beauty, grace, and architecture. These cathedrals were built much higher than older church styles. This required the Aries opposite quality of engineering in order to solve these problems, such as the invention of the external flying buttress.

With the new urban attitude education passed from the old monastery schools to the new urban cathedrals. While guilds sold their wares next to the walls of cathedrals the cathedral itself became the home of the new university. Libra rules literacy. As the new cathedrals were built they became a forum for an expanding liberal arts education as well as the traditional knowledge important to the guilds. Between 1200 and 1250 seventy new universities were established in Europe.

One of the more dynamic historical trends during this era was the creation of legal systems and the rise of national monarchies. Libra rules law codes. The Papal Monarchy, created in the Leo Era between 720 and 900, was revived in 1073 by Pope Gregory VII. It reached its height of power and splendor under Pope Innocent III (1198-1216). The driving force for this revival was the law. In the Virgo Era the primary Church concern was piety, purity, and religious devotion. Beginning with Libra, however, that concern changed to a legalistic focus. In this era the Church created the sacramental theory explaining the seven sacraments, thus creating a far-reaching social code of spiritual conduct that covered virtually everyone. The Church created laws governing every conceivable action or question and they established a system of legal judgment where all local decisions were overseen by Rome.

Any local decision could be appealed ultimately to the Papal court, including decisions rendered by secular courts throughout Europe. Through the law the Church controlled virtually every aspect of European life.

With the law as the new social yardstick increasing numbers of clergymen were running afoul of the law. Because of their positions within the Church, and because they could always appeal to the Papal court, they were almost always let off with a mild reprimand. As a result secular courts were powerless to bring those offenders to justice. Secular rulers, in response, were forced to strengthen their own legal systems to counter this problem.

In the middle of the 12th century England's Henry II instituted reforms that allowed either party in a dispute to call the sheriff to bring both plaintiff and defendant along with twelve citizens who knew the facts together before a judge. The twelve were then asked under oath if the plaintiff's statements were true or not, and the judge then issued his verdict on this basis. Out of this grew the trial by jury system of modern jurisprudence.

Henry also set up a system whereby local sheriffs were required to bring before the state appointed jurists who traveled around the country in order to apply the law uniformly throughout the country. They would be familiar with local conditions. These men, under oath, were required to report on every case of robbery, arson, murder, and any other crime they knew of since their last judicial visit. This was the beginning of the Grand Jury. To help him make these changes Henry gathered around himself a staff of the most eminent lawyers to advise him on which laws should be enforced. Like the Roman jurists of the Aries Era, the traveling judges began to set certain precedents based upon their decisions that came to supplant local customs. These precedents came to be known as English Common Law.

In 1164 Henry issued the Constitution of Clarendon, which declared that any clergyman accused of a crime must be taken to a royal court first. Thomas a' Beckett, the Archbishop of Canterbury, stood up against this constitution and was murdered. This act shocked England so severely that Henry's attempt to bring the clergy under secular law was abandoned. Henry's son, King John, was forced, in 1215, to sign into law the famous Magna Carta. This document holds that no man can be imprisoned or punished without a legal judgment by his peers or by the law of the land. It said in essence that the law is greater than the king. John of Salisbury further forwarded a legal theory that defined a person's right in such a judicial system, including the right to rise up and put a tyrant to death. The king's function was to administer the law, not to make it or change it at will.

In Germany Frederic Barbarossa abolished the traditional trial by ordeal replacing it with a strengthened royal legal system. Later in the era Louis IX of France established the right of appeal from lower courts to his own royal court.

The strength of the Papal Monarchy lay in canon law. Behind the national interest in strengthening their own secular legal systems, secular governments became more cohesive and national monarchies began to emerge. In 1152 Frederic Barbarossa officially established the Holy Roman Empire under that name completing the process begun by Charlemagne 350 years earlier. In England the rise to national monarchy was begun by Henry II in 1154. Phillip Augustus established a French monarchy in 1180.

This era also witnessed an explosion in literature. Libra rules literature. _The Poem of the Cid_ and _The Song of Roland_ were written in this era extolling the heroic ideals of the legendary heroes of the Leo Era. The Arthurian legends were compiled into one long literary cycle. The French poet Chretien de Troyes invented the Arthurian hero Sir Lancelot and added a Libran romantic twist to the story. He also took a Welsh myth about the lovers Tristan and Isolde and expanded that into a beautiful piece of literature. Later the German poet Gottfried von Strassburg would adapt and complete that story giving it its ideal medieval form. At the same time Wolfram von Eschenbach expanded upon the Parzival legend giving it what is considered its most perfect form. The foundations of modern literature were created.

Literature flourished in other ways as well. The Guliardi, followers of one Gulias, wrote pagan poems professing the joys of love and physical sensuality. Libra rules love, affection, and enjoyment. The continuing romance of Aucassin and Nicolette, somewhat on the bawdy side, was a favorite of the growing merchant class. And the Fabliaux were a series of short stories that were indecent and made fun of priests and monks.

These literary accomplishments were preceded by the songs of the Troubadours beginning about 1087 in Provence in southern France. They sang about romantic love and in their songs woman was idealized as a beautiful unattainable noble lady. From the songs of the Troubadours love as the central theme grew in potency to become the most powerful redeeming force in the universe. Controversy raged over whether this love was at its most harmonious as the faithful affection between husband and wife, or whether it could even be sustained by the strains of wedlock. Here true love must be between a knight and mistress. In any event codes of conduct were required between men and women.

While most men were off fighting in the Crusades women were left at home with more autonomy than they had ever known. Eleanor of Aquitane, Queen of France and England, her daughter Mary of Champagne, and her granddaughter Blanche of Castille set about the task of creating codes of etiquette and the art of manners. They established the Late Medieval Courts of Love, and through their efforts the position of upper class women in Europe were considerably elevated. These ideals became the backbone of a new code of Chivalry based on manners and an idealized love of an unattainable lady.

The Aries opposite to Libra rules war and fighting. This was the era of the Crusades. The Seljuk Turks were in control of the Holy Land and as trade returned to Europe and their horizon expanded Europeans began to think about bringing Jerusalem back to Christendom. Between 1096 and 1244 there were four major crusades and numerous minor ones, sent to relieve the Holy Land from the "evil" Turks. As European population increased during this era, fighting began to break out throughout the continent. One of the reasons for continuing the Crusades past the first one (the only successful Crusade) was that a crusade was very efficient for channeling much of the growing Aries energy towards a common outside enemy. Libra rules both marriage and open enemies. All too often these mob Crusades were sidetracked. European Jews were assaulted even before those Crusades left Europe.

Throughout this period the Church turned its focus directly on the law and became a legalistic institution. This focus forced secular governments to strengthen their legal systems forcing them to grow into strong national monarchies. Trade returned to Europe and literature flourished, as did education. After 1260 things would change again.

SCORPIO ERA: 1260 TO 1440

The sign of Scorpio is a very powerful and intense sign and the history of this era is very intense. Scorpio is symbolized not by one image but three, the scorpion, the serpent, and the eagle. These three together give an image of successive levels of transformation, which is what Scorpio is all about. At the bottom, living in the self-made hell of fear, prejudice, desire, greed, anger, and jealousy is the scorpion. The scorpion is enclosed completely within his hard protective shell, armed with two large claws and a venomous stinger. Above the scorpion the serpent is equally venomous, but he has shed the hard protective prison of his shell. The serpent is fluid and mobile. Most importantly it periodically sheds its skin as it grows giving the image of death and rebirth. It was traditionally seen as a powerful symbol of wisdom and the regenerative properties of the Great Mother, creatrix of all life. The snake was sometimes pictured as circling up in the form of a circle with its tail in its mouth symbolizing immortality within the never-ending cycle of death and rebirth. At this level death is no longer to be feared. The serpent represents the level of power, another Scorpio quality. The highest expression of Scorpio is the eagle representing the final transformation possible under Scorpio, breaking free from the limitations of life on earth. The eagle is traditionally seen as one of the most powerful of all birds, able to soar to great heights and possibly even to reach heaven.

The Book of Job in the Old Testament presents the Scorpio image , pictured as Satan not as an evil adversary to God, but as a trickster, a son of God sent by God (implied in God's willing acquiescence to Satan's request) to test how deep were the foundations of Job's spirituality. Only in the test can the true worth of a devotee or hero be known.

Scorpio is ruled by Mars, the planet that also rules Aries and gives to Aries the love of challenge and competition. Mars gives to Scorpio that same ability to rise to the greater Scorpio challenge of overcoming death and gaining the ability to regenerate and transform. In addition the recently discovered planet Pluto, which rules death and rebirth, was given co-rulership of Scorpio along with Mars.

This is a pivotal era in our history. This period marked the death of the medieval world and the beginning of the Renaissance. The word renaissance means rebirth, and it denotes a process of transition from one level of cultural accomplishment to another, higher level. The Renaissance is traditionally dated from 1300 to 1650 and entailed a rebirth of the old Greek and Roman ideals in art and literature. It didn't really flourish on a wide scale until the following Sagittarius Era after 1440. Here in Scorpio the individuals who hammered out new expressions of human concern and power did so in an environment of destruction, death and greed.

Giotto was the first western painter to bring a sense of humanism into painting in the 14th century. Chaucer with _The Canterbury Tales_ and its new focus on individual human beings, and Dante in _The Divine Comedy_ with its ready acceptance of the ancient classical world began the Renaissance in literature. Roger Bacon began the scientific Renaissance at the end of the 13th century with his insistence on direct observation of the natural world. In religion John Wycliff in the 14th century and John Hus, who was burned at the stake in 1415, advocated Church reform and began a religious reformation by trying to instill individual human devotional values into the Church.

The environment that this renaissance took place in was literally an environment of death. Scorpio rules death. By 1300 the agricultural expansion of the previous two eras began to slow down. The Crusades as a means of acquiring new lands in Palestine for the unlanded had proven to be a failure, and Europe was showing signs of overpopulation. Around 1320 several bad harvests kicked off an ominous rise in the death rate. Then came several epidemics and the mortality rate soared. The worst of the epidemics was the Black Death. It began in China in 1333 and first hit Europe from 1348 to 1360 wiping out one fourth of Europe's population. In some places one-third to one-half the population died. The Black Death masked several other diseases that came with it and it swung back and forth across Europe for the next 100 years decimating Europe even further. The French town of Toulouse went from a population of 30,000 inhabitants in 1335 to a mere 8,000 in 1435.

The Church began to change along with this new focus on death. Beginning in the last half of the 13th century cathedrals began to focus more on the funerary aspect of religion. Wealthy laymen and ecclesiastics sought to have their bodies put to rest within cathedral walls rather than in church cemeteries, somewhat reminiscent of the tomb building activity of the Age of Taurus, with its Scorpio opposite. By the 14th century cathedrals housed an ever-increasing number of chapels and alters for continuing rounds of soul-masses to be performed for those who could afford to pay. For those who couldn't afford the cost of Church burials, the Church instigated the mortuary. This was an exaction placed upon the deceased's property by the local bishop or abbot. The Church official could take the best possession of a dead individual in payment for his burial. In addition to the Taurus opposite ruling money, Scorpio rules loans, debts, profits, and taxation. The Church transformed itself from a legal institution to a rather blatant moneymaking institution during this era. The Church, through the increasing sales of indulgences, which allowed people to buy their way free from sin, and other exactions, created an environment of hatred towards the Church that would set the stage for the Protestant Reformation in the next era.

Merchants rose in power as money began to replace the Church as the source of power in Europe. At the beginning of this era merchants began investing their money in the growing Italian textile business. This opened up the possibility of increased profits on an unheard of scale. Capitalism was created in Europe. Italian states without avenues to the sea became middlemen between the Venetians and the Genoese, and the markets in northern Europe. In the north the Hanseatic League along with the new Stagle League transformed themselves from guild associations into powerful moneymaking organizations during the 14th century. Banks were created in this era for the first time in centuries. In the 13th century the first bills of exchange appeared in Italy, and with them the first true modern bankers. In 1407 the first modern bank was opened in Genoa.

National government no longer accepted services in trade for fiefs. Money replaced the vassal system of reciprocal services, and feudalism quickly died. Phillip IV, also known as the Fair, changed all remaining feudal dues into direct taxes. He taxed the income and property of merchants, and in 1302 he even attempted to tax the Church. Taxation increased heavily everywhere, both by king and local overlords. The unusually heavy taxation coupled with the plague and war created an unbearably dismal life of heavy Scorpio suffering for most peasants. Peasant revolts in the 14th century increased in both frequency and in violence.

As money became more prominent the traditional aristocracy gave way to wealthy merchants. Scorpio rules plutocracy and oligarchy. Wealthy families came to power as oligarchies became the predominant political institution. The Visconti family rose to power in Milan in 1311; the Habsburg family began their rule of the Holy Roman Empire in 1273; and Florence came under the rule of the enlightened plutocrat Cosimo de Medici. Greed became the overriding motivating factor in the vast bulk of political administrations. The acquisition of money became more important than either good government or a healthy spiritual foundation for religion.

This greed fostered the longest war in history, the Hundred Years War from 1337 to 1453. The fighting was not continuous. There were many truces as well as many bloody uprisings by townspeople and peasants. It began because the French feared that the English might make an alliance with Flemish burghers over economic interests they had in the woolen trade of Flanders. The French finally defeated the English rallying to victory because of the emotional death of Joan of Arc.

Scorpio also rules absolute and exclusive power. In 1294 Pope Boniface VIII, the last medieval pope, was elected to the Papacy, and in 1300 he proclaimed himself the supreme authority over all humanity. Salvation now required everyone to accede to that authority. By the end of Boniface's pontificate the shortcomings of the Church were coming under increasing criticism and condemnation for its failure to reform itself while screaming about its absolute sovereignty. In response Marsilius of Padua proposed the theory that the emperor had absolute authority over the Pope. In 1305 the French king Phillip the Fair moved the Papacy to Avignon where it remained until 1415. In 1378 Louis of Bavaria installed his own Pope, Nicholas V in Rome, and thirty years later a council in Pisa installed a third pope, Alexander V. The three ruled concurrently for six years before being deposed in 1415. At that time the Papacy was returned to Rome but by then it was too late. Antichrist became a favorite term for papal claimants and by 1415 the mystical power the Papacy held for Europe was dead. The conciliar period between 1415 and 1460 worked from the view that the ecumenical council at Constantinople had absolute authority over the pope. The Medieval Church was dead.

This era has been called the Age of Dislocations and Disasters by historians. It was a violent and destructive period that marked the death of the medieval world. Chivalry also died as social harmony and balance was replaced by the new Scorpio qualities of lust for power, manipulation, greed, passion, bestiality, sadism, and masochism. The ends justify the means became the unspoken motto for this era as rulers saw themselves as above the law, secular or spiritual, able to do as they pleased. Almost any form of self-advancement became justifiable. Pursuit of power, wealth, sensual pleasure, or the ruthless suppression of a rival became the ideal. Weakness was despised.

In the New World, in Peru, the Chimor kingdom centered at Chan Chan showed signs of an unusually harsh rule. There is evidence of human sacrifice there, especially in association with the burial of their kings. Around 1240 in the Yucatan, the Itza people settled at Chichen Itza and created the Mayapan Empire. Here also they established the cult of the sacred cenote, or pool, where human sacrifices were made to their gods. Farther up in Mexico the Aztecs created, around 1300, their own civilization. Their religion was also centered around human sacrifice and the Scorpio focus on death and suffering. They made war on their neighbors mainly for the purpose of acquiring a supply of slaves to be used as sacrifice to their hungry war god.

In this position, Scorpio as the eighth of twelve signs, time was allowed to go through a violent death process affecting all major social institutions of this age, and plant seeds of a new paradigm that would begin to flourish in the next era of Sagittarius.

SAGITTARIUS ERA: 1440 TO 1620

Sagittarius sits at the top of the zodiac right next to the midheaven line. In this position it indicates the height of cultural achievement, the flowering of human potential. It is symbolized by the centaur Chiron shooting an arrow into the sky. Centaurs were seen by some in Greece as magic shape-shifters and teachers to the Hellenic gods. Centaurs in general represent the animal nature of man running free and uncontrolled by the direction of the higher human spirit. Chiron was the only centaur able to subdue his animal nature, enough to acquire gentleness, knowledge and wisdom. He was famous for his knowledge of various disciplines such as medicine and music. He taught the use of medicinal herbs to mankind. He became instructor to the greatest heroes of his age including Achilles, Aeneas, Hercules, and Jason. Sagittarius is a fire sign, and like Aries and Leo, that fire energy lights the cultural sky creating golden ages called renaissances in honor of Scorpio.

The Renaissance began in Italy but it soon spread to every other nation in Europe. The Italian Renaissance flourished in the 15th and 16th centuries. The French, Spanish, English, and German Renaissances flowered during the 16th and 17th centuries. In Italy Leonardo da Vinci, Titian, Giorgioni, Tintoretto, Michelangelo, and Raphael led the renaissance in art. In Germany it was Albrecht Durer and Hans Holbein, and in Spain, El Greco. In the area of literature Rabelais and Montaigne led the French Renaissance, while in England in the Elizabethan period drama flourished behind the work of Christopher Marlowe, Ben Johnson, and Shakespeare. In Spain it was Lope de Vega, and Cervantes.

The Polish scientist Copernicus went to Italy in 1496, and along with Galileo spearheaded the Italian Renaissance in science. In Germany it was Kepler. Erasmus in Rotterdam led the Renaissance in the Low Countries in humanist philosophy. In England it was Sir Thomas More. There was even a Renaissance in religion separate from the Protestant Reformation. Its leaders were humanists rather than Protestants. Valla, Ficino, and Mirandola began a thorough reexamination of ancient Church writings developing techniques of objective evaluation in order to ascertain the authenticity of sacred literature. Through their efforts the New Learning began to see a natural religion underlying the philosophical and religious dogmas of the Church. The most notable leader of this religious Renaissance was Thomas a` Kempis.

Persia also blossomed into a golden age of culture during the reign of Shah Abbas the Great at the end of the 16th century. In China the Ming Dynasty ushered in a golden age of culture from 1368 to 1644.

In the New World in Peru, Pachacuti, the ninth Inca ruler, between 1438 and 1471, laid the foundations for a Peruvian golden age. He created laws that are still in use today. His social and political innovations still touch almost everyone's lives in Peru, Bolivia, and Ecuador. There arose with the Incas a distinctive style of pottery that was not seen before. Architecture arose out of nowhere fully matured with no Peruvian antecedent. They developed the first steepled roofs on top of two and three story buildings. They used huge polyhedral stone blocks that interlocked, needing no mortar. Cuzco was a well-planned urban center with public monuments, and inhabited by a diverse cosmopolitan people.

In Mexico the Aztecs also enjoyed a brilliant golden age with vast and beautiful architecture. The Spanish, upon seeing both the Aztec and Incan cities, were awe stricken with the accomplishments of these non-Christian "savages". There were few cities in civilized Europe that could even compete with these Indian cities. In addition, after the fall of the Mayapan, around 1460, a mild renaissance of Mayan art followed in the Yucatan.

Sagittarius rules religion, dogma, zealousness, and fanaticism. Sagittarius also rules excess. The violent mind of the Scorpio Era seems to have left a certain impression in the Sagittarius Era. The energy of this era seems to have expanded, in Jupiter fashion, some of the excesses of the previous era. The planet Jupiter rules Sagittarius. From the late 1400's into the early 1500's Europe was caught in an excessively violent period of treachery, abduction, fratricide, depravity, and sadism. Violent pogroms were instituted against the Jews. In 1506 in Portugal Jews were ordered to leave the country. They were deemed too slow in their response and in one night almost 4000 were slaughtered. Violent intrigue was endemic, even among the Popes.

Around the beginning of the 16th century a series of worldly Popes sat on the Papal throne. They became the worst despots in all of Europe. In this they were expressing the new Sagittarian worldly energy while still coming to terms with the previous Scorpio concerns with sex, suffering, and death. They were all lechers; they were the least compassionate, devout, or chaste of anyone within the Church. It is interesting to note here that the centaur is symbolically seen to represent the lower animal nature in complete control over the higher spiritual potential of man. Popes and cardinals hired assassins and often reveled in the sight of blood. These Popes often hosted recreational murder plays in which violent and bloody deaths were actually enacted in front of the Pope and others. They also hosted hedonistic Vatican orgies.

The Protestant Reformation was also an excessively violent revolution. In 1517 Martin Luther nailed 95 theses to the Wittenberg Church door complaining of Church abuses. In 1520 Pope Leo X issued a Papal Bull condemning Luther's teachings. Luther then burned the Papal Bull and was, in turn, excommunicated. Luther then took refuge behind the princes of Germany for support. The Protestant Reformation was born and northern Europe broke away from the authority of Rome.

As it turns out Luther was born full of hatred. He often saw Satan in visions and he constantly fought with the devil, in his own words, by farting and flinging "shit" at him. Luther's hatred was reflected in the emotional nature of all of northern Europe at that time. As Germany pulled away from Catholicism the populace saw an opportunity to strike back at their former Church oppressors. Fighting erupted across northern Europe, and not only between Protestants and Catholics. Protestants also fought against other Protestant Churches as they came into being. The 16th century was a very bloody century as people all over northern Europe sought release of their pent up anger and hatred. Christians slaughtered other Christians all in the name of Christ. Executions and mass butchery became commonplace. Within four years of the Diet of Worms in 1521, when Luther became a fugitive from Rome and Germany rose up in support of him, 250,000 Germans were killed or executed.

Protestants were, for the most part, angry and zealously dogmatic in their understanding of the Bible. Germany embraced Lutheran teachings. Calvinism became extremely popular in Western Europe because he gave to the growing interest in capitalism, important in Scorpio, a new Sagittarius theological foundation. Monetary success indicated that God favored an individual's course of action. In those nations in the west of Europe where trade and finance were the leading pursuits Calvinism seemed the most agreeable of the new religious philosophies.

The Gemini opposite to Sagittarius rules division. Like the Gemini Era, 360 to 540, Europe is split apart during this era. The Protestant Reformation split Europe in two between Protestant and Catholic. What was begun by religious reformers was now finished by the various states. This era saw a rise in national consciousness continuing the trend begun in the previous two eras. The oligarchies of Scorpio gave way to the rise of despotic governments in Sagittarius. In order to secure their own national governments these states tended to create of the new Protestant churches official state churches. The English state church was the new Anglican Church. Lutheranism became the official religion of Germany, Denmark, Norway, and Sweden. Presbyterianism, a Calvinist religion, was the new official religion of Scotland. Further, within the Catholic religion, the Catholic Church in Spain divorced itself from Rome and became a state religion. The Spanish Inquisition, used to fight Protestantism, was financed by the state.

The Protestant Reformation created a division within the Church similar to the east-west division of the Gemini Era. It also divided Europe politically between Protestant and Catholic states. With this division came a century of religious warfare between 1520 and 1640.

Gemini and Sagittarius both rule travel and movement, Gemini ruling short travel and Sagittarius ruling long distance travel. These religious wars instigated a period of mass movement all over Europe. People of various religious outlooks began to move enmass to other states, or even to other cities within a state where they would not be seen as minorities, and where they could continue to pursue their livelihoods. Catholics moved to Catholic states, capitalists moved to Calvinist states. Others were forced to move also. Jews and those designated as witches were often forced to move to areas more tolerant to them.

Sagittarius rules vision, higher education, and discovery. In 1453 Constantinople fell to the Turks. Byzantium then appealed to the West for aid and in the process western scholars gained access to ancient Greek manuscripts that were thought to have been destroyed long before. The Greek love of humanity served as a foundation for the new humanist learning. Humanists like

Erasmus began to search for a deeper more plausible explanation to spiritual questions. They saw a natural religion underlying religious teachings and it was here that they thought lay the correct answers. Science and astronomy flourished as people flocked to find answers directly from Mother Nature herself rather than accepting blindly the old answers of an abusive Church.

The invention of the printing press by Guttenberg fueled this humanist learning. In 1454 the first books were printed at Mainz and from there printing shops quickly spread to the rest of Europe. Printing technology and the New Learning of the humanists and scientists combined to create a revolution in knowledge. Because of the speed of production and the ability to mass-produce books in very large quantities, Church attempts to stop these ideas from spreading were overwhelmed. Education and learning were, for the first time, pushed down towards the peasant class. Education began to become more available than ever before. Towns began to establish their own schools attracting scholars of the New Learning. The Gemini opposite to Sagittarius rules basic education. Grammar schools were created as foundations for higher education.

In response to the Protestant Reformation the Society of Jesus, the Jesuits, was founded in 1540 by a Spanish soldier, Ignatius Loyola. Its chief weapon was education. The Jesuits established schools throughout Europe for the general education of all, not just the elite. Later Charles Borromea, Archbishop of Milan, created Catholicism's first seminary schools for the proper training of priests and clergy. Education from this era on would begin to replace belief as the foundation for humanity's search to know his and her place in the universe.

Called the Age of Discovery this era witnessed the Sagittarius need to discover and expand, to fly over the horizon in order to increase one's field of vision. Sailors and navigators began to expand their limited vision of the world and sail farther out into unknown territory in order to find a direct sea route to the East. In 1445 Dinis Diaz, sailing close to the coast of Africa, rounded the Cape of Good Hope and banished the theory that equatorial heat was so intense that no human could live there. In 1497 Vasco de Gama furthered this feat by sailing straight south, out of visual contact with Africa, until he rounded the Cape. He sailed to India and returned in 1499. In 1492 Columbus sailed west to prove that the earth was round. By this route he hoped to reach China by a more direct and supposedly shorter route. In the process he discovered, or perhaps rediscovered, the Americas opening up a whole new world for exploration. Later Balboa would discover the Pacific Ocean and in 1522 Magellan sailed completely around the world.

From China, in the 15th century, Ming Dynasty sailors began their own energetic era of sea exploration reaching as far west as Africa. At the end of the 15th century, though, they suddenly withdrew back into themselves.

Renaissances happened before in association with Sagittarius. Looking at parallel developments in the previous Age of Aries, the Sagittarius Era, 720 to 540 BCE, also saw brilliant renaissances among the Chaldeans, the Assyrians, and the Egyptians. Just prior to the height of Classical Greece Greeks were in their archaic period, dated to this Sagittarius Era. This period is considered by many archaeologists and historians to have been a brilliant renaissance of Greek culture not widely talked about because of the accomplishments of their Classical period.

CAPRICORN ERA: 1620 TO 1800

Capricorn lies at the top of the zodiac alongside Sagittarius. Like Sagittarius Capricorn also marks periods of significant cultural achievement. But Capricorn is different. Capricorn is symbolized by the goatfish, a symbol that implies mastery of both one's inner spiritual nature and the base outer world. Capricorn is an earth sign signifying the ability to remain grounded and create something solid and enduring. The goatfish symbolizes the Capricorn ability to achieve lasting goals here on earth by focusing the emotions of humanity towards the civic goal of achievement for the good of all members of society. Capricorn combines the earthy nature of the goat with the spiritual consciousness of the fish, of creative intelligence, the Greek Logos. In this balance Capricorn symbolizes the classical, perfectly and mathematically proportioned quality of civic life and art. Capricorn is ruled by the planet Saturn. Saturn rules discipline and austerity. Capricorn rules structure, reason, and natural law.

As we enter into the Capricorn Era the major historical thrust comes to revolve around the use of reason and the renewed appreciation of classical ideals. In the now past Sagittarius Era Western man, for the first time, gave a name to his own time. A Gemini opposite to Sagittarius tendency. In this Capricorn Era people from various parts of Europe again named their time, this time in terms reflecting Capricorn qualities. In one place this time was called the Age of Reason; in another area the Age of Enlightenment; in still another the Age of Philosophers and Kings. The human mind in Sagittarius had expanded itself out of the narrow Christian mindset and matured. Now man applied that mind towards finding and delineating the natural law of the humanists. Modern philosophy was born, with reason applied to observed scientific facts in order to reveal natural laws. Capricorn rules philosophers, wisdom, natural law.

This was the period of great Western philosophers. The modern constitutional government of England was based on the political philosophy of Thomas Hobbs. American democracy was built around the political philosophy of John Locke and the natural rights of man. Scotland's Adam Smith and his economic philosophy proposed capitalist enterprise as a necessary function of government. Italy's Cesare Beccaria created the foundations of modern penal practices with his philosophy on crime and punishment. In science Sir Isaac Newton created modern physics with _The Mathematical Principles of Natural Philosophy_. Hume and Berkley with their philosophy of the nature of the mind and the process of knowing helped lay the foundation for the modern scientific process of experimentation. Vico, a philosopher of history, helped create the modern discipline of history. Montesquieu pioneered sociology with his social philosophy. At the end of this era Rousseau introduced romanticism with his social contract theory. And the French evolution philosopher P.L.M. de Maupertius forwarded, in 1741, a survival of the fittest theory, predating Darwin's theory by 99 years.

Capricorn rules government. Political theory put forward by various political philosophers created a virtual revolution in government during this era. In 1625 Hugo Grotius stated that since government was established on natural law, the Church had no business in civic affairs. Soon afterwards the Catholic Church lost all of her influence in the politics of Europe. Secular governments began a period of administrative reform throughout Europe and Russia in the 17th and 18th centuries designed to strengthen government around natural law and efficiency in administration. In France this trend was in the direction of a stronger monarchy. Under Louis XIII the Catholic Cardinal Richelieu was more political statesman than priest. As Louis' chief administrator he set in motion a program of administrative reforms that helped centralize the power of the monarchy. This set the stage for the rule of Louis XIV, the Sun King, the ultimate absolute monarch in Europe. Under Louis XIV, from 1660 to 1685, France became the most powerful nation in Europe. Baroque art was subjugated to the glorification of the state, of government and of man's achievements. It reached its ultimate expression as a universal art style. Colbert, the king's chief advisor, built an administrative apparatus to support the Sun King and the monarchy. The aim here was to subject the thoughts and actions of the entire nation towards civic responsibility, a powerful Capricorn motive.

The Romanov line in Russia was established in 1613. Russia as a nation did not grow as other nations grew and matured. It was purposely and efficiently built into a powerful nation during this era. Under Peter the Great (1682-1725) Russia was quickly modernized and westernized. The old Duma of nobles was abolished and in its place a senate of appointed men was established. Peter attracted to his court experts in all fields of expertise, especially the more practical fields; shipwrights, gun founders, teachers, clerks, and administrators, and even soldiers. He set up schools to teach technical skills, and he founded an academy of science. Following him Catherine the Great (1762-1796) rivaled Peter in her efforts to build Russia into a powerful nation.

This era was also a period where many countries were experimenting with a new republican form of government. In 1641 the Great Rebellion racked England. Against the Royalists supporting the king Charles V, Oliver Cromwell and his Roundheads rebelled in defense of civil liberties. In 1649 the Roundheads won and Cromwell established the English Commonwealth, a representative republican form of government. Following Cromwell's death in 1658 the Commonwealth fell apart and in 1660 royal power was reestablished, but by this time the Parliament was too powerful an

English institution. In 1688 James II was dethroned and the English Parliament invited Queen Mary and her husband William of Orange to come from the Netherlands in order to rule England. William had to agree to certain stipulations before he could assume the throne, and thus contractual monarchy was born. The Crown and Parliament, especially the House of Commons, had to work together according to a written agreement. In the same year an English Bill of Rights was created to legally and politically insure certain basic rights for those to be ruled.

The direct result of these English governmental reforms was the founding a true democracy in the United States of America in 1776. Colonized by the English, the colonists began to insist upon those same rights guaranteed to those in England concerning representation in Parliament. They were refused and like Oliver Cromwell a century earlier they proclaimed themselves free from England. The American Revolution was fought to preserve their individual political liberties.

In America the position of king was abolished and replaced by an elective president designed to further insure that civil liberties would not suffer at the hands of one powerful man. The U.S. Bill of Rights, attached to the Constitution, was modeled after the English Bill of Rights.

Representative types of government were not limited to England and America. In this era republican governments evolved in the Dutch United Provinces, in the cantons of Switzerland, and in the republics of Italy. Finally in 1789 the French revolted against the royal monarchy built earlier in this era, powered by the ideals and success of the American Revolution.

Government expanded beyond the limits of politics during this era. Capitalism changed into mercantilism during this time. The Mercantile Revolution turned capitalism into a major economic and political power in the 17th and 18th centuries. Joint stock companies were created along with stock exchange, easier to carry paper currency, checks, and life insurance. The 17th century was a period of rapid commercial expansion with huge overseas empires being created. These companies were given certain overseas lands as their own, and in turn they became extensions of their national governments. As more mercantile companies were given colonies to exploit and collect natural resources, governments became more interested in these economic matters.

The Hudson Bay Company became the vehicle for British imperialism in North America. In India the British East India Company became so powerful that they established their own government to rule India. This was the period of the British Raj.

Neither Capricorn nor its opposite sign Cancer have anything astrologically to do with art. Yet Capricorn periods like this tend to be highly artistic. The Capricorn qualities of achievement, reduction to essential parts, and focus on natural law tend to converge in the creation of Classical art. The last time this happened was in the Capricorn Era of the Age of Aries, between 540 and 360 BCE, in Classical Greece. At this present time art again returned towards classical expression. During the Renaissance figures in art were often depicted twisting and straining, pushing the natural limits of the skeletal system perhaps as an expression of the Jupiter ruled Sagittarius need for expansion and freedom. In Capricorn, figures become more sedate and orderly. Painting becomes more classical in its attempt to portray the structure of natural law within the human form, and within the frame of a painting. In Europe this actually took two forms. The first is termed classicist. It is a reverence for the ancient Greek and Roman classical forms, and the resultant tendency to imitate those models. The second is termed classical. Here contemporary themes were imbued with classical concerns for structure and mathematical proportion.

The French painters Poussin and Claude Lorraine created the parameters of classical painting in the 17th century. Behind them the classical Baroque art style spread to become an international style. This classical tradition included Rubens, Van Dyke, Valasquez, Rembrandt, Vermeer, Frans Hals, Gainsborough, Reynolds, David, and Benjamin West. Rococo art in the 18th century was an adaptation of classical art, focusing on the ornamentation of natural forms.

Order and reason, the classical ideal, permeated drama and literature also with the works of Voltaire, Milton, Racine, Moliere, Dryden, Swift, Alexander Pope, Daniel Defoe, John Donne, Goethe, Gibbon, Fielding, Blake and Diderot.

In 1607, at the end of the Sagittarius Era, Monteverdi created opera, a whole ensemble of many singers, musicians, and set artists creating a dramatic baroque setting. Following this, throughout the 17th and 18th centuries, music became a major focus of experimentation. Modern musical instruments were invented and classical music and the modern orchestra was developed. Handel created the oratorio. Schutz created the first German requiem in 1636. Gluck transformed opera into noble drama that would recall the tone of classical antiquity. Bach stands out as perhaps the most classical of this era's composers. His works are very attentive to rational order and mathematical harmony. Haydn established, along with Mozart, technique and stylistic principles of symphonic construction and the symphony orchestra.

Architecture reflected the classical order. With the works of Bernini and Christopher Wren, building took on classical elements with domes, columns, and architectural sculpture. Baroque art began with architecture before spreading rapidly to the other arts. The supreme example of classical Baroque architecture was the Palace of Versailles in the court of Louis XIV. Built to express classical concerns for reason and order, it incorporated into its proportions precise mathematical equations that were designed to hit the eye of the viewer with a sense of supreme correctness. In the 18th century, while France was perfecting Rococo architecture, following the Baroque, England was working on an even more severe or precise classicism known as Palladianism.

In China the Manchurian Ch'ing Dynasty replaced the Ming in 1644. Under their rule China entered a period of what has been called classical achievement as opposed to the previous era golden age of expressive arts. With the Capricorn Era, 1620 to 1800 CE, came a period of classical achievement and government, especially under the reign of K'ang Hsi (1667-1722). At this time, borrowing from the West, Jesuit scientific knowledge was brought to court and built upon.

Capricorn is ruled by the planet Saturn. Saturn's Greek name is Kronos. In ancient Greece Kronos was considered to be the same as Chronos, Father Time, giving us the word chronometer for a device that measures time, a watch or clock. It also gives us the word chronology meaning the sequence within time for the unfolding of historical events. It is related to the Capricorn quality of structure and framework. Time became an important question during this era.

The natural religion seen by the Sagittarius humanist was still ruled by God. In Capricorn that god was now seen by some philosophers as an interfering god, with that interference being the cause of much suffering and excess, leading to the religious wars of the Sagittarius Era. As man began to look at nature and to discover her laws it became clear to the Capricorn mind that man, by ascribing to God the cause of every action, took no personal civic responsibility for his actions, opening the way for more violence in the name of God. This was irrational to the Capricorn view. Capricorn saw the world increasingly in structured mechanical terms, as a totality of causes and effects. It was theorized that God only created this universe, yet in sufficient complexity that it would run itself, and thus did not require constant intervention. God was thus described as a watchmaker who, after building the watch, merely wound it up and let it go. It was now up to man to study and learn how the watch worked in order to more efficiently function in harmony with that watch. This view, called Deism, became the predominant religious view in the 17th and 18th centuries. The ultimate expression of this reasonable Deism surfaced in France in 1793. The worship of God was abolished by the Commune of Paris and replace by a cult of reason.

The concern with time also surfaced in the problem of how to measure time on a daily basis. In 1656 Huygens invented the pendulum clock. Escapements that controlled the escape of a clock's driving force were invented in 1670. In 1736 John Harrison invented the first spring driven chronometer. Due to the superior accuracy of the Harrison chronometer the British Navy was able to navigate far more precisely than any other navy. The margin for navigational error was reduced immensely and the British navy thus was able to out gun every other navy on the high seas. The measurement of time to a high degree of accuracy enabled Britain to literally rule the waves, becoming the most powerful nation in Europe.

The Cancer opposite sign to Capricorn also powerfully affected the world during this era. Cancer rules land, food, community, and security. Following the Age of Discovery in the Sagittarius Era Europe now spread out around the globe in a vast process of colonization. The English were more successful at colonizing

North America than the French and Germans because England transplanted entire communities to the New World, including livestock with which to begin new and secure self-sufficient lives. These communities discovered among other things tobacco, and they began to cultivate it creating a valuable commodity allowing them to survive economically.

Cancer rules food. Following the discovery of many new foods in the previous era, this era intensified the transplantation of plants and animals all over the globe. Wheat was introduced to the Americas, bananas to the West Indies, potatoes to Ireland, and horses to America. Cassava, corn, and sweet potatoes were introduced to Africa. Coffee was introduced to Java and Jamaica among many other examples.

Sugarcane was introduced to the West Indies, but in order to more efficiently grow the sugar, as well as other crops in the South in the new American colonies, slaves suddenly became a valued farming tool. They lived in the hot tropics in Africa and thus were seen as the most suited to be sent to the Americas. Black slaves in the New World were used exclusively for agricultural and domestic service reflecting the Cancer energy. Slavery thus became a huge and profitable business in the 17th and 18th centuries.

In Europe food preparation underwent tremendous advancement during this time. France's first great restaurants were established, and to support these restaurants France created the concept of cooking schools such as the Cordon Bleu. The pressure cooker and the soup ladle were invented along with the idea of clean plates for each new dish served. Sir Francis Bacon experimented with the idea of refrigeration by stuffing chickens with ice in order to retard spoilage. At the end of this era Napoleon offered 12,000 francs reward to anyone who could devise a way to package or bottle food so that his armies wouldn't have to forage for food on campaigns. Vacuum packaging was finally invented in 1804.

Rum, which doesn't spoil, replaced beer, which does, for sailors on long voyages. The British also discovered that citrus fruits prevented scurvy in sailors. The British navy took to giving limejuice to their sailors, giving to them the nickname "limey". In addition to the advanced chronometers available to their navy British sailors were healthier than sailors of other countries. In battle they were healthier and more energetic giving them a tremendous advantage in any engagement.

Farming expertise increased through the 17th and 18th centuries. Around 1750 England spearheaded an agricultural revolution more far reaching than any other since the Neolithic Revolution during the Age of Cancer. Other nations came to England to learn new farming techniques and new improvements in animal husbandry that promised to increase yields on an unimaginable scale. By 1800 famine had been conquered as a large demographic disaster. Famines would now be confined locally within national borders.

The Industrial Revolution had its beginnings here in Capricorn. The heart of the new Industrial Revolution lay for the most part in the ability to make steel. During this era much of the industrial energy was spent in the process of making iron and steel rather than in the creation of an industrial economy. Cancer rules mining and what is mined from the land. The steam driven engine was invented in the 18th century but it remained uneconomical to use. At this time it was used almost exclusively in the mining of coal.

The only industry to thrive in this era was the textile industry, textiles and clothing being a Cancer concern. The Spinning Jenny was invented in 1764, the water frame in 1769, the spinning mule in 1779, and the cotton gin in 1792. Cotton came to replace wool for thread. Other industries that began to thrive in the latter half of the 18th century were those that supported the growth of the textile industry, such as chemical dyes, etc. Yet this mechanization was still not a true revolution.

The Capricorn practical focus on learning, wisdom, philosophy, and understanding natural law supported the establishment of academies of learning throughout Europe in this era as natural extensions of the Sagittarius-Gemini creation of schools and universities in the previous era. From the middle of the 17th century learning societies were created in many countries across Europe, among them the English Royal Society in 1662, and the French Academie des Sciences in 1666. In the 18th century academies multiplied and diffused down to smaller towns with more limited aims.

Women's roles were greatly relaxed by the 18th century. Cancer rules women. Their range of contact in the 17th and 18th centuries expanded out beyond the traditional family and religious context. They were allowed much more freedom to meet and even exchange ideas with other people. Unsupported by any royal court the first clubs were formed around 1700 and in the 18th century the salon, or lady's drawing room, appeared. Friends and acquaintances gathered there for intellectual conversation. Some French salons became important intellectual centers.

By the end of the 18th century Europe had entered an age of female artists and novelists. A woman's old age was not to be spent in a cloister anymore. In 1792 Mary Wollstonecraft began the feminist movement by writing on the rights of women as valuable members of society. Politically the 18th century produced some notable examples of women as rulers of nations. There was one English Queen, Queen Elizabeth, and five Empresses, four of whom were Russian, including Catherine the Great, who all ruled very successfully in their own right.

Again, looking back to the Age of Aries, the Capricorn Era, 540 to 360 BCE, was the great period of Classical Greece and the Athenian experiment with democracy as a new form of government. Their major rival was Persia, which was built around Capricorn classical efficiency and the ideal of the great enlightened monarchy as the ultimate expression of a more traditional form of government. The Persian Monarchy was a different type of kingly rule than had been experienced before, and would more closely resemble the monarchy of the French king Louis XIV, the Sun King of classical Europe. Going farther back to the Age of Taurus, the Capricorn Era, 2700 to 2520 BCE, Old Kingdom Egypt was at its height, a period of pyramid building, and what is called classical Egyptian art and architecture. Mathematical proportions became important in all that they accomplished. It has been noted by historians that the achievements of Old Kingdom Egypt were not equaled for over 2000 years, until the accomplishments of classical Greece.

AQUARIUS ERA: 1800 TO 1980

Aquarius is the sign of the water bearer. In esoteric language water is symbolic of consciousness. This consciousness is not merely wakefulness in our ordinary state of understanding. It is a deeper level of awareness where all knowledge becomes available. As an example it is the conscious awareness of the quantum reality that underlies and supports the shallower reality of classical physics. While the planet Mercury rules both Gemini and Virgo, it is said to be exalted in Aquarius. This means that Mercury has its most exalted form of expression in the sign Aquarius, as the play of pure awareness and consciousness expressed in the form of true genius and revolutionary ideas supporting the ideals of universal brotherhood. Aquarius is ruled by the planet Saturn. While we tend to think of Saturn as dull and drab, always limiting any expression of exuberance and joy in the name of teaching us lessons, ancient cultures indicate that the legendary golden age of humanity was an age ruled by Saturn. Saturn is the father of the twelve gods that rule Mount Olympus. He is a supreme creator god with only one other god higher than him, his own father Uranus. Uranus is also said to rule Aquarius giving to that sign electric creativity and revolutionary impulse. Together they give to Aquarius times the tendency towards revolutionary new directions and expanded consciousness.

What has made this Aquarius Era so much more powerful and revolutionary than Aquarius Eras of the past ages is that we are now within what astrologers call the orb of influence of the Age of Aquarius, which will dawn in 2160. We are feeling the coming Aquarian energy already. The recurring renaissances that happen at the top of each age are part of a cyclical changeover from one age to the following age. Scorpio supports the death of the prominent social constructs of the age it resides in. In Scorpio seeds of a new way of thinking are planted, seeds which tend to flower in the following Sagittarius Eras. Reflecting the larger cycle of the ages, the seeds planted in Scorpio are for the most part social ideas and directions that concern the next following age. For example in the Age of Aries, a major new direction of cultural inquiry lay in the realm of religion and spiritual thought. The Prophetic Revolution in Israel beginning around 700 BCE reflected the incoming Age of Pisces and Pisces' concern with the transcendent nature of religion. In India there was the Buddha and in China Lao Tzu introduced Taoism.

In our present Age of Pisces, Scorpio set the seeds for an Aquarian mindset. Aquarius rules science, so that as we approach the Age of Aquarius the Aquarius Era that we just lived through between

1800 and 1980 was intensified with Aquarian energy coming from two directions. Since the Scorpio Era, and more powerfully the Sagittarius Era, the energy of Aquarius was fructified and like the fetus within the womb, it has been growing stronger ever since. When we entered the Aquarius Era in 1800 the growth of scientific energy sped up beyond the capacity of society to comfortably absorb. Knowledge, tradition, and society began to come apart at the seams.

This era was revolutionary on all fronts. The most obvious revolution that characterized this era was the Industrial Revolution. Around 1800, during the Napoleonic war years, the demand for iron rose sharply. The steam engine invented by Watts was used in Robert Fulton's steam ship and sailed up the Hudson River in 1807. This venture was the first commercial success for any engine, and it proved that the Industrial Revolution could henceforth be successful financially. This was a turning point that insured the success of the revolution.

In 1800 Maudslay invented the industrial lathe and eight years later the world's first large scale mass production unit was in operation in England at the Portsmouth block-making yard. Skilled engineers came to America to escape the turmoil of the Napoleonic wars and in 1814 the Boston Manufacturing Company was formed. Traditional industry depended on workers performing various tasks from various locations, often from home. For the first time in history the whole operation of a company was centralized under one roof. The American system of manufacture was born. Eli Whitney was making interchangeable parts for muskets since 1798. In 1815 his idea was accepted by other industries and became the second part of the American System of Manufacture. In 1909 Henry Ford invented the assembly line where a worker dealt with only one small part of the product. The American System of Manufacture was now complete. Industry had become, in the 19th century, mechanized. This was a revolution in the creation of goods. In the 20th century workers became extremely specialized in their small part of the process of creating goods. This was an even more radical revolution.

The Industrial Revolution brought with it revolutions, for better or worse, in many very important and basic areas of our lives. One of these areas is economics. The means of livelihood for most non-farmers is the ability to create and sell crafts or other goods. With the change to industrialization traditional crafts industries died out to be replaced by machine made articles, many with replaceable parts. With the centralization of industrial operations people had to move to where the factories were in order to survive. Cities began to grow rapidly, both in number and in size. Factories and the factory smokestack replaced the church and steeple as the prominent village or city landmark. As cities grew so did poverty stricken slums.

Prior to the 20th century land had been the primary indicator of wealth. From the land came the food that kept one free from hunger and the raw materials for the small home based crafts industries. At the top of the social ladder the aristocracy tradition-ally was hereditary mainly because of large tracts of inherited land. It was a land-based economy. Industrial capitalism began to revolutionize that economy as the machines' ability to produce goods from raw materials became more important than the raw materials from the land themselves. Around 1890 finance capital-ism began to replace industrial capitalism. Money came to be seen as the most essential raw material in any industrial venture. The investment of money began to gain in importance, even over the needs of industry.

Industry was no longer there to fill a real need. The need had to be created in the minds of the purchasing public in order to support industry. Industry thus began to advertise their products, and department stores were created as centers where industry could show off their wares. An advertising industry grew up around the sales of new products and fashion.

The revolutionary idea of credit expanded the purchasing power necessary to support a hungry industrial appetite. In 1910 "Morris Plan" banks, as they were called after their founder, first began to make loans to private citizens. Following World War II personal credit began to spread out to the entire population. Today credit cards like Visa and MasterCard allow private citizens the revolu-tionary freedom of buying all sorts of manufactured goods and services far beyond our means of immediately paying for them.

A third area of revolution is transportation. The Watts steam engine provided a means of power other than traditional power sources such as animal, wind or water. In 1800 the high-pressure steam engine was invented, designed for over the road transportation. In 1812 the first steam locomotive was built, and in 1825 the first modern railway was built in England to transport heavy loads of coal from the Durham coalfield in Stockton to Darlington. In 1830 the first combined freight and passenger service was opened between Liverpool and Manchester. From there railway service expanded at a tremendous rate. In 1830 there was only a few dozen miles of railway track in the entire world. By 1840 there was 4,500 miles of track and ten years later, in 1850, there was 23,000 miles of track.

Around 1876 the internal combustion engine was invented. Following several attempts at building a personal passenger car Henry Ford built the first commercially successful automobile in 1908, the Model T. At the same time men were experimenting with the idea of flight. The Wright Brothers are credited with the first successful flight of an airplane in 1903 at Kitty Hawk. Humanity's speed and means of transportation has radically changed. We have even gone to the moon. Truly revolutionary.

The machine, and technology, has revolutionized virtually every aspect of our lives from communications and knowledge to the home, personal fulfillment, world interaction and culture, art, and warfare. Electricity, ruled by Uranus, was practically harnessed for the first time by Volta in 1800 with the invention of his storage battery. Electricity allowed the invention of the telegraph, the telephone, radio, television, and the personal computer. Access to knowledge has been revolutionized through the various mediums of radio, television and the computer. Avenues for personal fulfillment have been revolutionized through the vast expansion of a workplace and career driven by technology during this era. Even warfare has been revolutionized.

In 1803 Henry Shrapnel invented the exploding artillery shell replacing the solid cannonball. In 1866 Alfred Nobel invented dynamite, a much more explosive material that would replace black powder. With the increase in mechanization war began to change dramatically after the turn of the century. In 1904 the Japanese attacked Russian forces at Port Arthur in southern Manchuria launching the largest war ever fought to that date. This was the first war to employ armored battleships, self-propelled torpedoes, rapid firing artillery, modern machine guns, and land mines. Ten years later World War I, the war to end all wars, broke out in Europe. Tanks and aircraft, as well as toxic chemical weapons such as mustard gas were added to the arsenal. A mere three decades later World War II introduced even more revolutionary weapons to the list, including rockets and the atom bomb.

Industrialization has revolutionized family structure. In 1814 the Boston Manufacturing Company began hiring young farm girls as workers. Other companies found that they could cut costs if they hired women and children, replacing men as the breadwinner in family life. At the same time children began to learn trades other than those of their fathers. In an increasingly industrial and technological workplace knowledge was changing rapidly. Traditional knowledge held by parents and elders became increasingly less important. The value of parental wisdom was replaced by the new knowledge of science, and the news and stories transmitted through the new mediums of radio and television.

In 1800 the gas lamp was invented revolutionizing the work cycle of the modern man and woman. This invention allowed industry to work their employees' longer hours, and to eventually keep production going well into the night. This change has thrown the natural circadian cycle out of balance. We no longer work according to the rising and setting of the sun. We now live in a revolutionary new and artificial environment.

Food has undergone a radical revolution. In 1804 Nicholas Appert opened the world's first cannery, or vacuum-bottling factory, near Paris. Food processing would totally revolutionize the new food industry. In 1814 England's Donkin-Hall factory created the first foods to be sold in tins. In 1895 pasteurization was introduced in order to kill any harmful bacteria present in food to be bottled or canned. As the industry began to grow chemists in the 20th century created artificial flavors, chemical preservatives, free-flowing agents, and artificial colors to help create artificially tasty and convenient products.

Aquarius rules genius and science. Industry and technology have been fueled by advances in science during this era. The natural philosophers of the previous era, including Sir Isaac Newton, gave way to the pure scientist in this era. The scientist/inventors of the 19th century such as Volta, Samuel Morse, Marconi, Thomas Edison, and Alexander Graham Bell led to the true genius of modern science in the 20th century with the Theory of Relativity of Einstein, and Quantum Mechanics of Max Planck, theories that have radically revolutionized the way science looks at the universe we live in. We now know that we live in an expanding universe of uncounted galaxies, speeding quasars, and deadly black holes. We live in a universe where a particle of matter is simply trapped energy. We may also live in a universe containing more than ten dimensions.

Aquarius rules global communications and world culture. Napoleon structurally united all of Europe reorganizing European countries to conform to the organizational ideals of the French Revolution. He consolidated all of the old and confusingly disparate political patterns that had come into being throughout Europe into more manageable patterns. These nations then went on to create wholly new states with a new feeling of belonging to a new European cohesiveness of identity that would lead to a unification of the world that was unknown before. Europe opened China and Japan to a burgeoning new level of world trade. With the invention of the steam engine international and even global transportation soon became a reality. The telegraph began the push towards today's global communications network. An international money economy was developed to support international projects, along with the creation of multinational corporations.

Utopian ideals, brotherhood, equality, and progressiveness are all traits of Aquarius. Based on the civil focus on individual right's within government in the previous era culminating in the American Revolution in 1776, and the French Revolution in 1789, the political ideals of a basic right to the pursuit of happiness, liberty, equality, and brotherhood were born. America became the utopian ideal for much of the rest of the world with attractive images such as America's streets being paved with gold. The new ultimate dictatorship of this era, Communism, was created by Karl Marx writing on the utopian ideal of worker's communes, all toiling in the spirit of equality and brotherhood for the greater good of all. The Cold War during the last decades of this era was a war of utopian ideals between the utopian promise of capitalism of the West and that of utopian Communism in Russia for the hearts and minds of the technologically primitive Third World.

The Aquarian ideals of equality have spread to cover a wide range of people and of all life in this era. Beginning with "Fanny" Wright in 1824 women have fought for and gained a degree of equality to men in almost every area of life in the West. The Equal Rights Amendment was gaining ground until the end of this era, when the energy changed and it was then finally stalled. Slavery has been abolished and Blacks have at least legally been granted equal rights in this country, as have other minorities. The rights of the handicapped, both mentally and physically handicapped, are protected by law as are the rights of the poor and unemployed. Even the rights of prisoners are now protected by law. These rights have also been extended to domestic pets, through organizations such as the Society for the Prevention of Cruelty to Animals, and even to wildlife within national forests and state parks. The Environmental Protection Agency was established to further protect entire ecosystems, including plant life.

One of the most personally promising of Aquarian gifts is that of immortality. Immortality implies not only the lengthening of the average lifespan but also a reduction in the mortality rate allowing more people to survive into adulthood and beyond. Already, in this era, great strides have been made towards that goal. Since the beginning of the 19th century there has been a very dramatic drop in the mortality rate that has spurred a powerful increase in population growth. In Europe alone, in 1800, there were 190 million people. By 1900 there were 420 million. That same year worldwide there were 1.165 billion people. Today that number is over 5 billion. Over this same time period the average life span of an individual has dramatically increased, to almost double that of previous periods. The average lifespan today for both genders is in the upper 70s with many living well beyond that.

The population growth of these last two centuries has been seen as one of the most important themes of this modern era for it is linked to almost every other theme. It fueled the unprecedented rise in huge metropolitan cities and urban living. It created huge consumer markets making the Industrial Revolution profitable. Socially it created fertile grounds for strife and armed revolution as people competed to attain a decent standard of living. Increasing numbers of governmental social institutions were created for the deliberate amelioration of this increasing unrest.

The Leo opposite sign to Aquarius has given to this era the leonine quality of the divine right of rulership. This quality has been applied to the ideal of personal living. The world culture of the Europeans as it spread during this era propounded the individual rights of ethnic groups or nations to rule themselves. The French with Napoleon not only exported the unifying principles of cohesive administration as based on the French Revolution, they also exported the idea of nationality and self-rule creating an essentially modern Europe. In the 1950s European nations that still held overseas colonies began to unilaterally allow those colonies their freedom and self-rule. In the US our basic foreign policy in this era has been to help Third World countries to modernize and become contributing independent nations in the creation of an Aquarian worldwide economic marketplace. It does not matter that we have been overbearing meddlers in the process.

Leo rules heroism and the love of the fight. Any fight. This era supported the birth of a modern recreation and sports environment. In 1860 the first world heavyweight championship boxing match was held between the US champion Heenan and the British champion Sayers. That same year the longest bare knuckles fight in US history was held lasting four hours and twenty minutes. And in 1860 the first British Open golf tournament was held in Scotland. In 1867 the Marquis de Queensbury rules for boxing were formulated. In 1863 the rules for soccer were created and in 1868 badminton was invented. In 1869 the first intercollegiate US football game was played between Rutgers and Princeton. This was a variation on soccer with 25 men on a side. In 1874 the first modern game was played between Harvard and McGill using only 11 men per side. That same year lawn tennis was patented in England from a game traditionally played indoors.

Baseball was invented during this same time period and soon grew to become America's national pastime in the 20th century. Spectator sports have become extremely popular in today's world venting a lot of Leo's need for sometimes violent competition. On a relatively ominous and violent note that combativeness has spilled over into the two largest and most destructive wars in history being fought in the 20th century; World War I and World War II.

The creativity and legendary figures of the sign Leo can also be dramatically seen in this period. In the middle of the 19th century Impressionism dramatically and very creatively revolution-ized the course of Western art. We remember the names of these artists as legendary in the field of painting, names like Renoir and Monet among others. After that art became even more creative making legendary heroes out of the best artists. We are all familiar with Van Gogh, Cézanne, Picasso, Mondrian, and Jackson Pollack, among many others. Art styles have been eclectic, revolutionary, and highly creative with Post Impressionism, Pointillism, Dadaism, Cubism, Fauvism, Surrealism, and Abstract Expressionism leading to other expressions of Modern Art. In music there is Mozart, Beethoven, and Wagner. There is Elvis Presley and Bob Dylan, as well as the Beatles and the Rolling Stones. There are new and revolutionary music styles such as Rag Time, Blues, Jazz, and of course Rock and Roll.

Looking back to the Age of Aries, the Aquarius Era, 360 to 180 BCE, the Greek world changed from classical Hellenic Greece to a scientific Hellenistic Greece. Hellenistic thought was scientific and mathematical rather than philosophical. It was also international. Alexander the Great defeated the Persians around 330 BCE and began a period of conquest that would unite the various nations of the Near East into one cohesive world culture. The Greek language was adopted as an international language that kept the world as they knew it unified. The Hellenistic civilization was an interna-tional civilization that was supported by economic developments that are secondary in magnitude only to the commercial and industrial developments of our own Aquarius Era from 1800 to 1980. An international trade was opened up extending all the way to the Indus River in India. An international money economy replaced the agricultural economy of that era. Investment and speculation increased along with a sudden rise in industry. Trade and industry became major activities of government. The Ptolemy's in Egypt established factories and ships in nearly every village and town of their empire, owned and operated by the state. State owned banks were established throughout the Near East. Speculation, the cornering of markets, intense competition for markets, the resultant growth of advertising, the growth of large business houses, and the development of insurance were common practices during that era.

Around their industry came the growth of huge metropolitan

cities. Cities grew and new cities were formed almost as rapidly as they did in the 19th century in America. Farmers left their villages for the excitement of the city in record numbers. Many cities expanded to become huge metropolises with well over 100,000 inhabitants. Alexandria in Egypt had well over 500,000 inhabitants. Not even Rome surpassed it in size or magnificence. It contained well-paved streets laid out in an orderly fashion. It had magnificent public buildings including a museum and a library containing 750,000 volumes. It had public parks. And these cities also had growing slums similar to those we have today.

Around 360 BCE the focus on philosophy dissolved and a new focus on science entered the picture. Aristotle spanned both the Capricorn Era and the Aquarius Era. For most of his life, and especially after 360 BCE he was more of a biologist than philosopher. Much more wide ranging than his predecessors he spent many years studying the structure, growth patterns, and habits of various animals. He made many discoveries that would not be rediscovered until the 17th century of our own age. He examined the process of insect metamorphosis, the reproductive habits of the eel, and the development of the embryo in dogfish. Among scientists of that time astronomy, mathematics, geography, medicine, and physics all became very popular.

Aristarchus of Samos, called the Hellenistic Copernicus, deduced that the sun is the center of our solar system. Euclid was the first to present geometry as a rational and logical discipline. Hipparchus laid the foundations for plane and spherical trigonometry. Eratosthenes calculated the circumference of the earth to within 200 miles. Herophilus of Chalceon began the study of anatomy by being the first to dissect a human body. He described in detail the brain and he discovered the function of the circulatory system. Erasistratus created physiology as a discipline distinct from biology. He discovered the valves of the heart and the motor and sensory nerves. Archimedes of Syracuse created experimental physics as a science.

PISCES ERA: 1980 TO 2160

Finally we reach the Pisces Era beginning in 1980 and going to 2160 BCE. Pisces rules religion and mysticism, prophets and prophecy, and the fulfillment of prophecy. Pisces also rules false prophets, escapism, neurotic fears, lack of focus or direction, imprisonment, and dissolution.

All of the world's great religions focus on mysticism and prophecy. Those of the Orient deal heavily with mysticism and the process of finding heavenly awareness, glossing over prophecy. Pisces rules contact with other worlds, higher worlds. Christianity focuses much more heavily on prophecy. In our modern world the Protestant branch of Christianity, and especially Fundamentalist Christianity, has narrowed their focus even more towards literal prophecy, with almost no interest in mysticism. All other religions talk about the same prophetic future as does Christianity, and Christianity is also an otherworldly, heavenly, mystic religion; the focus is just different.

The religious tone of this age has been one of attainment of heavenly bliss, of the Messiah or the world savior, and of his return. Buddhists await the second coming in the Maitreya Buddha; the Hindus await the Kalki Avatar. The names are different and the religious trappings surrounding him and his coming are different. But, in this Pisces Age, as an incarnation of God, of the divine, the Son of God, he is the same. And now that we are in the Pisces Era of the Pisces Age the mystical and the prophetic energies are now intensifying. The second coming both as a single divine individual and as a worldwide personal transformation is getting very close to reality.

This is the positive Piscean potential that all religions have focused on over the last 2000 years. The rational secular vision, unable to believe in the mystical, has fallen prey to the lower chaotic energies of Pisces. The utopian promise of a technological paradise is already falling apart due to inflation, violence and escapism through drug abuse and mass entertainment. Violence is already epidemic within society and it is increasing. Depression, suicide, child violence, rape and family abuse are all at epidemic levels. There are 30,000 suicides each year in the US. It is estimated that ten to twenty times that number attempt it. The suicide rate is higher than the murder rate in this country, with three suicides for every two murders committed. While more women than men attempt suicide, men succeed more often, with 24,000 of the 30,000 suicides committed by men. The rate of depression is much higher. Pollution of various types still threatens us with extinction. And this era has just begun.

In the last Age of Aries, the Pisces Era, 180 - 0 BCE, brought with it social and political chaos on a large scale. The Late Republic in Rome was the most violent and destructive period of Roman history. A people who were, a century earlier, very industrious and practical, quickly became lazy and unproductive. A huge gap opened up between the rich and the poor. Large slum tenements were built. Civic pride was replaced by greed as the motivating factor for government service. Huge influxes of slaves displaced Roman citizens from many jobs; and usually slaves lived better than the citizenry. Street violence increased with gangs of slaves assaulting individual citizens. Roman armies fought each other for the prize of foreign conquest. Senators murdered fellow senators. The Roman leader Sulla used gangs of slaves to enforce his view and he even had senators openly murdered.

In China, the Early Han Dynasty, 200 to 0 BCE, was undergoing similar social and political breakdown. During the previous Age of Taurus, the Pisces Era from 2340 to 2160 BCE, supported similar trends of social and political chaos and breakdown both in Egypt and Mesopotamia. The difference today is the widespread availability of technology, of deadly automatic weapons and the existence, everywhere, of various forms of pollution, drugs, and processed foods that affect the overall psychology of society. This Pisces Era is in the Pisces Age. The energy is doubled in intensity both for good and for evil. In all likelihood, given our present non-spiritual technological culture, it becomes almost a certainty that the worst of Pisces will emerge in a vast Biblical end-time scenario of destruction before we make it into the promise of the Age of Aquarius.

THE SIGNS OF THE TIMES
SMALLER TIME
THE PHASES

The phases help define an astrological era. Each era goes through the same life cycle of twelve stages of development that the ages do. These phases are smaller in duration and as a consequence not as powerful, generally, as are the eras.

A brief look at the phases of the Aquarius Era, 1800 to 1980 CE will help us to understand these phases and to project forward into the future. Because this Aquarius Era is so close to the Age of Aquarius, due in 2160, the effects will be quite pronounced.

The Aries Phase, 1800 to 1815, was a period of almost worldwide war, a precursor to the World Wars of the 20th Century. The Napoleonic wars were waged in every part of Europe, in North Africa, on the high seas in the Atlantic Ocean and affecting the Americas. It even caused uproars in India. America went to war with England again in the War of 1812. In 1808 Latin American and South American countries began the fight for their own independence from Europe.

In the Taurus Phase, 1815 to 1830, money and economy again became a focus, as did peace, and building, all Taurus concerns. The Second United States Bank was founded in 1816 marking a period of economic growth and banking concerns. It was founded to curb unsound banking practices and inflation. The bank supported the financial operations of the government and acted as a repository for government funds. It also compelled state banks to limit the number of notes issued and maintain them at full face value. The US unified and stabilized her economy creating a single US currency. In 1816 the first American savings bank was founded in New York. The Philadelphia Savings Fund Society became the first US savings bank to actually accept deposits. And the Providence Institution of savings in Boston became the first bank to receive a corporate charter. In 1825 the New York Stock Exchange, the economic center of this country, opened its doors for the first time.

In Europe Napoleon was defeated in 1815 and the major powers of Europe sought to enforce a peace upon the Continent for the next 15 years. The Quadruple Alliance consisted of the four most powerful nations in Europe; England, Russia, Prussia, and Germany. They agreed to use their military power to prevent France from ever again disturbing the peace and tranquility of Europe. Their aim was to support peace and prosperity. They sought to restore the status quo of European rulership in Americas as well as in the Europe following the fight for independence pushed by the Latin and South American nations. The US responded by issuing the Monroe Doctrine insuring the freedom and peaceful independence of these new world countries.

Gemini rules the mind and travel. The Gemini Phase, 1830 to 1845, was a period of intense inventiveness. The Industrial Revolution began in earnest in Europe. The Napoleonic Wars had halted all industrial activity and expansion during the previous Aries Phase, and Taurus is not an industrial or inventive sign. But now, in Gemini, an inventive sign, Europe quickly entered the industrial age of expansion. Travel increased dramatically as people in Europe immigrated in huge numbers to the US. Large numbers of people left Europe for the Americas. In the single decade between 1830 and 1840 the US accepted 599,000 immigrants. This was a sharp increase over the 400,000 immigrants accepted during the previous four decades combined. People in the US and European immigrants further created a huge movement west. In 1830 Jedediah Smith led the first wagon train west to the Rocky Mountains. Soon after that the Santa Fe Trail and the Oregon Trail were opened. Railroads became popular as a means of transportation. The first modern railroad was built in 1825 in England. In 1830 the first combined passenger and freight railway service was opened in England. In 1830 there existed only a few dozen miles of railroad track in the entire world. By 1850 there were 23,000 miles of track. This phase witnessed a rapid rise in the number of steamships, with the first transatlantic voyage of a fully steam powered ship completed in 1838. In 1839 the first real bicycle was invented, and the first street cars were built.

The communication of Gemini strongly affected this period. The telegraph was pioneered by Joseph Henry in 1831. In 1832 Samuel Morse began work on the electric telegraph, which was completed and demonstrated in 1837. His assistant Alfred Vail devised a way of communicating over the telegraph using dots and dashes that would be called Morse Code. Telegraph lines also crossed the continent and lines were laid across the Atlantic Ocean to Europe.

The printed word exploded reaching mammoth proportions. Books, pamphlets, and leaflets flooded the country. In 1833 Ben Day founded the New York Sun creating a revolution in two areas of news. He sold his papers for a penny, down from the going rate of three pennies, offering news to the masses at an affordable rate. He also hired newsboys to go out on the streets to hawk his papers. In 1835 James Bennett founded the New York Herald as the prototype of the modern newspaper. In 1841 Horace Greeley followed with the New York Tribune. Behind the brilliance of such writers as Charles Dickens prose began to replace poetry as the dominant form of literature.

Gemini rules education. This phase saw the establishment of the first public supported schools. There followed a mass movement towards education on all levels. In 1837 the world's first kindergarten was opened in Thuringia in Europe. In 1836 Arkansas was admitted to the Union under the stipulation that 1/16th part of every town would go to the support of schools. Academies and colleges were rapidly established in the western towns along the Mississippi River.

On an ominous note, Gemini rules division. The national unity of America began to show signs of a basic division between the industrial North and the traditional cotton growing South. The slavery question further tended to divide the country along those same North-South economic lines. This division would erupt eventually in the Civil War during the Leo Phase.

During the Cancer Phase, 1845 to 1860, land, community, housing and food became a prime focus. In Europe Karl Marx published his Communist Manifesto in 1848 based on the concept of communal living and shared ownership of land and food. In the US the concept of Manifest Destiny was put forward in 1845 that theoretically gave the American people the "right" to possess and settle lands of the American continent all the way to the Pacific Ocean. The migrations of the previous phase passed over the Great Plains on their way to California and Oregon. In this phase the agricultural and cattle raising potential of the plains became vitally important to the US. In the Indian Territories, Indian treaties were broken, one after the other, in order to open up the Indian lands to US settlers. The question of free homesteads, especially in these Indian lands, became a very popular issue. In 1854 the Kansas-Nebraska Act was signed and white homesteaders were officially allowed to homestead the Indian Territories. This area would become America's Breadbasket. With the new interest in land the US Department of the Interior was created in 1847.

Farming was revolutionized and mechanized during this phase. The California Gold Rush in 1849 pulled so many farm hands off farms in the East that farmers found themselves alone, with no farm help. They were subsequently forced to purchase the new McCormack harvesters in order to harvest their crops. Cancer rules mining and all things dealing with the land. Gold comes from the land, as does oil. The California Gold Rush in 1849 was only the most famous of many such gold rushes. In 1851 New South Wales in Australia had her own gold rush. In 1859 the Colorado gold rush began, and at the same time the Comstock Lode in Nevada struck both gold and silver. In 1854 the Pennsylvania Rock Oil Company was founded which would begin the new petroleum industry. In 1859 petroleum production began.

Digging into the land in another area, archaeology began to flourish as a science. The British archaeologist Layard began his excavations at Nimrod in Iraq. Six years later he discovered the Assyrian remains of Nineveh. In 1856 Neanderthal Man was discovered in the Neander Valley in France.

Cancer rules houses and the home, architecture, construction, and real estate. Modern construction techniques and materials were begun in this phase. In 1849 concrete reinforced with iron bars was invented. Three years later Elisha Otis invented the safety elevator in 1852. This invention would lead to the modern high-rise building. In 1847 James Bogardus invented the first prefabricated cast iron and glass curtain wall buildings in New York. His prefabricated buildings soon sprang up in Philadelphia, Baltimore, St. Louis, and other cities. In 1850 a fifty-year period of tenement building on a large scale began in New York. In 1857 large plate glass windows were pioneered at Mentmore Towers in Buckinghamshire, England.

Technology during this phase was focused inside the home as well as around construction. In 1850 the first White House cooking stove was installed replacing the open fireplace. In 1855 the first domestic gas stove was introduced, as well as a military stove capable of providing enough cooked food for an entire battalion. The mason jar was patented in 1858 that allowed a family, for the first time, to preserve their own food for winter months. That same year a Frenchman, Ferdinand P. A. Carre, built the first mechanical refrigerator. The first sewing machine was invented in 1843, and was patented in 1846. Four years later Singer invented the popular Singer sewing machine in 1850.

At the same time food and food adulteration became a growing problem. The year 1848 saw violent food riots in countries throughout Europe. Patent medicine became increasingly popular throughout this phase following the medical promises of Hostetter's Stomach Bitters, a 44% alcohol cure-all. While nothing was done about food adulteration in the US, England was finally forced to pass a food adulteration law in 1860.

Cancer also rules women, nurturing, and survival. In this phase, in 1848, the first women's rights convention was held. By 1852 women's suffrage began to gain ground. In 1855 the first college to grant degrees to women was founded at Elmira, New York. In 1857 Britain created the concept of alimony payments to women in divorce cases. The focus on women during this phase began to improve their health. Beginning around 1850 there is seen a dramatic drop in the mortality rate of children.

The Leo Phase, 1860 to 1875, was the period of American glory. Leo rules legendary figures, glory, and romanticism. The Old West was popularized by dime novels. In 1860 Anne Stephens wrote the first dime novel, _The Indian Wife of the White Hunter_. Through this medium the Wild West became highly romanticized carrying with it many of America's most popular heroes and antiheroes. The James Brothers, Frank and Jessie, along with Cole Younger, rode with Quantrill's Raiders in 1863. In 1872 they robbed their first train on their way into American lore. In 1863 widespread cattle rustling began in Texas. In 1865 the first train robbery took place and in 1866 the first cattle drive north along the Chisholm Trail took place. The Wild West towns of Abilene and Dodge City were founded. The new Colt .45 six-shooter and the Winchester repeating rifle became famous for their regular use in the Old West. And Stetson created his famous 10-gallon hat, used widely in the West, and commonly remembered with affection even today.

Leo rules the love of the fight and self-rule. In 1861 the famous Apache Indian chief Cochise began his attacks on white settlers in earnest. In 1862 the Sioux Indians under Little Crow rose up against whites settlers. And in 1864 the Cheyenne, supported by the Arapahoe, Comanche, and Kiowa went on the warpath against the whites. The high romance of Cowboys and Indians began. This period has remained, to this day, one of the most legendary and romantic periods in all of American history.

In the east the Civil War broke out giving a Leo warrior expression to the divisions within the union. And it also remains one of our most legendary and romantic wars, with great American heroes on both sides. We easily remember such figures as Robert E. Lee, Stonewall Jackson, Ulysses S. Grant, General Sherman, and Admiral Farragut. President Abraham Lincoln easily stands as our most legendary president. South of the border the legendary Benito Juarez was leading the Mexican fight for independence against the French rule of Emperor Maximillian. In Germany Emperor Wilhelm I and Chancellor Otto von Bismark established the Second Reich during this period.

In other areas of the east and in Europe sports became very popular as forms of organized competition and fighting. In 1860 the world's first heavyweight boxing championship was fought. That same year the longest bare knuckles fight in US history was fought lasting four hours and twenty minutes. In 1867 the Marquis de Queensbury rules for boxing were formulated. Football was invented during this phase as a variation on soccer. In 1863 the rules for soccer were created. Baseball was invented during this time as was badminton, and lawn tennis, adapted from an old game traditionally played indoors. In late 1859 a Frenchman named Leotard presented the first flying trapeze circus. P.T. Barnum created his Greatest Show on Earth in 1871. He built a huge building to support his circus, called Barnum's Hippodrome. It would later be renamed Madison Square Garden.

Legendary figures emerged in the business field as well. In 1860 John D. Rockefeller entered the oil business and inaugurated a period of intense speculation and the creation of financial monopolies. Rockefeller, Carnegie, Vanderbilt, and others known collectively as the Robber Barons engaged in heavy speculation and the cornering of markets, business as a game of chance where the fight itself is important, in the creation of America's first financial empires.

Leo rules creativity and gambling and this energy invaded the world of business and finance. The fortunes of Rockefeller, Carnegie and Vanderbilt were based on the gambling nature of speculation. Not only were fortunes made, they were also taken away. In 1866 this gambling nature created a financial panic in London on May 11th creating a Black Friday for the first time. In 1869 Wall Street experienced its first Black Friday behind the speculation of Jay Gould and James Fisk. Trying to corner the gold market they destroyed half the banks and businesses in New York. This need to gamble and speculate even entered politics. The administration of President Grant was renowned for its corruption. The infamous Tweed Ring that ruled New York was exposed by cartoonist Thomas Nast in 1869 revealing a history of economic and political manipulation and corruption.

As a fire sign period European art entered into a golden phase of innovation. Behind the work of such legendary artists as Monet and Renoir Impressionism in Europe revolutionized the art world with its light filled impressions of how sunlight (Leo is ruled by the Sun) created the visual image. This set the stage for the evolution of modern art into the 20th Century. This phase is in the Aquarius Era, and Aquarius is the opposite sign to Leo. Aquarius rules revolution.

The Virgo Phase, 1875 to 1890, has been called the Second Industrial Revolution as inventiveness again flourished on a large scale. A sharp increase in the number of inventions and industrial advances is seen in this phase. Virgo rules study, analysis, and methodical mental acuity. Edison, Bell, Marconi, and Tesla all created the foundations for the widespread use of electricity for home and industrial use. In 1875 Alexander Graham Bell invented the first telephone. A year later Thomas Edison was hired by Western Union to improve on Bell's telephone. With $40,000 he built the first research laboratory. The next year he invented the hand crank phonograph, and ten years later the motor driven phonograph. In 1878 he invented the electric light bulb, and in 1883 he pioneered the radio tube. In 1888 Nikola Tesla invented the alternating current motor.

The first pathology laboratory in the United States was built at Bellevue Hospital in New York in 1877. In 1879 the Russian scientist Pavlov performed his now famous experiments with dogs. The first American agricultural experiment station was founded at Wesleyan University in Connecticut in 1875. In 1882 psycho-analysis was pioneered by a physician who used hypnosis on a patient. He told of his success to Sigmund Freud who then began his own work in seeking out the pathways of the mind. The Virgonian analytical science and Mercury inventiveness of this phase laid the scientific foundations for the explosion of science and technology in the 20th Century.

Virgo also rules disintegration, separation, and division into small compartments. The Old West began a process of settling down. Barbed wire was used after 1875 to cut the open range into small parcels of farmland. The once powerful Native American tribes were finally defeated and herded onto small reservations. In 1875 the Nez Perce Indian Territory was opened to white settlers. The Comanche chief Quanah Parker ended his hostilities and retired to a reservation. In 1876 the Apache leader Geronimo left the reservation and began his own last ditch war against the whites with a small band of warriors. That same year the Indians of the northern plains achieved their greatest, and last, victory at the Battle of the Little Big Horn. In 1886 Geronimo was captured and the last major Indian war ended. In 1889 Oklahoma Territory was opened to white settlers. The following year the Sioux chief Sitting Bull was killed at Grand River. In December of 1890 the Battle of Wounded Knee, a very un-heroic massacre of unarmed men, women, and children, ended all Indian resistance. The Sioux lands were opened to white settlers. Indian nations were now all crowded onto small and inadequate reservations.

The Wild West was also coming to an end in this phase. In 1876 Wild Bill Hickok was shot in the back. The Northfield, Minnesota raid by the James gang proved to be their last raid. The Younger brothers were caught and Jessie James retired under an assumed name. He would be shot in the back in 1882. In 1881 Billy the Kid was killed by Pat Garrett, and a few months later the Earps fought the Clantons at the O.K. Corral. Law and order was coming to the West. In 1883 the Wild West was revived in the form of a show, Buffalo Bill's Wild West Show, at Omaha, Nebraska.

New battles now centered on the Virgo question of labor, and labor relations. Work and working conditions became a major focus of this phase. In 1877 government regulation of private business gained legal support in the Supreme Court decision Munn vs. Illinois. The US Civil Service Commission was established in 1883. Civil Service applicants would henceforth have to take an examination in order to prove their ability to work in a particular government position. A Bureau of Labor was created in 1884 within the Department of the Interior to more effectively deal with the question of work. The question of labor and working conditions was so strong that the Bureau was elevated to the status of Department of Labor a mere four years later in 1888. That same year the Interstate Commerce Commission was established to regulate trade between states.

The attempt at creating labor unions in the Gemini Phase between 1830 and 1845 now reemerged creating permanent crafts guilds and labor unions in this phase. Labor strikes, often violent, plagued this period. In 1881 Samuel Gompers organized the Federation of Organized Trades and Labor Unions in Pittsburgh. In 1886 he founded the A.F. of L., the American Federation of Labor. In 1877 and 78 railroad strikes on the Atchison Topeka and Santa Fe, the Pennsylvania, and The Baltimore and Ohio railroads ended in violence and federal troops were called in to quell the violence and force the strikers back to work. In 1882 a huge wave of strikes for higher wages struck all across the nation. These strikes increased in number until 1886, the peak year for labor strikes, as workers went on strike in order to get an eight-hour workday and improved working conditions. That year the US Labor Movement got her first martyrs in the Haymarket Massacre in Chicago.

In 1879 Germany ended her free trade policy in order to protect her own workers. In 1880 Britain passed her first Employers Liability Act to aid injured workers. That year the word "boycott" entered the labor lexicon in a dispute between the Irish Land League and absentee British landowner Charles Boycott. The League of Struggle for the Emancipation of Labor was founded in Switzerland that would eventually create a Russian labor movement.

Labor concerns in the US entered the area of politics with the creation of the Union Labor Party, the Socialist Labor Party, and the Greenback Party in 1888. The major US presidents of this time, Cleveland and Hayes, in Virgo fashion were both unpopular but were known for their efficient administrative reforms.

The planet Mercury rules the sign Virgo, and like Gemini, also ruled by Mercury, movements of people again affected US history. The US experienced another heavy period of mass movements of people into this country. In 1879 a large exodus of blacks from the South headed to Kansas. In 1880 550,000 English and 440,000 Irish entered the US. A year later Jews in Russia became the scapegoat for the assassination of the Czar. Pogroms were started spurring an immense emigration of Jews over the next 30 years. Over those next few decades 1.5 million Russian Jews, along with 500,000 Romanian Jews joined with Jews from other Eastern European countries would enter the US. Mercury rules travel and movement.

Libra rules social interaction, love, and enjoyment among other things. The Libra Phase, 1890 to 1905, supported the joyous and highly social period of the Gay Nineties. Trade, amusement parks, the building of great hotels and the joy of a social city life became important. Social interaction became a major focus of this phase. Hotels, restaurants and museums became popular as a new interest in leisure travel entered our consciousness. This phase marked an intense period of hotel building. The first world-class hotels were built here and in Europe, and many restaurants began a process of upgrading their services, becoming more elegant and formal. Restaurants began to hire well-known chefs. Entertainment became extremely popular at this time and many theaters, including Carnegie Hall, were built to serve the rapidly increasing numbers of people that were interested in going out to socialize.

The New York and the Chicago Symphony Orchestras were founded as was the London Symphony. For the less elegant tastes Vaudeville theater was created as was the new medium of film entertainment.

The first theater showing of a motion picture as well as the first commercial showing of a film took place in 1895. In 1903 the Great Train Robbery was the first film to tell a complete story.

Amusement parks became very popular and increased dramatically in number. The boardwalk at Atlantic City was built into one long continuous walk from three smaller boardwalks. In 1898 the Atlantic City Steel Pier was opened with amusement park attractions. Between 1897 and 1907 Coney Island expanded to become the greatest amusement park in the world. In 1893 the first Ferris wheel was installed for the Chicago World's Fair. That year in France the first striptease dance was performed in the artist's quarter in Paris. In 1896 Little Egypt began her famous sexually stimulating dances.

In support of this new casual and leisurely lifestyle the hamburger was invented using chopped "Hamburg" steak between two slices of bread. Chocolate and milk chocolate candies were pioneered in the previous Virgo Phase. They became extremely popular in this phase as candy and soda shops proliferated. In 1895 the first US pizzeria opened in New York, and in 1904 the ice cream cone was introduced.

At this time and in this process the position of women rose sharply. In addition to the introduction of the striptease dance women began to reveal more of their feminine charms by wearing bathing suits at the beach. In 1895 Cold Cream was introduced as a feminine beauty aid to improve complexion and attractiveness to the opposite sex. In 1902 the brassier was invented in France, perhaps as an aid to making the bust appear more appealing. And Cartier began creating beautiful jewelry for women. Women were first given the right to vote in New Zealand in 1893. And in 1896 women's suffrage was granted in Idaho by a constitutional amendment.

World trade became important as the US and Europe expanded their trade contacts with the Orient. Libra rules public relations, trade, and interaction. In conjunction with Libra the Aries opposite rules war. In war Japan defeated China in 1895 with the result that European countries rushed into the void to carve out trading colonies of their own on Chinese soil. In 1899 the Open Door Policy was put forward for European powers to agree to honor the trading rights of all countries without discrimination within their own spheres of influence. To maintain a harmonious international trading atmosphere the US took on the role of world policeman at this time. Following the Spanish American War the US found herself with foreign colonies of her own to contend with. The US acquired Puerto Rico, Cuba, and the Philippines. In the Libran manner of compromise and balance Cuba was granted her freedom in return for a military base on her soil and a promise not to enter into treaties with other foreign nations. The Philippines remained a colony with the promise of full independence at some indefinite later date. The Philippines was retained because it allowed the US a military presence in the newly opened Oriental market.

In the Western hemisphere the US now began to enforce the Monroe Doctrine, using her growing power to force European interests to accept Libran mediation rather than resorting to the old expedient of armed conflict. Latin and South American countries owed much to European banks. The Roosevelt Corollary to the Monroe Doctrine in 1904 gave to the US the task of keeping Europe out of the Americas while at the same time helping the economically poor Latin countries to pay their debts. Mediation became the preferred way to deal with differences, and using her military might to force mediation the US became a world power.

In 1896 following America's insistence on mediation between Britain and Venezuela, America and England entered a long period of Anglo-American cooperation. Other countries took up the vision of mediation as well. As world interaction began to increase throughout this phase neutral countries began acting as mediators in international disputes. As a result the World Court at The Hague was established in 1899 to act as a channel for mediation. Libra rules compromise, arbitration, and intermediation.

The Aries opposite to Libra rules engineering. Throughout this phase automotive engineering skills flourished for both private and military applications. In 1897 the S.S. Turbinia became the first vessel to be propelled by a steam turbine engine. That same year the first submarine able to operate successfully in open waters was launched. In 1896 aviation was pioneered by Samuel Langley. He launched a steam powered model airplane on a flight covering 3000 feet, the first mechanically powered aircraft. In 1900 Zeppelin created the first rigid airship in Germany, and in 1903 the Wright Brothers flew the first successful manned flight at Kitty Hawk. Karl Jatho in Germany claimed that he flew successfully four months prior to the Wright Brothers.

In the private sector the gasoline powered automobile was successfully built and automobile companies proliferated. In 1893 the first Ford Motorcar was road tested and two years later the Lanchester Motorcar was introduced in Britain. The Paris-Bordeaux road race was begun in France and the first US road race was held between Chicago and Milwaukee. In 1896 the Haynes-Duryea was the first motorcar put up for public sale. There were a total of 25 cars on US roads. In 1897 the first large US automobiles were built by Winter Motor Carriage Company. In 1898 automobile production reached 1000 cars per year, and would climb to 2500 the next year. British Leyland was founded in Britain along with British Daimler Company. The Stanley Steamer was built in Massachusetts, Renault was founded in France, and Fiat in Italy. As other car companies were being founded, including Mercedes, Oldsmobile, Packard, Pierce, Studebaker, and Cadillac, the motorized bicycle was also created. In 1903 the Harley-Davidson Company was founded.

An interesting parallel emerges here in the creation of mechanically powered vehicles. Engineering is an Aries trait. The Aries Phase, 1800 to 1815, saw the first economically successful use of a steam-powered engine in Robert Fulton's steamship in 1807. From that time steam engines were put into increasing numbers of steamships and locomotives. During this Libra Phase, with its Aries opposite, gasoline replaced steam as a fuel and the gas-powered automobile proliferated.

Building also benefited from Aries engineering. Much of the new building of this phase was centered on a new engineering feat creating tall skyscrapers for the first time. In 1890 the first true skyscraper was built in St. Louis utilizing an unbroken sweep of vertical line from top to bottom. Skyscrapers quickly began to appear in other cities. That same year the Manhattan Building in

Chicago was the first skyscraper to use a steel superstructure. In 1903 the Ingalls Building in Cincinnati was the first skyscraper to utilize a new steel reinforced concrete frame. The Eiffel Tower was built in Paris in 1899. City landscapes would now reflect the Aries ideal, in Pisces, of reaching for the stars, overcoming the challenge of being earthbound. This effort parallels the innovative and skyscraping building accomplishments of the great Gothic Cathedrals, like Chartres, during the Libra Era, between 1080 and 1260, with its Aries opposite sign.

Beginning in 1905 the period we call the Twentieth Century began. I use the year 1905 rather than 1900 because it signals the beginning of the Scorpio Phase. The Scorpio Phase, 1905 to 1920, was a pivotal period for our modern world. Like the Scorpio Era of the Age of Pisces, indeed of any age, this period marked the death of traditional thought in many areas. Ruling death and rebirth this was a transitional period signifying the death of the older classical world and the birth of what we call the modern.

Art is a vivid marker for this resurrection of culture. Until this time art had adhered to the classical ideals of representation. From the beginnings of this phase all that began to dramatically change. The Fauvists Matisse, Derain, and Vlaminck shocked Paris audiences and critics in 1905 with wild and electric colors applied to pictorial imagery. In 1907 Braque, Leger, and Picasso introduced cubism further shocking audiences. In 1908 the first exhibition of analytical cubism was staged in Paris. In 1912 Braque introduced collage as an art form. In 1910 Kandinsky produced the first nonrepresentational paintings and in 1915 DuChamp created the first Dada style painting. The following year Dada expanded with Hugo Ball, Jean Arp, and Tristan Tzara performing chaotic presentations of form and language designed specifically to destroy, in Scorpio fashion, any and all preconceived ideas of what art and artist should be. In 1917 Mondrian created pure abstract art using horizontal and vertical lines in black, gray and white as the only three colors.

Scorpio rules mystery, penetration, and the discovery of hidden knowledge. It is concerned with the underworld and the powerful energies that lie beneath the surface of what we perceive around us. This drive to penetrate to deeper levels of reality lies behind the transformation of art in this phase. This drive also affected science, especially physics. Newtonian physics dealt with the surface appearance of the physical world. Now physicists began to push deeper into the unseen world, to the very roots of matter, to reveal a revolutionary universe (the Scorpio Phase of the Aquarius Era). In 1905 Einstein published his Special Theory of Relativity. He showed that light responded to gravity, and theorized that the universe was curved because of that bending of light around planets and stars. Light traveling across the universe would be affected by gravity and eventually return to its starting point. In 1911 Rutherford created a nuclear model of the atom with a positively charged nucleus and negatively charged electrons. In 1913 Niels Bohr of Denmark devised a new model of the atom by combining Max Planck's quantum theory with Rutherford's nuclear atom. His model violated classical electromagnetic theory, but it accounted for the results of the hydrogen spectrum that was found in the atom. Classical Newtonian physics was replaced by Quantum Mechanics as scientists turned inwards to seek out the deep inner nature of atoms and the immense Scorpio power residing there. In 1916 Einstein again revolutionized the field of physics with his General Theory of Relativity.

Other areas of science underwent equally powerful transformations. Modern medicine was created with the introduction of powerful chemical medicines, chemotherapy, and the introduction of the hot-cathode x-ray. Freud transformed psychotherapy into a science with his theories of subconscious sexual urges. Scorpio rules sexuality. Carl Jung introduced his psychological theories based on the power of primitive mythological archetypes as they affect our psyches in 1906. Research took on a new importance in this phase.

Scorpio rules violence through its connection with the Mars rulership of this sign. Scorpio rules death and destruction. This phase saw a marked increase in the use of terrorism as a political tool. For several decades terror as a weapon had gained some limited popularity in Russia. In 1905 the suffragist Emmaline Pankhurst began using sensational terror tactics such as arson, bombing, window smashing, and hunger strikes to gain her ends. Also that year the IWW, the Industrial Workers of the World, was founded. The "Wobblies" as they were called, favored violent terrorist direct action tactics to protest their positions. In 1907 "Big Bill" Heywood, president of WFM, a mineworkers union, was tried for the murder of Idaho's former governor Steunenberg. In 1910 a bomb exploded at the LA Times newspaper to silence opposition to labor organizers. In 1915 Joe Hill, IWW organizer, was executed for the murder of a Utah man and his son. Political assassinations increased during this phase. In 1910 the trench coat, with rings inside for the purpose of carrying hand grenades, was introduced.

War had been raging in the Balkans since 1912. The Austrians were looking for any excuse to fight in the war and in 1914 their crown prince Archduke Franz Ferdinand and his wife were assassinated by a Serbian terrorist. Austria declared war and the Scorpio insanity was on. Because of the increase in international treaties from the previous phase Europe was tied together by various treaties of defense. Germany declared war on Russia and France, and neutral Belgium was invaded. Britain later entered the war, and Japan declared war on Germany and Austria. Over the next couple of years other nations declared war, and in 1917 several American nations including the US declared war. The First World War was indeed the first war in history to include the entire world in its scope. And it was one of the dirtiest.

Airplanes and submarines expanded the arena of death bringing destruction from unseen places, hidden beneath the sea and from the sky. In 1916 the first armored tanks were introduced into the arsenal of warfare. And in that year the bloodiest battle in world history was fought. The Battle of the Somme followed the largest artillery barrage in history. 1,437 British guns fired 1.5 million rounds along an 18-mile front for seven days. In that battle the Allies lost 794,000 men. The Central Powers lost 538,888 men. Poison gas was introduced as a weapon in 1915 when Germany used chlorine gas at the Second Battle of Ypres. World War I ended after killing over ten million men, and blinding, maiming, mutilating, and crippling or permanently shell-shocking another 20 million.

Worse still was the return on a large scale of deadly disease. Disease and epidemics have been a constant companion to mankind since the Neolithic Revolution. Yet, it seems, that in Scorpio, disease and epidemics tend to take on an added deadly importance. Disease became more violent in this phase. In 1907 the bubonic plague, always a threat, killed 1.3 million people in India. In 1910, in response to a change in Paris fashion towards imitation sable and sealskin fashions, Chinese workers trapped marmots that carried the bubonic plague virus. 1.5 million people died in China and India over the next nine years. In Russia a typhus epidemic hit in 1917 killing three million people over the next four years. This all lead up to the worst pandemic to hit humanity since the Black Death in the Scorpio Era in the 14th century. In 1918 the Spanish Flu pandemic, which began in China, hit the world killing, over a six-month period, 21.64 million people worldwide. Half a million Americans died, 19,000 in New York City alone. World War I ended in part because the Spanish Flu left the Germans so weak that they finally surrendered. Within hours of signing the armistice the flu broke around the world and the pandemic was over.

We tend to honor Scorpio disasters more than those of other times. The 1906 San Francisco earthquake is perhaps the most famous earthquake in US history. So, also, is the sinking of the Titanic in 1912 the most celebrated sea disaster.

Scorpio rules corporations, joint stock, corporate resources, and taxation. In the area of business the US government began to break up large trusts with the result that they reorganized themselves into larger and more diversified corporate systems where outright ownership was replaced with majority interest in stock holdings. The Robber Barons of earlier phases began to create corporate plutocracies. In this phase John D. Rockefeller became the world's first billionaire. By 1917 the US had 40,000 millionaires, up from 4000 in 1892. This phase marked an increasing trend towards wealth concentrating in the hands of the few.

The Taurus opposite to Scorpio rules money. Scorpio rules manipulation. American politics entered a period of Dollar Diplomacy. President Taft sought to extend American markets overseas with the idea that through economic interests we could more effectively control foreign politics. Dollars would replace bullets. To bring more money into the treasury Britain, in 1909, created her first income tax, or super-tax, on incomes over 5000 pounds, along with a very steep estates tax. That same year the US put to the states for ratification the 16th Amendment authorizing an unapportioned income tax. In 1918 the British income tax was doubled over the 1915 level, from 15% to 30%.

To further increase the corporate marketplace credit was extended to private individuals for the first time. In 1910 the first "Morris Plan" bank, the Fidelity Loan and Trust Co., opened in Virginia. The increased importance of money was supported by new ideas relating to economics. In 1911 economic price "indexing" was pioneered by economics professor Irving Fisher. He stated that prices rose in proportion to the supply of money and the velocity of that money's circulation. Money related not to goods and services but to itself, a very Scorpio-Taurus view. In 1913 Charles Beard wrote *Economic Interpretation of the Constitution*, a history of the American Revolution indicating that economic factors played the major role in our founding fathers decision to declare independence.

This phase ended, during the last few years, with inflation and price increases hitting all of the industrial countries of Europe and America. During the war, food rationing became a necessity that was hampered by tremendous rises in prices for the little food available.

This phase marked a dramatic change of culture, a transformation so vast that it is known by the name the 20th Century. The modern world would henceforth be worlds away from the relatively primitive accomplishments of even the science of the Industrial Revolution. And the science of the Industrial Revolution was itself a huge leap over the accomplishments of the previous world.

From the seeds planted in Scorpio the Sagittarius Phase, 1920 to 1935, brought with it expansion and exuberance. Radio and TV were invented. Sagittarius rules vision, broadcasting, and publishing. This phase witnessed an explosion in education and the transmission of knowledge because of the invention of radio and television. Like the invention of the printing press in the Sagittarius Era between 1440 and 1620 radio and television expanded the available pathways of knowledge beyond people who were literate to include for the first time illiterate peoples. In 1920 the first radio station, KDKA, began broadcasting in Pittsburgh. Hundreds of radio stations soon followed across the country. In 1921 the BBC was founded in England, and in 1923 the Zenith Radio Corporation was founded in the US. By 1927 NBC had so many radio stations in its lineup that they were divided into a Blue Network and a Red Network. FM radio was introduced in 1933.

This was the beginning of the Golden Age of Radio.

In 1926 the first successful television demonstration was given and by 1928 the first regularly scheduled television shows were aired in Schenectady, New York. *The Jazz Singer* was aired in 1927, the first successful full length talking movie, and that same year the Academy of Motion Picture Arts and Sciences was founded and presented its first Oscars. As people flocked to the increasingly popular movie houses people became increasingly aware of international news through the inclusion of newsreels in the show.

Sagittarius rules freedom, expansion, discovery, and long distance travel. The symbol of Sagittarius is the centaur shooting his arrow high into the air. This phase was one of the exuberant expansion of flight. In 1919 the first transatlantic flight was completed in a flying boat. Later that year the first nonstop transatlantic flight was made by John Alcock and Arthur Whitten-Brown. The race was on to push the limits of flight. US Army Lieutenant Doolittle flew the first coast-to-coast flight in one day in 1922. Two years later the first flight around the world was made by two US World Cruisers. Charles Lindbergh flew across the Atlantic in 1927, and Amelia Earhart followed in 1928. British aviatrix Amy Johnson was the first woman to fly solo from London to Australia in 1930, and Wiley Post became the first to fly solo around the earth in 1933.

This phase saw the explosion of commercial aviation. In 1920 KLM Royal Dutch Airlines and Quantas Airlines were both founded. In the following years Aeroflot, Pan Am, TWA, Northwest Airlines, Delta Airlines, Lufthansa, United, American Airlines, Braniff, and Continental Airlines were founded among others. Airports were built along with aircraft companies like Douglas, and Northrop. Between 1927 and 1929, a mere two years, air miles increased from six million to 30 million, and passenger numbers increased from 37,000 to 180,000.

Beginning in 1920 the enthusiasm of Sagittarius exploded in the phenomenon known as the Roaring Twenties. Sagittarius rules indulgence, excess, optimism, opportunity, and cultural participation. In spite of Prohibition the Roaring Twenties refused to let a law forbidding alcohol ruin their joy for life. Opportunity and expansion allowed organized crime to quickly grow into a huge multi-million dollar criminal business during this phase. Prohibition gave the Italian Mafia the opportunity to supply the

Sagittarius drive for fun with their own supplies of alcohol. The Mafia grew into a major facet of modern culture.

Music and dancing flourished. Here we find the First Youth Rebellion where students disregarded the practical direction of their parents in order to dance and party away their lives. The Roaring Twenties was a decade of dancing and music. This period is also known as the Great Age of Jazz, also called the Negro Renaissance, with such greats as Duke Ellington and Louis Armstrong. Irving Berlin then took black jazz and made it popular for a white audience, and for the rest of the world.

Sports also flourished in the expansive Sagittarius energy. In 1920 Babe Ruth was acquired by the Yankees from Boston. He began a 14-year stint as the "King of Swat" elevating baseball to the position of "America's game". The Yankees became the first team to draw one million spectators in a single season. Beginning in 1921 basketball began to be seen as a respectable sport behind the play of Nat Holman, and in football Red Grange and Knute Rockne electrified football fans. Athletic attendance broke all records and the stars of each sport became national heroes whose faces and accomplishments were more widely recognized than heads of state.

This phase was a period of Sagittarian boom and an expansive bust. The stock market crash of 1929 was easily the worst economic crash in our history. It expanded rapidly with the resulting depression spreading to the rest of the world within a couple of years. The Great Depression lasted ten years. In 1930 the Smoat-Hawley Tariff Bill raised America's tariffs to their highest levels ever. Other countries followed suit and a general worldwide depression set in. Trade declined, production dropped, and unemployment dramatically increased.

The causes of the Crash of '29 and the resultant Great Depression lay in the unconstrained Sagittarian search for good fortune and the tendency to excess and indulgence. Get rich schemes became popular. In 1920 Charles Ponzi offered get rich quick schemes to thousands of Bostonians, robbing them of their savings. A period of schemes and con artists began as people on all levels sought to grab a piece of the American dream.

Americans practiced almost no restraint in their buying habits. Credit became extremely popular as people rushed to mortgage their future for more immediate desires. The American industrial system promised vast opportunity for everyone and in an environment of exuberant optimism, installment plans increased five fold in seven years, opening up vast new vistas of individual ownership. By 1928 stock prices had soared beyond the limit of safe return. The desire for overnight fortunes pushed the market too high and in 1929 it came crashing down with Sagittarian gusto. The expansiveness of Sagittarius, and of Jupiter, the ruler of Sagittarius, can express itself in any direction, good or bad. It fueled the early economic boom of this period, but when that boom went too far, it continued in the direction of expanding the resulting depression into a worldwide phenomenon.

Then came the Capricorn Phase, 1935 to 1950. This period was one of great government. Capricorn rules government. Beginning in 1933 American government as a social institution began a revolutionary change that would alter American society. Big business was ineffective in countering the Great Depression, and when Franklin Roosevelt became president in 1933 he inaugurated the New Deal, a program of increased government control in practically all areas of public life. Legislation was passed by Congress at a dizzying pace in order to help stabilize the economy. The Emergency Banking Act, the Federal Emergency Relief Act, the Civil Works Administration, the National Recovery Administration, and the Agricultural Adjustment Administration were only a few of the many pieces of legislation and federal organizations created by the federal government beginning a long period of American big government.

Beginning in 1935 the US government began subsidizing the American farmer by buying surplus grains, by paying the difference in prices between overseas markets and the higher home market, and by paying farmers to not grow crops. In 1936 John Maynard Keynes strengthened governmental policy with the power of philosophy in his work "*The General Theory of Employment, Interest and Money*". He stated that depressions are not a necessary part of the economy. What is needed is government action in the form of investment in public works, in encouraging capital goods production, and in encouraging consumption in order to stabilize the market. There is a parallel here to the Capricorn Era between 1620 and 1800 where government control and civil liberties were paramount. Roosevelt expanded the duties of a democratic government to include the welfare of its citizens in times of emergency.

Government in other countries began a period of increased involvement and control as well, but more along the lines of total monarchy. In 1933 Adolph Hitler became dictator in Germany, restoring German political influence. That same year Austria became a dictatorship, and Portugal became a dictatorship under Salazar. In 1936 Franco began his rise to power in Spain, and Stalin in his bid to strengthen the Russian central government began his Great Purge. With Mussolini in Italy and Winston Churchill in England this was a period of powerful and well known national leaders.

In 1938 Mexico nationalized foreign oil investments in order to bring the money generated into the Mexican economy. The Mexican government had been pushing an agrarian revolution since 1934 in order to try to stabilize and strengthen the country. In 1946 she elected her first civilian head of state, who then began a program of electrification, irrigation, and improved transportation.

In 1942 Britain outlined a post-war government controlled cradle-to-grave social security system for her people. Following WWII she began to nationalize various services such as electricity production, transportation and railroads, and the iron and steel industries. In 1948 South Africa solidified political power in the much-hated Apartheid program. And in 1948 the Zionist political dreams of the Jews were finally realized, after close to 2000 years, in the creation of Israel, a Jewish political state.

World War I was fought because of revenge for an act of terrorism, an assassination. Scorpio. World War II was fought to stop Hitler's need for German "breathing room" to gain more land, a Cancer opposite to Capricorn concern. Cancer rules land, boundaries, and agriculture. The German geographer Karl Haushoker published his book, *Power and Earth*, in 1934. He professed a modern German manifest destiny, similar to our own Manifest Destiny put forward in the Cancer Phase between 1845 and 1860, stating that a powerful Germany had the natural right, by their position in Europe, to rule Eurasia and dominate the coastal countries. Hitler evolved his idea of German breathing space from this work. It gave him the validation he needed to begin his conquest of Europe which began WWII. Cancer rules foundations, home and family, and community. It is the sign of the mother. Hitler's idea for his conquest was the creation of the Third Reich, the Thousand Year Reich, an enduring government of German supremacy. In 1935 the German SS began a breeding program encouraging pure young German, Aryan, women to mate with SS officers in order to create pure Nordic children for the Fatherland.

Cancer energy also helped greatly in the Allied victory over Germany in the war. It has been argued that the war against Germany was won at home. This war effort was a community effort. Everybody sought ways to get into the action, and the Federal government utilized that feeling to the fullest. Considering that Allied and Axis armies were roughly equal to each other in abilities the difference then lay in the speed with which America was able to arm both herself and her allies. In 1939 only two percent of the gross national output was in armaments. In the year following the attack on Pearl Harbor armament production quadrupled, and by 1944 US arms production was 50% higher than the combined Axis arms output. By 1944 3.5 million women worked alongside 6 million men in American factories.

Material drives unified America and gave the common individual a sense of being a communal part of the war effort. By 1942 the Boy Scouts had collected 150,000 tons of paper. That same year one Seattle shoemaker gave 6 tons of rubber heels to the drive, and 5000 tons of rubber tires were acquired from the city of Los Angeles. Children dutifully saved their toothpaste tubes for scrap metal drives. These drives were immensely successful because Americans gave everything they had beyond basic necessities. The material drives, the largest scavenger hunts in history, were so successful that the government was hard pressed to handle the material collected. The enemy, in the long run, was simply crushed under the weight of US weaponry.

Food was also part of this Cancerian effort. Victory Gardens were planted so that food grown by farmers would be free to feed "our boys" overseas as well as the English. These gardens produced one third of all US vegetables consumed. Refusing to surrender the English began to "Dig for Victory" planting their own backyard gardens for food.

Cancer rules women. Women entered the war effort in record numbers. Women military branches were formed; WAVES for the Navy, WACS for the Army, Women Marines, and SPARS for the Coast Guard. 300,000 American women served in the Armed Services from America to Bataan in the Philippines. Women pilots ferried planes to England, and drove trucks, anything to support the men fighting on the fronts.

WWII was the most communally unified war in US history. Even the Japanese living in this country tried valiantly against American fears and prejudice to prove in any way they could that they were 100% American and supported our fight against the Japanese.

In Japan the non-combatant population was just as supportive of their own government. The decision to drop two atomic bombs was arrived at because it became increasingly clear that the Japanese people would fight to the last man, woman, and child in defense of their country.

This same feeling of national civic pride fueled the Russian people through the German invasion of Russia in 1941. The Germans advanced so rapidly that British Intelligence predicted the fall of Russia in ten days. During the worst winter in Russian history the Russians held the Germans at bay at Leningrad and by spring the remnants of some 22 German divisions surrendered in 1943. In the 17-month siege Leningrad lost 2.5 of its 3 million people, mostly to starvation and cold. But rather than surrender the Russian people chose to hold out at all costs. Of the 54.8 million people who died in WWII approximately 25 million of them were Russians.

The Final Solution to the creation of Hitler's master race was also based on Cancer energies. To allow breathing room for the creation and nurturing of a new racial community of Nordic Aryans, "inferior" races, as they were called, needed to be contained and dealt with according to this view. Beginning with his Aryan breeding program Hitler then turned to the Russian example of the concentration camp. In 1937 Buchenwald was opened to political prisoners of all faiths. That year German Jews were barred from industry and public recreation areas, and forced to wear the Jewish Star of David as a racial insignia. Romanian Jews were also barred from professions and from land ownership. The following year, as Germany began her territorial expansion, anti-Jewish sentiment spread with her. The largest pogrom in German history was begun and Jews were sent to concentration camps. In 1941 gas ovens were installed in those camps as part of the "Final Solution" to Europe's "Jewish problem".

Jews were conscripted into labor gangs, military brothels, summarily machine-gunned, sent to camps, or, where camps were unable to handle them, simply herded into inadequate ghettos and walled off from the rest of the population. By the wars end, the Nazi genocide had very efficiently, in Capricorn manner, killed 14 million "racial inferiors", 6 million of who were Jews. Other groups who suffered were the Poles, the Slavs, and the gypsies, all of who were also considered inferior. The "Final Solution" reflected a decidedly Satanic Cancer vision applied with Capricorn efficiency at its very worst.

Nature played her part in the drama of this phase. America's breadbasket, the Midwest, entered a dry period in 1933 creating a disaster known as the Dust Bowl. In 1934 Okies and Arkies from Oklahoma and Arkansas began a five year period of migration to California. By 1935 dust storms were turning midday to darkness in the West. 350,000 people moved to California over a five-year period only to find no jobs for the vast majority of migrants. This forced the US to focus on farming practices. A Green Revolution ensued based on the work of the Rockefeller Foundation and their efforts to reorganize the faltering Mexican agricultural system. This revolution promised to wipe out hunger worldwide using new high yield grains and chemical fertilizers among other advances. The Green Revolution stands as one of the top three agricultural revolutions in all of history. The other two were the Neolithic Revolution of the Age of Cancer, and the agricultural revolution created in England in the Capricorn Era, 1620 to 1800, with its Cancer opposite energy, that finally halted the constant threat of recurring and widespread famines that had plagued Europe for much of this age.

The Aquarius Phase, 1950 to 1965, was another period of great and revolutionary science. This was the beginning of the atomic age, the age of computers, and the space age. It was a time of transistor technology and the search for genius. America had a monopoly on atomic weapons since 1945 when they dropped two atomic bombs on Japan. In 1949 Russia broke that monopoly with her own atomic bomb test. The atomic bomb used over Hiroshima had a limit to the potential for energy release. The next level was the hydrogen, or H-bomb, first tested in 1952 at Eniwetok. Using nuclear fusion rather than fission there was now no known limit to the amount of destructive energy available. The Russians soon detonated their first H-bomb and the atomic, or nuclear age was born. The revolutionary potential for total global self-destruction had been realized for the first time in history. As a result, and in Aquarian fashion, the world entered into a revolutionary new type of war. The US and Russia became superpowers because of their nuclear weaponry and engaged in an ideological but deadly Cold War that lasted the entire phase.

The invention and application of the transistor replacing glass vacuum tubes created a technological revolution as powerful as any scientific revolution in history. It allowed dramatic advances in technology during this phase. It allowed scientists to create the first intercontinental ballistic missiles, known as ICBMs, capable of delivering nuclear warheads anywhere around the globe. In 1956 the Polaris missile, which could be launched from a submarine while submerged, was built. Transistors allowed mankind the ability to explore space for the first time in history. In 1957 the Soviets launched the first man-made satellites, Sputniks I and II, and in 1958 the US launched her first space satellite. In 1961 Yuri Gagarin of Russia became the first human to orbit the earth from outer space. That year Alan Shepard Jr. became the first American shot into space and the next year John Glenn became the first American to orbit the earth. The race for space had begun. We had entered the Space Age extending humanity's reach, impossibly, to the edges of space.

In the early 1950s IBM, International Business Machines, began to compete with Rand in manufacturing computers. In 1951 the Univac computer was introduced to businesses on a commercial basis, and in 1953 IBM introduced their model 701. In 1954 only 20 computers were shipped to businesses. By 1957 that number had jumped to 1000. In 1959 RCA introduced the first fully transistorized computer as a booming data processing industry was rapidly growing. In 1960 computer typesetting was introduced in Paris. We had entered the Age of Computers and the revolutionary potential of artificial intelligence.

Aquarius is a mental air sign. It is intellectual. The planet Mercury rules the signs Gemini and Virgo. In these signs thinking and thought processes become important. The sign Virgo even rules the quality of science. Looking back at our history the first industrial revolution may have been the invention of crafts industries covering every conceivable craft and need during the Age of Gemini between 6480 and 4320 BCE. During our most recent complete time period, the Aquarius Era from 1800 to 1980, we see another level of science altogether. While ruling Gemini and Virgo, Mercury is exalted in Aquarius. Here it gives to Aquarius the qualities of genius, revolutionary science, and the attainment of the impossible. The Aquarius Era, beginning in 1800, brought with it the Industrial Revolution as a successful way of life. The Virgo Phase between 1875 and 1890 saw another spurt of scientific invention that has been called the Second Industrial Revolution. Then after 1905, as we entered the high point of the Aquarius Era cycle, the period associated with renaissance and rebirth, the world entered into the truly revolutionary science known as the period of the Twentieth Century. Now, as we entered the Aquarius Phase between 1950 and 1965, of the Aquarius Era, humanity took it another step higher creating a technological revolution. We entered space, and we harnessed, as well as we could, the impossibly high energies of the atom, and atomic fission. And we began to build a whole new and revolutionary society based on a completely new and revolutionary type of technological computer intelligence. We have expanded our human intelligence, the ability to collect, remember, and process information with the addition of computer technology.

In 1950 television sales began to increase rapidly opening up a revolutionary period of mass media. TV brought world news and fashion directly into the home on an unprecedented scale beginning a process of uncontrolled mass education (ruled by Aquarius) about the outer world that created a more cosmopolitan outlook in the average American. Aquarius rules the collective, the unity of mankind, a cosmopolitan outlook, global communication, mass media, and mass education. Through the use of media, radio and especially television a mass culture was created around the educational as well as the mind-numbing entertainment fare of television. Television radically altered the process of political power. In 1950 TV gave popular power to Senator McCarthy and his hunt for Communist sympathizers in the US. It made Senator Kefauver a national hero in 1950 by televising his Special Committee to Investigate Organized Crime. In the early 60's Senator Kennedy defeated Richard Nixon for the presidency largely because of his greater public appeal through the medium of television.

In a totally revolutionary manner we accomplished the impossible. We no longer had to go out into the world to experience it. We brought the world into our own homes to experience the world from our own armchairs. More people than ever before were exposed to more personal ideas about holidays, excitement and self-help solutions to problems through the medium of television. This had a revolutionary effect on the family. Normal family life began to seem dull and uninteresting.

Romance, from the Leo opposite to Aquarius, began to replace duty as a goal of human fulfillment. Leo rules romance as well as children. Combined with the introduction of oral contraceptives the family began to break apart through a dramatically increased divorce rate, and the rebellion of young people against parental control.

Wearing tight jeans and leather jackets motorcycle gangs were created, quickly gaining a reputation as mean and troublesome, as warrior gangs. Leo rules the love of the fight. In suburbia young people, again in tight jeans, built hot rods and hung out at the local hamburger stands looking tough, and looking for others to race against. Street gangs grew in number in inner city slum areas as more young people, again in tight jeans and leather jackets, took to the streets rebelling against the depression of their living conditions. Exemplifying this trend was the movie idol James Dean who, in the movie _Rebel Without a Cause_, portrayed a troubled teenager who rebelled without any specific reason except the need to rebel. He died in a racing accident in 1955 and became a national teenage idol.

The planet Uranus rules, along with Saturn, the sign Aquarius. Uranus, as well as Aquarius, rules rebellion against the strictures of social norms. It seeks to break free from any inhibiting rules or regulations. This energy seeks the bizarre and unusual.

This phase has been focused socially and politically on the creation of a unified world community of nations rather than a world of separate and often conflicting nations. In 1949 a Council of Europe statute was signed beginning the process of creating a unified Europe. Initially ten European nations signed the statute. Eight years later, in 1957, the Treaty of Rome established the European Common Market as a unified economic community. Russia annexed Eastern Europe at the end of WWII and in 1949 these Communist countries created the Council for Mutual Economic Assistance while the Western nations created the North Atlantic Treaty Organization, NATO, as more nations began a period of establishing collective international organizations. In 1958 Egypt, Sudan and Syria established the United Arab Republic. In 1960 the oil-producing cartel of OPEC met for the first time. In 1961 the African Charter of Casablanca created a NATO type of organization between Ghana, Mali, Guinea, Morocco, and the United Arab Republic. A year later an organization of African states was established by 20 nations while those ministers who signed the Casablanca charter boycotted the meeting. They agreed to establish an African Common Market, a development bank, and a payments union. In 1963 the Federation of Malaysia unified Malaysia, Singapore, Sarawak, and North Borneo. A Latin free-trade association was established in 1961 and the Alliance for Progress helped spur economic and social development in Latin America in cooperation with the US.

Following the war America poured millions of dollars into rebuilding both Japan and Europe. This created the foundation for the idea of building a unified global economy based largely on the American dollar. In this process English emerged as the universal language of diplomacy.

Russia closed off Eastern Europe into a collective Communist Bloc and began a period of actively exporting Communist ideals as an Aquarian system that promised to unify the globe in a prosperous utopian collective. The US countered by presenting American capitalism and industrial know-how in a similar vein, as the path to a utopian life of technological luxury and ease. As each country sought to unify humanity behind their own ideals a cold war was created. China became Communist behind Mao Tse Tung. The world began to collectivize itself from many different and separate nations into three major camps, two of them being the Free World versus the Communist Bloc. The third camp became known as the

Third World, undeveloped countries that were seen as ripe targets for the spread of Communist or capitalist ideologies.

In this environment of Aquarian brotherhood and equality the British Empire, totaling 40 nations, began a period of self-induced decline by granting freedom to her holdings in Africa and the West Indies after 1952. Britain was reduced to only 12 closely related nations. Other European countries followed suit by granting independence to their own colonies in Africa. France finally granted independence to her colonies in 1958. By the end of 1960 almost all of Africa was comprised of free nations, except for the independent white states of Rhodesia and South Africa. By the same time almost all of Southeast Asia was also independent.

Freedom was taking another turn within the US during this phase. In 1948 the NAACP began to push, for the first time, for full integration into white society kicking off a phase of increasing racial unrest and civil rights activism. By 1954 Aquarian brotherhood and the Leo love of the fight resulted in the first of many victories for black people. That year the Supreme Court ruled, in Brown vs. the Board of Education, that segregation in schools was unconstitutional. The next year racial segregation was knocked down for public golf courses, parks, swimming pools, and playgrounds as well as for interstate busses, trains, and terminal waiting rooms. In 1956 Martin Luther King Jr. stepped forward to lead blacks to demand their new constitutional rights from a white population that refused to acknowledge the Supreme Court rulings. In 1957 the first Civil Rights law since the Civil War reconstruction days was enacted by Congress. It established a Civil Rights Commission and provided federal safeguards of voting rights. In 1960 the first sit-in demonstrations by blacks were held in lunch counters in Greensboro, North Carolina. A new Civil Rights law was passed by Congress that year, and the Justice Department brought America's first sweeping civil rights suit charging a plot against black voters in Tennessee. In 1961 the "Freedom Riders" began demonstrating on Birmingham, Alabama buses. Other demonstrations soon followed throughout the South. In 1963 President Kennedy asked Congress for new far-reaching civil rights legislation banning segregation in privately owned facilities that were open to the public. That same year President Kennedy federalized the Alabama National Guard to face down Alabama Governor George Wallace's opposition to blacks.

By the end of this phase President Lyndon Johnson called for his war on poverty with the Economic Opportunity Act coordinating the new Job Corps, the Neighborhood Youth Corps, VISTA, the Head Start Program and various community action programs. These programs were largely targeted to help minority populations to better themselves and find an integrated place within society.

In the US the federal government supported the integration of blacks into American society against the fears and prejudices of the white population in true Aquarian fashion. In South Africa the vote went the other way. In the early 50's the South African Supreme Court ruled for blacks, that apartheid was illegal. The South African government quickly passed a resolution that made the executive branch the highest legal authority in the country with the power to censure the court. The only legal rulings allowed were those that supported white supremacy and the status quo.

The largest minority in the world, women, also increased the fight for their equality with men during this phase. To reward American servicemen for their duties in WWII the US built large tracts of houses for these men. Suburban living became popular, complete with Bar-B-Qs and cocktail parties. Laborsaving devises flooded the home insulating the housewife from social interaction as never before. The old tight-knit urban neighborhoods were left behind, both friends and relatives, to be replaced by the virtual social interaction of television in suburbia. More people became disillusioned and began to look beyond marriage for fulfillment. In the 50's the divorce rate began to rise drastically. More women turned to the male oriented career work world. By 1960 34% of American women over 14 were in the work market, and 31% of American married women.

Extra-marital affairs increased. In 1952 the first oral contraceptive was produced. In 1960 contraceptives were refined enough, and the sexual climate was relaxed enough, that Enovid 10 was marketed as the first commercially available, over-the-counter oral contraceptive. It was marketed as Conovid in Britain the next year. With readily available oral contraceptives, women found themselves free from the fear of pregnancy and the accusations from family and friends due to extramarital pregnancy. Casual sex offered women the option of equality with men in the arena of sexual conquest. It allowed women to explore their own sensual fulfillment, an area that had been lacking in our puritanical, patriarchal culture.

Feminism was coming of age. In 1963 Betty Friedan, in her book *The Feminine Mystique*, wrote that women were deluded into thinking that their fulfillment lay in their husbands and family, that true fulfillment resided in the world of career and sexual freedom.

Beginning around 1965 the utopian ideal of the Twentieth Century began to dramatically fall apart. This was the Pisces Phase, 1965 to 1980, of the Pisces Era and it marks another dramatic turning point in modern history. Pisces rules prophecy among other things and it seems as if, quite suddenly, all the ancient prophecies of doom began to emerge on the historical stage. The world had come close to creating at least the image of a utopian society in the US with the American Dream of a chicken in every pot and a car in every garage. During the decade of the fifties that utopian dream was almost at the point of becoming a reality, or at least so we thought. We had rebuilt the world after WWII and were in the process of trying to remake the world according to the ideals of American capitalism and good old-fashioned American know-how. Everything had the utopian appearance of success and prosperity stamped on it. It was a glorious period of history. Yet dark forces lurked beneath the surface, forces that carried with it the power of prophecy.

As stated before each age contains twelve astrological eras. In the course of an age's evolution, as it proceeds in time through each of these eras, every age reaches a period where the essential social constructs are torn down and the next age is recognized. This last era has historically been one of social and political breakdown. Pisces rules dissolution, the process of dissolving, or washing away all the old dirt, and the Virgo opposite sign rules disintegration.

Historically the world entered into the last era, the Pisces Era, in 1980. This will last until 2160 when we will then enter into the Age of Aquarius. Leading up to this final dissolving era we experienced the Pisces Phase of the Aquarius Era between 1965 and 1980. What happened then was almost Biblical in the social destruction it began to bring with it.

The Gulf of Tonkin Resolution gave the President of the United

States, in 1964, the power to escalate our involvement in Vietnam. Unfortunately for our national unity, this phase also brought with the Vietnam War a Piscean sense of martyrdom and pacifism that seriously tore at our anti-Communist resolve. It also saw the disintegration of our national sense of purpose. In 1965 the first American combat troops landed in Vietnam. Almost at the same time resistance to the war began to increase. After 1966 with the dramatic increase in the draft, there arose an equally strong draft evasion effort. By 1968 10,000 American youths had fled to Canada. In the fall of 1967 there were 204 college campus demonstrations, the vast majority of them anti-war. In 1970 National Guardsmen fired on these demonstrators at Kent State University. Following the Tet Offensive in 1968 even some Senators and newspeople began to turn against the war effort.

In 1963 President Kennedy was assassinated in Dallas, Texas. From that moment on, America slipped into a period of Piscean paranoia and irrationality that almost left the country in shambles. Pisces rules insanity, irrationality, fear, and paranoia. That same year, 1963, NAACP leader Medgar Evers was murdered following a civil rights broadcast by President Kennedy. In 1964 America entered a period of devastating race riots. Harlem and Philadelphia erupted in 1964. In 1965 Malcolm X was killed and race riots tore apart Watts in Los Angeles. In 1966 race riots hit Cleveland, Chicago, and Atlanta. In 1967 race riots spread far and wide tearing at the soul of 127 cities, with Newark and Detroit as the worst hit. The next year Martin Luther King Jr. was assassinated and race riots immediately erupted in dozens of US cities. That same year Robert Kennedy was assassinated in Los Angeles, and in 1972 George Wallace was shot and crippled by assassins. Racial fears between blacks and whites intensified.

A strong disillusionment in our country and our leaders hit rather suddenly between 1965 and 1966 as the race riots broke out. The Vietnam War seemingly had no real reason behind it, and no foreseeable end. By 1970 a deep disenchantment had set in along with a credibility gap between youth and those in power. Student riots closed down dozens of colleges and universities. New Left radical groups were created beginning a policy of terrorist bombings in order to halt government activities. In 1969 the Weathermen changed their name to the Weather Underground and began bombing public buildings.

Fear even entered the individual home on an unprecedented scale. In 1962 the Boston Strangler began killing women until he was caught in 1964. That year, 1964, Kitty Genovese was attacked and killed in Queens, New York while her neighbors looked on. Not wanting to get involved the police were not called until 30 minutes after her death. In 1966 Richard Speck terrorized Chicago with the murder of eight student nurses. In 1969 Charles Manson and his followers made headlines with the brutal Tate-La Bianca murders. During the 70's serial rapists and murderers became a horrifying part of the city environment. Serial murders increased dramatically with the Son of Sam murders, the Hillside Strangler, and the Zodiac killer as perhaps the more infamous.

City schools were also affected. As drug use became more prevalent some students became more violent. More students, and younger, began carrying weapons to school with the result that schools soon became barricaded battlegrounds. Students attacked teachers killing some and raping others. Vandalism increased dramatically and schools responded by putting up chain link fences for protection. Parent-child violence increased as did the suicide rate among children and teenagers. Runaway children and teens became a serious new problem for American families.

Violence and paranoia were increasing on all sides. The 70's became known as the decade of fear as more people barricaded themselves in their homes. The crime rate climbed steadily and by the end of the phase prisons were dangerously overcrowded and prison violence on the increase. Prison riots became commonplace. Many criminals convicted of minor offenses were let off without a jail sentence because there was no place to put them. Pisces rules prisons and large institutions.

Pisces rules karma, or spiritual or cosmic law, and law enforcement. Throughout this phase law became a central issue in American life. In 1966 the Miranda decision required that all persons arrested for a crime be read their legal rights. Confessions obtained without those rights being explained were held to be inadmissible in court. Soon other decisions further limited police powers, protecting the rights of citizens, criminal or not, against unlawful searches, and limiting the scope of evidence to narrow constitutional guidelines. Against this trend President Nixon sought to increase police powers in the early 70's with his "no-knock" anti-crime legislation. Crime began to rise dramatically. As crime increased so did revelations of police brutality and false arrest. Respect for the law sunk to an all-time low. During the 70's police, or pigs as they were now called, were constantly under fire from blacks and white New Left groups such as the SLA and the Weather Underground. In highway pursuits of black militants in inner city areas, like the Black Panthers, police would break off pursuit once offenders reached the safety of their own neighborhoods. It was too dangerous to go any farther.

Violence spilled onto the international stage as well. Terror became a preferred weapon of various Arab groups. Terror is linked with Scorpio, but here it is the Pisces paranoia that was the astrological driving force. In 1968 the first jetliner was hijacked to Cuba. Other hijackings soon followed. In 1970 a Pan Am jetliner was hijacked to Beirut. There the hijackers brought aboard explosives and flew to Cairo. Unloading the passengers they then blew up the plane. That year Palestinians hijacked a TWA jetliner, a Swissair and a BOAC jetliner and blew all of them up. In 1972 Lod Airport was shot up by Palestinians, and the terrorism increased. In 1972 the summer Olympic games at Munich was the scene of a PLO terrorist assault on the Israeli Olympic team, killing 11 Israeli athletes.

Paranoia and fear surfaced elsewhere also. In 1966 Mao Tse Tung inaugurated the Great Proletarian Cultural Revolution in China and unleashed his Red Guard army of Chinese youth on an unsuspecting Chinese public. Following the end of the Vietnam War the Cambodian government under Pol Pot terrorized her own people sending her intellectuals and artists off to rural "killing fields" for re-indoctrination in Communist theory. In France in 1968 universities were closed due to student riots, and industrial strikes created an economic crisis. And beginning in 1973 Argentina experienced a rash of assassinations and kidnappings as government death squads became common in South America. Fear increased everywhere.

The economy was affected as well. Welfare began to increase rapidly as America slipped quickly towards becoming a welfare state. In 1965 New York City welfare rolls hit 480,000. Ten years later it would be 1.2 million people and require 3.4 billion dollars of the city's 12 billion dollar budget. Inflation began to rise steeply wiping out any advantages that pay increases promised. An energy crisis gripped the world in the early 70's and by 1973 that energy crisis and soaring grain prices created a worldwide monetary crisis followed by a world wide economic recession that was the worst economic crisis since the Great Depression. By the end of the 70's even middle class white collar workers were showing up on welfare rolls as the economy closed down around us. Unemployment climbed.

Pollution became a major issue of this phase. Pisces rules pollution, as well as confusion and lack of direction. In 1966 the first rare and endangered species list was compiled by the Department of the Interior. It listed 78 species in danger of extinction. In three short years that list was expanded to include 89 species close to extinction. That same year, 1966, California imposed automobile smog limits to take effect in 1969. And mercury contamination of fish suddenly became a major concern over the pollution of our food. By 1969 evidence was mounting concerning the harm caused by the pesticide DDT. By 1970 the Environmental Protection Agency was established to oversee the protection of various wildlife species and habitats. Pollution related crises created doomsday scenarios that were potentially more dangerous than nuclear war because of their pervading presence in the environment around us. Air pollution, smog, and acid rain affected the air we breathed. Water pollution, constant oil spills, toxic industrial waste dumped into our rivers, streams, and lakes affected the water we depend on for drinking and cooking. During the 70's one revelation after another brought our attention quickly around to the serious problem of toxic waste dumps near populated areas. One of the most famous was Love Canal where people were constantly getting sick and dying due to the toxic waste buried in the ground beneath their homes. Disposing of nuclear waste created in nuclear power plants also became a major concern in the 70's.

Pisces rules escapism, drugs, and alcohol. During this period the Hippie movement, around 1967 and the Summer of Love, popularized free love and drugs. Drug use has since expanded to become a major social and criminal problem. Pollution and species extinctions became ecological warning signs for disaster. Terrorism spread as a political and as a national weapon as violence expanded within society. Race riots and prison riots became common. A general atmosphere of fear settled over residential America during the 70's as crime became a major social problem. During this period the phenomenon of the serial killer and serial rapist became common. Economic inflation began to rise rather steeply. Welfare began to increase to immense proportions. Children began to run away from their families in increasing numbers. Unemployment and homelessness began to rise. The cost of these social ills has been depleting, at a rapid rate, the ability of most Americans to afford the promise of a technological utopia. The utopian promise of the American Dream suddenly began to fall apart all around us. Utopian promises quickly turned to doomsday warnings.

On a more promising side Pisces rules contact with other worlds. In 1965 the Gemini two-man space program was begun, and in 1967 Apollo II landed a man on the moon for the first time. Science had entered the realm of science fiction. We had actually set foot on another world. In 1972 the Soviet spaceship Venus 8 landed softly on the surface of Venus, and the American Voyager 10 was launched towards a photographic and electronic analysis of Jupiter. Other spaceships would soon be launched to study Saturn, Uranus, Neptune and, eventually, Pluto. Astronomers discovered quasars at the outer edges of the universe, pulsars, and black holes.

In 1960 less than 5% of the ocean floor had been explored. Even by 1965 scientists admitted that they knew more about the far side of the moon. After 1965, however, an intense push to understand the ocean was begun. By the end of that phase Jacques Cousteau and other oceanographers had discovered the mid-Atlantic Ridge that pushed the Old and New Worlds apart. They had studied the Great Barrier Reef around Australia and had peered deep into the Marianna Trench. Knowledge of our oceans grew rapidly. Pisces is a water sign.

The 20th Century had been a century of religious retrenchment. World War I in its devastation, along with the Spanish Flu Pandemic of 1917, offered no easy answers for those seeking religious reasons for what was happening. The Great Depression affected everybody and pulled the rug out from under any Church attempt to assign fault based on belief in God. Archaeological finds dating back millions of years destroyed man's belief in Old Testament chronology. The earth was far older than what the Bible led us to believe. Science was finding logical causes for phenomenon previously thought to have had magical spiritual origins. Psychology began to replace religion with their logical explanations of mental processes. People began to turn away from religion in increasing numbers. This phase marked a rather dramatic reversal of that trend.

In 1965 the spiritually hungry youth subculture known as the hippies began. That year Timothy Leary published his book _The Psychedelic Reader_ in which he presented the psychedelic drug LSD as the yoga of the western world. Love and dropping acid became the backbone for a western spiritual revival. LSD could chemically expand one's "consciousness" and bring visions, or revelations, and a feeling of oneness with the spiritual that the scientific technological world could not. By 1967 the Hippie movement had gained worldwide media attention. Children began running away from the harsh realities of their homes and families to the West Coast, to San Francisco and Los Angeles, seeking to find the love and non-judging acceptance that this movement promised. Most Americans viewed the Hippies as dirty, degenerate, and cowardly yet their lifestyle was based upon the Piscean Christian ideals of universal love, non-aggression (turning the other cheek), peace and happiness. Their movement affected the entire world, showing the technological West the shortcomings of an overly materialistic way of life, and opening the doors wide to the introduction of Oriental meditation practices. Their downfall was their use of drugs in order to experience their spiritual highs. After the Hippie movement died the drug addiction remained. Beginning with the Hippies drugs became extremely popular throughout all levels of society. Drug addiction and the violence it has generated became a major contributor to the climbing crime rate of the 70's.

Many in the Hippie movement, as well as others, were hungry for real spiritual experience. They became the main audience for Eastern spiritual techniques. In 1965 the International Society for Krishna Consciousness was founded in New York based on chanting as a non-addictive and safe means of experiencing the mystical side of existence. Hare Krishnas, as they were called, were found at all major airports wearing saffron robes and shaved heads selling their books to all who were interested. Maharishi Mahesh Yogi had introduced Transcendental Meditation, known as TM, to the West in 1955. Around 1967 the Transcendental Meditation Program suddenly experienced a massive increase in popularity. Other techniques and systems were also becoming very popular.

Not all groups may have been spiritually so evolved. The Moonies, the group founded by the Korean teacher Sun Myong Moon, gained a lot of negative press due to their heavy handed cult-like practices concerning money and total control of an individual's life. Baghwan Shree Rajneesh introduced a tantric sexual system that combined western psychological thought with traditional Eastern concepts. Before he was evicted from the US he was traveling with armed bodyguards around his compound in Oregon.

In 1968 an anthropology student named Carlos Castaneda published his first book _The Teachings of Don Juan: A Yaqui Way of Knowledge._ This book, along with others such as _Black Elk Speaks_, signaled a Piscean revival of indigenous Indian religious culture and practices. Native Americans began to fight for their religious rights and their cultural integrity often in violent confrontations with federal authorities.

In the late 60's and in the 70's Christianity witnessed a strong revival of faith as well. Evangelism increased and spread like wildfire. Christianity, and Islam as well, began gaining converts in large numbers. Both religions experienced a spurt of growth not seen within the last century. Televangelism, by the 70's, had grown into a multi-million dollar business. The Church embraced the new Born Again Christian movement as a popular vehicle for Christians that were rediscovering their faith. "Jesus Freaks", as they were called, equaled other groups in their zeal for preaching the glories of experiencing the Christ consciousness within.

The downside of this growth of religious fervor lay in the reviving strength of Fundamentalism. Both Christianity and Islamic Fundamentalism is based on a literal but arguably shallow translation of their respective holy books. Too often these literal translations remain wide open to fear, to judgmental and prejudicial views. Western influence in the Middle East was now being interpreted as a satanic materialistic influence luring Moslems away from the traditional practice of their religious life. International terrorism against the West can be seen as an Islamic fundamentalist attempt to rid Islamic countries of this satanic Western influence. On the other hand the Arabic use of terror caused the

West to view extremist Islamic groups as also satanic. The Middle East became an ugly and extremely violent battleground at the same time that extremist Islamic groups were planting bombs in public places throughout Europe.

The Pisces Phase led directly into the Pisces Era in 1980. The beginnings of the social ills and the chaos we face in this era were already beginning in devastating fashion in the Pisces Phase beginning 1965. What was begun then will intensify as this era progresses unless personal steps are taken to counter them utilizing the positive energies involved.

PART 2

THE END-TIME CYCLE

Time flows in cycles. We have just measured these cycles astrologically. The large end of this spectrum has been the cycle of the Precession of the Equinox, a cycle that completes one revolution every 25,920 years. Within that there are smaller cycles that direct human consciousness and history. There may also be larger cycles of time than these. In these cycles there are regularly scheduled periods of cleansing. There exists a regular end-time cycle that is a necessary period of reorganization within these cycles. In this section we will look at mythological and archaeological evidence to suggest the existence of periods of mass destruction that punctuate these cycles. These periods support the existence of an astrological end-time cycle. They give support to the prophecies of the millennial end-time that we are confronted with today.

In the cycles discussed earlier in this book there exists a process of rising up and of falling. At the end of each age, along the Pisces-Virgo axis, there are times of varying degrees of destruction, dissolution and disintegration. This very same process may well happen on a much larger scale. This larger cycle of destruction may have given rise to end-time mythologies; extinction of most life on earth that have happened in the past.

MYTHS OF THE FALL

Mythologies of most if not all cultures around the world tell us that indeed there have been in the past world destructions caused either by fire or by flood, or both. In our own Judeo-Christian tradition we remember well the story of Noah and his ark, an enclosed vessel 300 cubits by 50 cubits by 30 cubits, with a roof (or window) on top and a door in its side. The masculine and feminine halves of all of creation, two by two, were kept safe within while the Lord caused it to rain 40 days and 40 nights. World destruction by flood.

Almost all other cultures, great and small, advanced and primitive, say the same thing; that the world was destroyed in the past. Among the Australian aborigines Old Man Pundyil once burned mankind by opening the door of the Sun letting out a stream of fire. The Eskimos relate that during the fiery destruction the Arctic Ocean evaporated. The Spurinas of northwest Brazil tell us that very long ago the Sun, a boiling water cauldron, tipped over to roast a scalding flood upon earth. The Washoe Indians of California and Nevada tell of an all-encompassing volcanic upheaval that included several volcanoes. The stars melted and fell from the sky from the intensity of the heat. The Yurucari of Bolivia relate that the demon Aymasuni was responsible for the fall of heavenly fire, which destroyed everything on earth. Only one man escaped. Foreseeing the event he hid himself along with some food in a cave.

The Voguls of the Northern Ural Mountains in Russia tell of a holy fireflood, which burned and destroyed everything on the earth except for a few men who escaped on a raft. The reason for the flood was the destruction of the devil, Xulater by Num Tarem, the Fatherly. The Babylonian Epic of Gilgamesh speaks of a fire rain let loose upon the earth by the Anunnaki rushing across heaven with lit torches.

The Maoris were once a people who inhabited the entire Pacific Ocean from New Zealand to the Americas. Today the Maori are centered in New Zealand. Their culture hero, Maui, was in need of fire at one time. He was told how to get it by his blind Grandmother. It was guarded by Makuika, the giant, who acted as the guardian of the flame. Maui tricked the giant into a wrestling match and through the use of magical wands he eventually caused the death of the giant. He grabbed the fire but it was too hot and slipped from his grasp. The world began to burn.

The Tuleyone Indians of California remember Wek Wek the falcon who stole fire from heaven and carried it back under his wing. It fell out and scorched the earth. The Yana Indians of California tell us that their ancestors sent five men to obtain the fire-treasure. Coyote, the one who carried it naturally dropped it and the earth immediately burst into flame and the waters evaporated.

From Greece there is the story of Phaethon the son of the Sun God Apollo. Extracting a promise from Apollo to let him drive the Chariot of the Sun he soon found he could not control the solar steeds. They ran wild through heaven scorching the constellations and destroying our earth, which was saved at the last minute by a thunderbolt thrown by Zeus at the solar child, killing him and ending the tragedy.

In our own Judeo-Christian tradition the story of Sodom and Gomorrah may be a vestige of an older world destruction by fire story. Because of their evil the Lord rained fire and brimstone down on them from heaven. Only Lot and his two daughters were saved. They went up into the hills and dwelt in a cave, and because there was "not a man on earth to come into us after the manner of all the earth" (Gen. 19:31), the two daughters lay with their father in order repopulate the earth.

In many stories a flood or tidal wave comes to quench the fire. In many others the flood itself is the sole mechanism of catastrophe. We are familiar with Noah and his flood. The Chinese have a tradition where they see themselves as descendents of a lone individual, Nu-wah, the survivor of the Great Flood that destroyed the world. Are Nu-wah and Noah the same?

The Ahom tribe of Burma tell of their ancestor surviving the Great Flood in a gigantic gourd. Among the Annamese the vessel was a tom-tom. The Voguls were saved when Num Tarem built them a metal ark with a roof of seven-fold sturgeon hide. Among the Mandans of the U.S. a dove brought back a willow twig as a sign that the waters were receding. On the ark of Noah it was an olive branch. The Babylonian Noah was called Utnapishtim.

Anthropologists have counted over 500 flood stories from every corner of this earth. Many of these traditions tell of more than one world destruction, implying the existence of a repeating pattern within time. The history of this world, according to the Hopi, contains three destructions, and a fourth very soon to inundate us. To the Hopi there are nine worlds. The two highest worlds belong to the creator and to his nephew. There are seven worlds left that humans must evolve through. We are at present at the end of the fourth world.

The first world was a world of golden age proportions. There was no sickness until the end when evil entered the hearts of the people. Its mythic color was yellow and its sacred mineral was gold. Here the First People were pure and happy. Mother Earth gave everything to them without any work or hardship whatsoever. After forgetting the Creator, the first world was destroyed by fire. Those who still remembered the Creator were saved within the womb of Mother Earth.

The second World was created and land and water were alternated, continents were sunk and ocean lands were raised up. The Second World was like a silver age. The color was blue and its mineral was silver. Everyone was very spiritual but people were no longer able to communicate with the animals. They had to work for their food and shelter. Eventually they became greedy and evil came into the world. This Second World was destroyed by a pole shift and the world froze into solid ice. Those who were still spiritual were saved by living with the Ant People inside Mother Earth.

The Third World was created and a bronze-like age began. The mythic color was red and their sacred mineral was copper. On this world people had to work harder for their livelihoods. They built cities and civilizations and they multiplied very rapidly due to increased sexuality. They became wholly engrossed in their own ways. The power of sex was used in evil ways such as prostitution. War machines were built such as flying shields to attack other cities. This world was destroyed by a Great Flood. Those still spiritually pure were saved in hollow reeds, which eventually landed in this Fourth World. This world is kind of an iron age. The mythic color is yellowish white and the mineral is a mixed mineral called sikyapala. In this world work is very hard. It is ruled by opposition and duality. From these opposites we must learn to choose our own way, choices that will determine whether this world will also be destroyed.

The Aztec and Mayan traditions also speak of a similar series of world destructions. From the Greeks the poet Hesiod, in his WORKS AND DAYS, also tells of five ages, four of which parallel the Hopi story. Hesiod placed the Iron Age as the fifth and inserts an extraneous age as the fourth age of man. The Roman poet Ovid also speaks of four worlds that are nearly identical to the Greek and the Hopi stories.

A remnant of this same story is found in the Bible in the Book of Daniel. The dream of Nebuchadnezzar revolves around the image of a great man with five parts. The head is gold, then follows silver, brass, and iron with feet a mixture of iron and clay. The interpretation of the dream by Daniel reveals that the five parts are kingdoms. These kingdoms may represent time periods, one following the other as things worsen for the king.

The Greeks tell us that there were three world destructions. The Flood of Deukalion and his wife Pyrrha after the destruction of the Bronze Age follows two older world destructions associated with the hero/survivors Ogygos and Dardanos.

Plato, The Greek philosopher, in his work TIMAEUS related that the Egyptians know of many other destructions; that in fact there is a regular cycle of these destructions. Solon, the old Greek philosopher and lawgiver went to Egypt a couple of centuries prior to Plato's time and confronted, in his journeys, an old Egyptian priest who related the Egyptian history of repeated destructions.

In the very ancient culture of India the Jain religion outlines fourteen ages in all, seven descending ages and seven ascending ages, descent and ascent measured in terms of moral and spiritual qualities and in the physical stature of human beings. We are now in the lowest age.

The Hindus see history as an ascending and descending cycle of four ages set within larger cycles of time that surpass our present ability to fully comprehend. The four ages, or Yugas, are described in terms of the Greek and Hopi model. Satya Yuga was, and will be again, a pure Golden Age. Treta Yuga was a silver age. The Dwapara Yuga was a less brilliant bronze or copper age of life and finally the Kali Yuga we are now in is a hard warlike iron age.

The Kali Yuga is 432,000 years long; the Dwapara Yuga is 864,000 years long; the Treta Yuga is 1,296,000 years; and the Satya Yuga is 1,728,000 years in duration. The Kali Yuga is one-fourth as long as the longest Yuga, Satya Yuga. These numbers accord well with this astrological model of history.

The Kali Yuga is exactly 100 times as long as two astrological ages (2 x 2160 years per age =4320). The Dwapara Yuga is one-half as long as the Satya Yuga, or 200 times as long as two astrological ages. Treta Yuga is three-fourths as long as Satya Yuga, and 300 times longer than two astrological ages. Satya Yuga is 400 times longer than two astrological ages. Altogether they comprise one Mahayuga of 4,320,000 years. The mathematics of these cycles corresponds exactly to our shorter astrological cycles. And from here the cycles continue to build upon each other.

71 Mahayugas equal one Monvantara. This is also called one Manu. 14 Manus make up one Kalpa, also called one day of Brahma. At the end of this day of Brahma all of creation is destroyed whereupon we enter a night of Brahma, of equal length. There are 365 days in a year. 100 years of Brahma equals one life of Brahma. Beyond this 1000 lifetimes of Brahma equals one life of Vishnu. 1000 lifetimes of Vishnu then equals one life of Shiva. And 1000 lifetimes of Shiva equals one life of the Divine Mother. The Eternity of Absolute Being is made up of countless lifetimes of the Divine Mother.

The modern metaphysical discipline of Theosophy, presented by the mystic Helen Blavatsky in 1848 states that humanity today is of the fifth root-race of the fifth round of creation. The ancient

Etruscans record seven bygone ages. The Greek philosopher Aristotle outlined what he called a supreme year where all the planets and the sun and moon would return to their original positions. Within this supreme year there was a great winter he called kataklysmos, which means deluge, and a great summer, ekpyrosis, which means combustion. The world through its cycles is alternately burned and flooded. Heraclitus gives 10,800 years as a cycle after which all is burnt. Five astrological ages equal 10,800 years. The sixth age would then be the age of destruction.

From Tibet and from the Bengal Sea we are now in a fifth age following four previously destroyed ages. The Bhagavata Purana speaks of four pralayas, cataclysms, that ended four previous ages. The Buddhist Visuddhi-Magga tells of seven ages each separated by one of three different cataclysms. The Persian Zend Avesta also speaks of seven ages. The Chinese remember ten perished ages prior to the time of Confucius.

Hawaii and Polynesia speak of nine past ages, as do the Icelandic Eddas. And the Jewish rabbinical tradition says that God had made six earths prior to our seventh earth. He had destroyed them all. The Tower of Babel was in the fourth world. The names of these earths are Eretz, Adamah, Arka, Harabah, Yabbashah, and Tevel. The name of our present earth is Heled. Perhaps Heled is somehow related to the Christian term hell, with this last earth being the lowest of all the earths, a place of suffering and pain that parallels the Hindu Kali Yuga as well as the Greek description of the Iron Age as an age of fighting, opposition, and suffering.

The various religions that these mythologies have come from all warn that we are again at the threshold of a world cataclysm. From our modern Christian Fundamentalist perspective we tend to think of such change, an end-time, as a period of relatively few years, if that long, wherein dramatic changes culminate in a single cataclysm. Dealing with very long time periods it may well be that end-time periods themselves are an entire age of 2160 years. The entire Age of Pisces may be the end-time of Judeo-Christian prophecy, from the warnings of Christ all the way through to this final days period we are now in. Christ himself warned that before "this generation" was done, from his time until ours, all prophecy would come to pass. In this respect he may have been speaking about the generation of Pisces, not a generation of human length.

The Pisces Era then becomes that last Final Days of Christian prophesy, from AD 1980 to 2160.

In addition to the process of very slow geological changes due mainly to weathering and erosion there exists periods of punctuated equilibrium where sudden changes happen very fast within a geological scale. These periods in many cases may be associated with the Pisces-Virgo axis acting as an astrological trigger for sudden cataclysmic changes that increase in intensity through the age until a climax is reached. This Pisces-Virgo axis is important as a trigger for end-time scenarios. Pisces rules dissolution, a watery cleansing or washing away of accumulated social dirt. Virgo rules disintegration and extinction, a similar process of breaking down into dirt and dust, and of life coming to an end. The two act together, Virgo breaking down into dirt, and Pisces washing the dirt away.

People and cultures everywhere have mythological memories of an end-time cycle. It is only our modern western linear historical perspective that discounts these memories as fantasy even though there is ample archaeological evidence to support these claims.

EXTINCTION

Archaeological evidence supports the possibility that the collective memory behind all of these end-time mythologies may in fact be true. We are, at present, still in the Age of Pisces. Using the convenient starting date of 0 BCE we count backwards in time to calculate the approximate dates for the ages that will be examined.

Neanderthal Man dominated the world stage for a hundred thousand years prior to the emergence of homo sapien sapien, or modern thinking man. Neanderthal Man as it turns out was not brutish at all. It is proposed that he may have even gone unnoticed on the sidewalks of any of our major cities today. As early as 78,000 BCE, during an Age of Scorpio, ruling death and rebirth, we have one of the earliest finds of hominid burial indicating a possible concept of an afterlife. From Shanidar Cave in Anatolia archaeologists have found a Neanderthal grave that contained flowers and articles valued by the deceased indicating a process of sending one on his or her way, to a better life. Two and a half cycles ago, between 38,000 BCE and 37,000 BCE, during or close to an Age of Virgo ruling extinction, (38,880 to 36,720 BCE) Neanderthal man for the most part died out. This wasn't a sudden event. It may have taken several thousand years to complete but it seems to have begun as a noticeable event during this time.

As Neanderthal man died out homo sapien sapiens, modern man, came to prominence around 35,000 BCE, during an Age of Leo (36,720 to 34,560 BCE). He created a technological revolution (Aquarius opposite to Leo) in the Mediterranean around southern France, in Cantabrian Spain, in the Don Basin in the Ukraine, the

Lena Basin in Siberia, and in Matupi in Zaire. Flaked stone blades replaced heavy rock-like blades and knives were now used instead of hand axes.

Humans were on the rise, for the first time according to present archaeological theory. Or maybe we were rising from the ashes yet again. Extinctions happen all the time at low levels. One species or another is in the process of becoming extinct at any given time. Larger scale extinctions, where many species combine to become extinct in a single period, happen much less frequently. At the top of this extinction pyramid there have only been five mass extinctions that have come close to eliminating all life on earth. These are called the Big Five. The last of these included the dinosaurs.

Examining the record of major extinctions, below the Big Five in intensity, over the last 250 million years, one researcher reports that he found a cycle of major extinctions happening every 26 million years like clockwork. Every 26 million years a major extinction has taken place. The astrological precessional cycle of the earth's axis takes 25,920 years to complete one cycle. It therefore seems that every 1000 precessional cycles a pressure point is reached that triggers a major extinction.

With extinctions happening all the time at varying levels of intensity has mankind or civilization existed farther back in time? Are the myths of Atlantis and Lemuria true? Beyond the extinctions of plant and animal life there is indeed evidence of cataclysmic changes that have acted to hide from view a possible human history that is different from what we are willing to accept today. Because there is no acceptable framework in which to place these findings these artifacts are classified as out of place artifacts and stored away and forgotten about. Yet they indicate the possibility of the actual existence of mythological civilizations such as Atlantis and their total destruction.

Let's list some of these finds. Since 1968 there have been numerous finds of man-made structures that today lie underwater in the Bahama Banks and Bimini up to depths of 100 feet of water. In the Bahama Banks there are giant constructions of walls, squares and crosses along with other geometric shapes. There are archways and even pyramids all covered with fossilized shells. One wall was made of huge rectangular stone blocks weighing approximately 25 tons each. This wall may have been a dike surrounding the islands of

North and South Bimini.

At regular intervals there have been found three to five foot sections of fluted columns, some still standing. Near this wall was discovered an archway twelve feet underwater, a flat topped pyramid that had a base measuring 140 by 180 feet, and a large circular stone construction that may have been a water reservoir.

Andros Island near Pine Key was the site of another discovery made in 1969 by airline pilots flying over the site. They photographed a 60 by 100 foot rectangular shape with the eastern side and two western corners sectioned off. This construction appears to be an exact replica, both in design and size, of the Mayan Temple of the Turtles in Uxmal, in the Yucatan.

Near the mouth of the Orinoco River in Venezuela there is a sea wall 30 feet high under the waters of the Caribbean that runs in a straight line for miles. Off the Cuban coast there is the remains of a city covering five acres. There are sunken buildings off the coast of Hispaniola, one of which is 240 by 80 feet. There are several stone causeways that lie 30 to 100 feet below the surface of the Caribbean. These leave Quintana Roo, Mexico and Belize, and British Honduras, and run out to sea towards an unknown destination. Near Cay Lobos there is a sea wall running along an underwater cliff. Near all the Keys there are large stone squares, rectangles and crosses. All of these finds would have to have been built prior to 10,000 BCE when these areas were above sea level.

From a cave near Lussac-les-Chateau carved stones were found that date to the Magdalenian period, around 15,000 BCE. They show men and women in modern, civilized clothing, including boots, robes, coats, belts, and hats. These engravings also show well-tailored pants along with moustaches and well-groomed beards. One young woman seems to be sitting and watching a scene with something resembling a purse on her lap.

There is evidence that we are even older than this. In 1961 in Olancha, California three men searching for geodes discovered what looked like a 500,000 year old spark plug. In 1967 an article in the January issue of "Scientific Research" on "The Budapest Skull" reported that a skull was found in a quarry near Budapest that was determined to be a 500,000-year-old remnant of a true homo sapien sapien, or modern man. This is far older than archaeologists are willing to date the existence of human beings.

There are even older findings of civilized human activity. In 1851 in Illinois a businessman dropped and broke open a piece of auriferous quartz found in California. Split open it revealed an iron six-penny nail that was perfectly straight. Only slightly eroded its age was judged to be in excess of one million years.

In 1967 at the Rocky Point Mine in Gulman, Colorado human bones were found 400 feet below the surface embedded in a vein of silver. Found with these bones was a well-tempered copper arrowhead. This find was estimated to be several million years old.

In 1865 a two-inch long metal screw was discovered embedded in a piece of feldspar also several million years old. Although it had oxidized the form very clearly remained in the stone.

In 1958 the New York Times carried an article entitled "Discovery of Italian Skeleton Suggests a More Advanced Human Ancestry." Found 600 feet deep in an Italian coalmine the skeleton was estimated to be ten million years old. Dr. Johannes Huerzeler of Basle University in Switzerland concluded that the skeleton was humanoid rather than ape. It had a flat face rather than the snout of an ape. The front teeth were flat in the jaw rather than pointing outward as seen in apes. There was no simian gap between canines and adjacent teeth. The canines were smaller than ape canines. The lower molars were human and not apelike. And there was a hole that carries a nerve through the lower jawbone that is human.

Humanity may be even older. In 1885 in Austria a block of coal from the Tertiary period revealed embedded within it a steel-nickel alloy metal cube measuring 2.64 X 2.64 X 1.85 inches. The edges were still straight and sharp. Two opposite sides were convex with the other four sides perfectly flat. A deep groove ran around the cube. It was thought to have been machine made, possibly part of a larger machine. The Tertiary period is dated from 1.8 million years to about 65 million years ago.

In 1844 in a quarry near Rutherford Mills in England, workers blasting granite out of a pit discovered a gold thread. The thread appears to have been artificially made or manufactured. This thread was eight feet below the surface embedded in a rock that geologists estimate to be an incredible 60 million years old.

In 1845 a nail was discovered in Kingoodie Quarry in Britain half embedded in a granite block. The granite was also estimated to be 60 million years old. This is far older than the accepted view that early hominids began their ascent to humanity only about 2 million years ago when we first supposedly began to walk erect.

In 1999 Pravda reported the discovery of stone slabs in the Ural Region in Russia that made up a three dimensional relief map of the entire region, made with an unknown technology, that have been dated at an astonishing 120 million years old. With the map were inscriptions in an unknown hieroglyphic-syllabic alphabet. The map showed engineering works such as power dams, weirs, and a system of channels that covered about 12,000 km.

These out of place items, along with many others, indicate that our present view of man's history might be lacking some very important chapters. One of these chapters might be that of the "mythic" land of Atlantis. Because the myth of Atlantis has been so persistent archaeologists and historians have tried to shoehorn it into the present historical bias by giving it a late date and relegating it to a small island, Thera, in the Mediterranean, which blew up in the largest volcanic explosion in recorded history. Located north of the island of Crete its explosion would have been felt everywhere in the ancient Near East.

Plato talks of Atlantis in his work *CRITIAS*. According to Plato the older Greek Solon took a trip to Egypt where he met a priest who told the story to him. The priest said that Atlantis had sunk under the ocean, not the Mediterranean, 9000 years earlier. This would place the sinking of Atlantis at around 9500 or 10,000 BCE. This date corresponds to the sinking of the archaeological finds in the Caribbean. In addition 10,000 BCE lies close to the end of the Age of Virgo, along the Pisces-Virgo axis.

These archaeological finds, along with the mythic universality of cycles of destruction, indicate a strong possibility that humans did indeed reach high levels of civilization at one or more times in our past. If we indeed did achieve a high level of civilization and technological achievement more than once in our past then that would indicate a cycle of rise and fall is at play. We have already seen that within each age there is a similar rise and fall cycle inherent in the zodiac cycle of history. The signs naturally located at the bottom half of the zodiac, Aries through Virgo, correspond to historical periods that have been relatively neutral in terms of historical significance. In this Age of Pisces this period corresponds to the slow dissolution of the Roman Empire and the emergence of the Dark Ages throughout Europe, 0 BCE to 1080 AD. The top half of the zodiac gives rise to cultural high points. Libra brought with it the reemergence of trade and increased social interaction. Scorpio focuses on the destruction of the old forms of social structure. After this we saw evidence in each age of a recurring Renaissance followed by a classical period, and a scientific period. Culture rises and falls in a regular and astrologically ordered fashion.

Evidence indicates that humanity has risen to the heights before. Evidence also indicates that there have been periods of fall in the past. The earth spins like a top within an electromagnetic field. Our planet, within this field, has gone through magnetic reversals in the past where the North and South Pole changed polarity. Scientists have found evidence of 170 polar magnetic reversals covering the last 80 million years. Scientists say that we are in another period of magnetic reversal right now. Over the last 2500 years the earth's magnetic field has weakened by more than 50 percent. It is now less than half of its normal strength. And it is deteriorating at an increasing rate that will result in a magnetic pole reversal around the year 2030. Is there a connection between this and the increasingly destructive climatic changes that have plagued us over the last few decades? There has been a dramatic increase in volcano and earthquake activity. There have been massive changes in weather patterns, including increasingly destructive El Nino cycles, that have adversely affected many areas of the world. There are ozone holes over the South Pole. Tornadoes and hurricanes have recently become more powerful and destructive. Species extinctions are increasing to the point that some researchers warn that earth may be at the threshold of a Sixth Big extinction of almost all life.

The period of zero magnetic field may last decades. The mass extinction of entire species of simple forms of life in the past has been shown to correlate with these magnetic pole reversals.

Geologists are now beginning to see the possibility that ice ages may be evidence of cataclysm. In the last one million years there have been at least nine ice ages in Europe and North America.

Over the last one billion years ice, covering most of the globe, occurred approximately every 250 million years. This appears to be a somewhat regular cycle within this period that may correspond to the precessional cycle of 25,920 years and the possible cycle of major extinctions occurring every 26 million years within the last 250 million years.

We normally expect ice ages to proceed from the artic downward into Europe, Russia, and North America. But this is not usually the case. Evidence for huge ice sheets the size of continents exists in temperate to tropical zones. Ice ages have occurred in Africa, Madagascar, India, Argentina, Guyana, and in southeastern Brazil. The ice flow in some of these areas flowed out from the tropics and up into the higher latitudes, indicating the tropics as centers for those glaciers.

Perhaps the only logical explanation for this type of phenomenon would be a pole shift, as Compte de Buffon suggested in the 18th century. At one time India, or Brazil, lay at the North Pole and the extreme cold quickly built up a layer of ice thousands of feet thick.

One such event occurred at the end of the Pleistocene period where over 40 million animals suddenly died in the northern hemisphere. Entire herds of animals are found together, killed in their prime. From Asia to North America there are places where many thousands of animals, all at the same time, were quickly exterminated.

Upon examination of many of the remains biologists have found that food plants in the stomach, just eaten, were quickly frozen and preserved. In normal freezing conditions internal body temperatures will remain warm enough to break down food before freezing. This normal freezing change did not happen here. The food found within animal stomachs were flash frozen. The temperature required for this to happen would be well below 150 degrees below zero Fahrenheit. And it would have had to have been a sudden temperature shift, perhaps brought about by a sudden pole shift.

One of the most famous finds of this type of quick freeze is the Berezovka mammoth found in northeast Siberia. It has been recovered whole, with little sign of decomposition. In its mouth were still unchewed buttercups, a temperate zone flower, and grass. In its stomach was still undigested vegetation. In that same area in Russia there are also found trees from a temperate climate still rooted in the ground. There are fresh water shells that also indicate a much milder climate than exists there today. In the New Siberian Islands there were found whole trees belonging to the plum family complete with ripe fruit and leaves intact. Those trees today do not grow within 2000 miles of those islands.

The sudden flash freezing was accompanied by evidence of extremely violent forces. In the Alaskan muck pits the remains of mammoth and bison looked as though they were torn apart and twisted by some great cataclysmic event. Trees were also ravaged and piled up in great tangles and covered by a fine muck. This was all frozen solid. It was as if the earths pole shifted at a very rapid rate and suddenly stopped. Everything on the earth's surface was thrown around with tremendous force.

Carbon 14 dating of various animal remains indicates that not all animals died in the same event. There may have been a series of events. These dates vary from 48,000 BCE, plus or minus 3000 or 4000 years, to 10,000 BCE. The Berezovka mammoth is dated to 42,000 BCE. These dates are astrologically interesting.

The American psychic Edgar Cayce gave a series of readings concerning the continent of Atlantis. Atlantis broke up in three different events. In his reading the first cataclysm to strike Atlantis occurred around 50,000 BCE, right around the end of an Age of Pisces (51,840 to 49,680 BCE). Archaeological dates are approximately 48,000 BCE for the earliest event in this series of animal extinctions, close to the end of the Age of Pisces, along the Pisces-Virgo axis. The last date Cayce gives for the sinking of the island remnant that was Atlantis is 10,000 BCE, corresponding closely to the end of the Age of Virgo (12,960 to 10,800 BCE). The date 42,000 BCE for the Berezovka mammoth corresponds to an Age of Scorpio (43,200 to 41,040 BCE), while the second cataclysm affecting Atlantis Edgar Cayce gives as 28,000 BCE at the end of an Age of Taurus, the opposite sign to Scorpio.

It seems that Pisces and Virgo have a hand in cataclysmic events. In the zodiac the astrological axis that corresponds to the signs Pisces and Virgo, especially the ends of those periods, acts as a trigger for the release of destructive energies and the rebalancing of the cycle. Dissolution, disintegration, and extinction. Scorpio rules death and disaster. It may be that the sign Scorpio, and perhaps the Scorpio-Taurus axis, is another trigger for cataclysmic events.

The psychic Aron Abramson adds to Cayce's visions with pole shift visions of his own. According to Abramson a major geological pole shift occurred around 68,000 BCE. This date corresponds to an Age of Scorpio. Prior to that he places a major pole shift around 145,000 BCE, during an Age of Scorpio (146,880 to 144,720 BCE). And before that a pole shift occurred around 198,000 BCE, again corresponding to an Age of Scorpio (198,720 to 196,560 BCE).

Historically Scorpio time periods have brought about increased human concerns of death and suffering. In our most recent Scorpio Era (AD 1260 to 1440) the Black Death ravaged Europe and Asia, swinging back and forth across Europe for almost 100 years. That period has been called the Age of Disasters and Dislocations bringing with it the death of the medieval world. More recently in the Scorpio Phase of the Aquarius Era (AD 1905 to 1920), World War I introduced humanity to a new level of industrial and chemical warfare that killed 10 million combatants. In 1917 the Spanish Flu Pandemic became the second deadliest pandemic in history killing over 20 million people worldwide in a fraction of the time.

All of Aron Abramson's pole shift dates lie directly within Scorpio Ages. Within the inclusive dates of 48,000 BCE and 10,000 BCE a second cataclysm supposedly ravaged Atlantis around 28,000 BCE. This corresponds to the end of an Age of Taurus at 28,080 BCE, opposite to Scorpio on the Scorpio-Taurus axis. There seems to be a valid astrological connection here, connections that humanity may have incorporated into their ritual life.

END-TIME RITUALS

As above so below was a maxim important to the ancient world. During the early building phase of civilization, during the Age of Taurus, life was centered around a divine plan. Cities were built with outer walls facing the four directions. The temples, large and solid pyramid structures, stood in the center of the city acting both physically and socially as the hub of all life. Around this center society evolved highly stratified social structures. Everyone was assigned a place within society, possibly around an early astrological system of social placement.

Beyond the possible astrological arrangement of individual cities, with walls facing the four directions, societies and nations were often built around a twelve-tribe system. Throughout the ancient world nations and cultures divided themselves into twelve tribes, each tribe having their own tribal homeland. These twelve tribal lands were placed in a circular manner around a thirteenth central territory that acted as the sacred center to the entire nation.

In addition to ordering society along this astrologically divine geographical and social plan ancient man also structured his time astrologically. One such time was the sacred time of the New Year. The mythologist Mircea Eliade has made an in-depth study of celebrations of the New Year as they were performed throughout the Near East. These celebrations were in honor of the yearly end-time, and renewal of the yearly cycle. He found that regardless of the method of measuring the year, or of the dates assigned to the beginning of the year, the New Year holy days were universally regarded as very sacred and of the utmost importance. Everywhere people and society understood the importance of the ending of the year and the creation of the New Year.

One major theme of these celebrations was that of the purging of sins and diseases and the expulsion of devils and demons. The basic elements of this type of ceremonial view were fasting and other types of purification of the body and soul consisting of an internal struggle with demons or an expulsion of demonic influences using noises and cries. People then chased these demons through the streets yelling at them. A ritualistic aspect of this process was the use of a scapegoat. In this ritual an animal, usually a goat, or sometimes a man, was chosen as a vehicle upon which all the sins of the community were placed. It, or he, was then chased out into the desert carrying all of the year's accumulated sins with it. This aspect of the New Year ritual emerged into historical promi-nence with the crucifixion of Christ as the scapegoat carrying the sins of all humanity on his shoulders into the wilderness of death.

At times there were ritual combats between two groups that may have represented good and evil. There were also group orgies. Processions of masked men representing gods and ancestors wound through the city. It was at this sacred time of New Year that the initiation of young men into the sacred mysteries was performed.

Myths of the eternal return, as Mircea Eliade calls it, date to at least 3000 BCE.

The rituals of the New Year further included the prophetic reading of omens for the coming twelve months of the next year. At the beginning of the festivities, prior to the New Year, the king was dethroned and humiliated. In his place a "carnival" king was put on the empty throne. The entire social order was overturned and a number of excesses were allowed, even orgiastic excesses. Strict morality and sexual debauchery were played out on the streets side-by-side. Fasting and gluttony, grief and joy, chastity and sexual excess were all enacted, perhaps to portray the range of life from spiritual to secular, perhaps as a process of release for pent up emotional blocks accumulated from the past year.

At the beginning of this period the sacred flame was extinguished.

The people were, during this period, without their sacred light. They were thrown into darkness. At the end of this ceremonial period, after the New Year had dawned, the true king was re-installed on his throne and the sacred fire relit.

This ceremony sounds remarkably like a blueprint for the Age of Pisces and the founding and subsequent history of the Christian religion. All the great religions that have grown up around this Pisces energy are religions of duality, celebrating the great battle between good and evil. This battle was honored in the ceremonial battle between opposing groups of people during the New Year ceremony.

Christianity is overwhelmingly concerned with expunging Satan and his demons within the hearts of man. This expulsion of demons was not specifically a New Year ritual yet it had coincided everywhere in antiquity with the New Year Festival.

Christianity was created around the life of Christ. Christ was dethroned and ignored as the awaited Messiah, and it has been prophesied that he will come again, the Second Coming, and regain his place as the true king. The Buddhists await this coming in the form of the Maitreya Buddha. To Hindus he is awaited as the Kalki Avatar. To Moslems he will be seen as the Mahdi. And to many Native American peoples he will be seen as the return of the Pale Prophet, the Lost White Brother.

At the beginning of this age Christ came to this world as the true king. He was historically dethroned and humiliated and sent out into the wilderness of death. In addition his life was the focus of prophecy. Mystics, sages, saints, and yogis from religions around the world began receiving prophetic images of the end-times in great quantities, a reading of omens for the coming year. The Magi came from the mystical East to honor the "true king" and the advent of the age of the end-time. The Christian religion opened itself up to excess, greed, murder, sex, and political power at the same time it immersed itself in strict pious activity.

As an end-time the entire Age of Pisces can thus be seen as an unfolding of end-time historical expressions. The end-times are therefore 2160 years long and this last era of 180 years then becomes perhaps the Final Days of that end-time.

Mythology suggests that we have been here before. Archaeological and geological evidence supports this assumption. Ancient New Year ritual comes alive in the historical expression of this Age of Pisces giving us mythic evidence that we have come to this threshold yet again.

REVELATIONS

The single most important text that Christians refer to when thinking about the Apocalypse or the End-Times is the Book of Revelations, the last book in the Christian Bible. Revelations professes to give humanity an accurate prediction or prophecy concerning the historical events or trends that would affect us all during this last age. The question is, does it really tell us what is to be? Surprisingly the answer is yes. And we may have already been living through the greater part of those prophetic plagues for most of the last 2000 years.

Revelations begins its description of the events to take place in these End-Times in chapter 6 with the opening of the seven seals. The first four seals are collectively described as the unleashing of the Four Horsemen of the Apocalypse. The first horse is white and brings with it a man with a bow to conquer. This image has been interpreted as the rise of false prophets. The second horse is red and the rider has a great sword with which to kill. It has been interpreted as war. It might also be seen as murder, genocide, and execution. The third horse is black and its rider has a scale or balance in his hands. This has been seen as famine, but I might add the greed of business and capitalism as well seeing that the image presented is one of buying and selling. The last horse is a pale horse, yellowish in color, and his rider is named Death and it is said Hell follows after him. He is said to bring pestilence.

Disease increases with alterations in the environment. The Neolithic Revolution brought with it an increase in disease because of the creation of domesticated herds of food animals with their own viruses and parasites, as well as a starch heavy diet in the domestication of grains. After 4000 BCE, with the creation of cities, zymotics or herd diseases were introduced into human living conditions. These are crowd diseases where living conditions allow for the rapid and widespread movement of contagious disease to larger populations. Infection now became the leading cause of death among human beings. Here it is interesting to note this began with the Age of Taurus, after 4320 BCE, and the opposite sign of Scorpio, which rules death. These new diseases were small-pox, measles, mumps, flu, scarlet fever, typhus, bubonic plague, syphilis, gonorrhea, and the common cold.

Epidemics continued at a slow pace for the next 4000 years, until the Age of Pisces. The Virgo opposite sign to Pisces rules health. As towns started to grow into huge cities in the last century or two of the Age of Aries just before the Age of Pisces, population densities created a new environment for massive death rates. People began flocking to cities after 300 BCE creating the first large-scale metropolitan cities such as Alexandria in Egypt. By the second and third centuries in Rome, and in Europe, disease began to increase in virulence and occurred more often. The Plague of Orosius in 125 began in Africa. It killed 800,000 people in Numidia and 200,000 in North Africa. Soldiers brought it back to Rome killing 30,000 soldiers and an unknown number in Europe. This was only the beginning. In 166 the Plague of Antoninus, which may have been the first plague to come to Rome and the West from Asia, began a 14 year long scourge of Italy killing one-fourth to one-third of Italy's population. It killed 4 to 7 million people in Europe. This was a plague of measles and smallpox.

In the middle of the next century, beginning in 250, another return of these diseases ran through the Roman world killing one-half of its victims. At the height of this epidemic 5000 people a day died in the city of Rome. This disease, or diseases similar to it, returned to kill on a periodic basis over the next 300 years. This period marked the emergence of the world's first pandemics. Pandemics are epidemics that spread over much of the world. They are no longer confined to localized populations.

Evidence suggests that India also experienced huge mortality rates in these early centuries of this new age of pandemics. China similarly experienced a sharp population die-off between 200 BCE and 200 CE. Both China and Japan were plagued by severe epidemics for centuries afterwards with 50% mortality rates at times.

The Plague of Justinian may have triggered the onset of the Dark Ages in Europe. This was a pandemic of bubonic plague that ravaged India and China as well as Europe. It began in Egypt in 540 and from there it went to Constantinople. It caused one of the worst death rates in history killing 50% or more of those infected by the fifth day of infection. A cold weather form of this plague is called pneumonic plague. Without modern antibiotics it is 95% fatal. Up to 10,000 people a day died in Constantinople, killing 40% of the population. It spread west devastating Spain, France, Germany, Britain and Denmark for the next six years. It returned frequently for the next 40 years and then, in smaller outbreaks for another 150 years. One-half of Europe's population died. The warmer Mediterranean may have fared worse. The Near East and the Balkans were hit as hard as Europe. The Middle East and Africa were savaged by the plague. The plague traveled to Persia, India, and Southeast Asia. It appeared in China in 610 and for 200 years sporadically ripped at the fabric of Chinese life.

In the Roman Empire so many people were killed and those that survived were so demoralized that Europe entered a period of history that has been called the Dark Ages.

Covering the period roughly between 400 and 1000 the Dark Ages brought some respite from huge pandemics after the Plague of Justinian only because there were so few people left alive that diseases never traveled far. The Dark Ages were just that, dark. Recurring epidemics kept the population down. Rickets afflicted the survivors and malnutrition was the norm. Famines were a constant companion appearing on the average of one every four years. Peasants were always on the verge of having to sell everything they owned to survive. This included their clothes. During the hardest times they were forced to eat bark, roots, and grasses. Cannibalism was even part of the mix. Travelers were sometimes killed for the flesh of their bodies. Public hangings at times served as sources of potential food for those in attendance.

The average man in Europe stood at a little over five feet tall and weighed only about 135 pounds. Women were shorter and lighter. One-half of all Europeans lived only about 30 years. Young girls could expect to live only 24 years before they died. If a man reached 45 he most likely would look as if he was 80 years old, ancient and feeble.

Violence and death was endemic, and at times epidemic. As Europe experienced the huge die-offs that came with the new pandemics her farmlands reverted to forests and impenetrable scrub. Outlaws in increasing numbers flourished killing and robbing from the safety of those dark vast forests. Homicides were twice as frequent as death by accident, and only one in a hundred murderers were ever caught and brought to justice.

After about 1000, as the European population slowly began to increase, pandemics began to return. Beginning around 1250 a heavy cycle of recurring famines began in Europe. Add to this Europe's Little Ice Age began around 1300 creating more havoc with crops. In the decade of the 1290's especially heavy rains created severe crop failures and famines. Another cold front moved through Europe in 1309 creating the worst decade of famine in European history. Between 10 and 15 percent of the population of many cities died of starvation. Cold, wet summers continually rotted crops in the field and fueled the continuation of famine until 1325.

In 1333 China was hit by severe drought and famine followed by storms, earthquakes, floods, locusts and epidemics. In that decade the plague spread from central Asia to China, India, and the Middle East inaugurating the worst pandemic in human history, the Black Death. In 1347 Genoese traders brought the plague to Italy. Once it hit one fourth to one half of Europe died. The Byzantine Empire collapsed under the devastation of the Black Death. Islam lost one-third to one-half of her people with similar ratios killed in India. China lost 1/2 of her population, 65 million people to the plague. The Mongol Empire dissolved under the ravages of the disease.

In Europe another half dozen major plagues struck before the end of the 14th century. These often struck alongside other epidemics, and returned, in places, for 200 years or more. The death rate was so high that the medieval world collapsed opening the way for the new learning of the Renaissance. The workforce of Europe was so depleted that Europeans turned to slavery as a means of replenishing herself. As bad as this was, worse was yet to come.

During the Age of Discovery Europeans spread their diseases around the entire globe. They took disease with them everywhere, disease becoming their main ally in their conquest of the world.

European diseases were the worst in the New World with smallpox the worst of the lot. A major epidemic of smallpox hit the Spanish ports of the West Indies in 1518. It killed up to one-half of the Arawok Indians on Hispaniola before spreading to Puerto Rico and Cuba. Cortez had left Cuba for Mexico before the epidemic arrived there. After he met Montezuma and the Aztecs Spanish reinforcements from Cuba brought the disease with them. Cortez attacked the Aztec capital Tenochtitlan in 1521 with 300 soldiers and some Indian allies. When the city fell three months later one-half of the Aztec defenders had already died from the epidemic, including Montezuma and his successor. The canals were literally filled to overflowing with Aztec bodies. The Spanish resistance to the disease totally demoralized the survivors who then fled, sure that Spanish gods were after them. By 1530 the smallpox epidemic had leapt far ahead of the conquistadors covering the Americas from Argentina to the Great Lakes in the US. When Hernando de Soto marched through the land of the Mound Builders virtually no one was left alive. He encountered empty towns with corpses stacked in large houses.

Measles followed smallpox, killing two-thirds of the remaining survivors. These two diseases wiped out entire cities and tribes. And it kept coming back for more throughout the 16th century. Other Old World diseases followed such as mumps, typhoid, flu, diphtheria, and scarlet fever. Perhaps close to 100 million natives died from Old World diseases brought from Europe. There may have been many more uncounted deaths. The mortality rate due to disease here was higher than the Black Death in Europe and Asia, but it was spread out over 400 years.

Cholera became the new disease of the 19th century as cities grew into huge metropolises. In 1817 the first cholera pandemic began in Calcutta, India. Traders took it to China, Japan, and Southeast Asia, Arabia, and East Africa. It lasted six years. There were six cholera pandemics before the end of the 19th century. A seventh cholera pandemic began in Indonesia in 1961, and spread to Asia and Africa by 1970 with death rates around 10% of all infected. By 1991 it was the longest cholera pandemic ever recorded spreading rapidly to South and Central America. In 1993 a new strain emerged in India and Bangladesh killing 5000 people, spreading quickly to Southeast Asia. It may be the beginning of an eighth cholera pandemic hardier than all other cholera strains before, able to kill within hours.

Typhus broke out at the beginning of World War I with a 70% mortality rate in some places. Between 1917 and 1921 it infected 20 million people in Russia, killing 3 million. At the same time the Spanish Flu Pandemic, the second worst pandemic to hit humanity, second only to the Black Death, struck in 1918 killing over 20 million people in only six months.

Today, since the 1960's, there has emerged a very large tide of new and resurgent diseases around the world that has recently become a rising "epidemic of epidemics". New diseases have emerged from the Third World such as Hantavirus, Ebola, Lassa Fever, and a whole list of hemorrhagic fevers which cause fatal internal bleeding.

One of the most well known new diseases is AIDS which kills in the millions each year. It became a pandemic in 1985 with tens of millions of infections worldwide. It is almost always fatal, and it is mutating, becoming resistant to known therapies. It is also combining with other AIDS strains expanding into potentially new lethal variants. With its RNA core it could easily mutate into a highly contagious airborne disease with the potential of becoming the most deadly pandemic in history.

Dengue hemorrhagic fever is a new and very lethal variant of dengue fever that came out of the Philippines and Southeast Asia in the 1950's. The mosquitoes that carry it entered the US in 1985. They are a very aggressive species called the Asian tiger mosquito. It out-competes native varieties for a dominant place in the ecosystem. It is a dangerous epidemic waiting to strike the West. DHV, as it is called, is only one of many new hemorrhagic diseases to appear since World War II. Hantaan virus, one of many Hantaviruses, mostly infects human populations in Russia and much of Asia, infecting 200,000 a year and killing some 20,000 people each year.

Hepatitis B virus infects 200 million people around the word today. It kills more people each year than AIDS does. It was first discovered in the 1960's. In 1982 an effective vaccine was created and in the decade that followed the number of cases doubled making it the only disease that increased after a cure was found. Hepatitis C also became pandemic in the 1960's. It is even more common, infecting more people than hepatitis B and kills even more people than hepatitis B.

Other diseases are making dramatic comebacks as they become immune to all known medicines. Sexually Transmitted Diseases, or STD's, have spread like wildfire by the 1980's, many to pandemic levels. Tuberculosis is on the increase again infecting 1.7 billion people around the globe. This is one-third of the total human population. It kills more than 3 million people annually, far more than does AIDS.

Famine and pestilence on an apocalyptic scale have been an intimate part of human history since the second century.

The message given by Christ to love thy neighbor and to turn the other cheek was lost in the rising fear of Satan. Christians saw Satan everywhere they looked infecting the hearts of men. The Church turned away from the loving teachings of Christ and became a fear driven religion whose main concern was rooting out the evil that they perceived to be all around them. They saw life as a battle between good and evil that required, on their part, the use of violence and torture. Prejudice spread everywhere infecting the Church to its foundations. St. Augustine sanctioned the use of torture and murder in the name of God, setting the theological grounds for all future Church sponsored violence and hatred against Christians as well as "pagan" non-Christians. Accusations of heresy often led to execution. St. Augustine also created the doctrine of Original Sin using it against women. It was never a part of the teachings of Christ yet it took on an importance that fed the growing fears of this age and overshadowed the real message of Christ. Over the centuries of Christian domination women were often more feared by men than was Satan. They were hunted down, accused of witchcraft, and burned at the stake. Their only socially acceptable position in society was being married to a man who could watch over them, punishing them when necessary, which was deemed to be quite often. They could very easily be murdered by their husbands without any fear of being brought to justice. They came to be seen as the intimates of Satan in his battle for a man's soul, and were declared to have no souls of their own.

If God created humans in his own image, both male and female with sexually charged bodies, then the doctrine of Original Sin becomes one example of a false teaching created in the mind of a "false prophet".

The term "Satan" or "devil" literally means opposer or prosecutor. The earliest references to Satan, in the Book of Job, are more as the process of opposition or challenges put in the way of an individual in order to test them. This is a natural process inherent in the physical world. A basic principle of Newtonian physics states that for every action there is an equal and opposite reaction. Duality and opposition. The highest heaven reflects a state of unity. As the world was created different aspects of creation were separated out from unity, such as light being created and separated out from the darkness of the waters of the Deep. This separation created a world of increasing duality and opposition, a world where the process of Satan eventually became operative. Satan as an angel, a son of God appears as the tester, come to test Job to see how deep his spirituality really went.

The Christian Church, in its use of violence, torture and murder, and in its highly judgmental disdain for all other religions, whom they branded as pagan, reflects the emergence of the First Horseman of the Apocalypse, that of false prophets. We can gain some perspective on this view by looking at the message to the second church in Asia, the Church at Smyrna, presented at the beginning of Revelations. There it is stated that the angel tells those of that church that Christ knows the blasphemy of those who say they are Jews (Christians) but are actually followers of the synagogue (Church) of Satan.

The opening of the Fifth Seal, the seal that unleashes the tribulation, further illuminates this view. John looks and sees under the alter the souls of all the uncounted godly saints that were slain for their beliefs, and no retribution or judgment was passed on the murderers. The Church sees those saints as the early martyrs that died at the hands of Rome. This might easily be true. But we must add here all those "pagan" peoples that Christian zeal and fear butchered in later centuries. Included also are women, many of whom were branded as witches. And then there are those who were

Christians themselves who were unfortunate enough to go against the politically motivated catholic or orthodox view. It is now understood that we teach by our actions, not by our words. The Christian Church during pre-modern centuries has proven to be arguably an organization of False Prophets.

In 330 the First Council at Nicea was held to resolve a doctrinal dispute between Arius of Alexandria and the orthodox views of the Catholic hierarchy. The dispute was not resolved and Arius was put to death for his heresy. His followers rioted, 3000 of them, at the injustice and were mercilessly put to the sword. This event accounts for more Christian deaths at the hands of Christians than all Christian victims at the hands of Rome in the previous 300 years. Christianity has since been far and away the most violent and bloody religion in history.

During the Fourth Crusade, before the crusaders reached the Holy Land, they turned aside and sacked the Christian city of Constantinople in 1204. They raped and massacred its Christian inhabitants.

From the late 13th century into the 16th century violence throughout European society, and even within the Church, grew. By the late 15th century violent intrigue had already become a constant part of life. Weakness was despised, and those with handicaps were terrorized and tortured. The murder of anyone, even family, who was perceived as a threat to one's own power, was tolerated at all levels of society. This included the Catholic hierarchy up to and including the Pope. Five Popes, the Worldly Popes, who sat on the Holy See during the first part of the 16th century were the worst despots in all of Europe. All were depraved lechers, and all were ruthless in their quest for power. Popes and Cardinals commonly hired assassins, sanctioned torture and even reveled in the sight of blood. These Popes sponsored spectacles of recreational murder, often within the Vatican, where fights were enacted that portrayed actual fights to the death. The Vatican also sponsored regular orgies, and one Pope, the Borgia Pope, fathered a child on his own daughter, Lucretia.

The Protestant Reformation was born in violence, not a good omen for any religion. Martin Luther, the father of this movement, was filled with hatred from birth. As Protestantism gained ground other protestant religions sprang up, all angry and repressively dogmatic and doctrinal. John Calvin, the founder of Calvinism, was the most repressive of them all. He had his daughter executed for sleeping with a young man. As these religions took root there followed a vicious civil war within Christendom between Catholics and Protestants, and even between different churches within the new Protestant faith. Christians were killed and executed on the slimmest of reasons all in the name of Christ. Mass butchery was everywhere. Within four years of the Diet of Worms, the birth of the Protestant religion, 250,000 Germans were executed or butchered.

Following the hellish insanity of these religious wars science began to slowly replace religion as a means for understanding the universe. Reason replaced zealous prejudice and created a much more rational worldview. But Pisces rules spirituality. Science simply became another false prophet by rejecting anything spiritual or anything that resembled the insanity of the religious mind that infected Europe for the last 2000 years. False prophets have combined with severe internal violence through much of this age creating often hellish living conditions for most people. The Four Horsemen of the Apocalypse have run roughshod through this age already defining this age as an end-time.

Science presents us with yet another possible connection with Revelations. In chapter 13 of Revelations a beast rises up out of the sea with seven heads, and with ten horns on his head, and ten crowns on those horns. This beast is known as the Antichrist who is given power to war with the saints and win out over them for 42 months. With this beast there arises also a second beast up out of the earth with two horns. He is the False Prophet and he performs miracles and great wonders, and kills all those who don't worship the beast. It seems that a strong case can be made that the miracles performed here might well be those of science and technology. These miracles, and the scientific theories that they are based upon, have lead us away from our spiritual center and farther out into the relative world of physical creation. One of the main markets for this new science has been the military and the creation of a huge military industrial complex that stands in stark contrast to the nurturing ideals of spirituality. In the context of spiritual knowledge this process of science and physics, or the study of the physical world, then fits the definition of being anti-religion, anti-spirituality, and thus anti-Christ; the opposite to Christ.

It seems as if much of the prophesy of the Bible, and of the Book of Revelations has already been visited upon us throughout the last 2000 years. Perhaps the last seven plagues are representative of the potential we see before us as we head into the last era of this age.

FINAL DAYS

The Age of Aquarius lies just over the horizon, less than one era away. Astrology promises an amazing new period in world history when we finally get to that time. Hindu yogis tell us that we are about to enter a golden age beyond our wildest imagination. They say that we will finally create heaven on earth. Christian prophesy says that this coming age will be the glorious Millennium of Christ. But before we get there we still have approximately 150 years of this last era to go through.

This entire Age of Pisces has been an age of hardship, violence, pestilence, and famine, of the stampede of the Four Horsemen of the Apocalypse through history. Now the energy of Piscean dissolution has doubled in intensity now that we are in the Pisces Era of the Age of Pisces. To understand the power of this time it might be valuable to look at the transition of time into the Pisces Era of the last Age of Aries, 180 to 0 BCE.

Around 360 BCE, at the beginning of the Aquarius Era of the Age of Aries, the classical Hellenic period of Greek philosophy gave way to the world culture and science of the Greek Hellenistic period. Science flourished throughout the entire Near East. Great Metropolises were built, and within their boundaries were also built great libraries and museums. In all of its aspects life in this early Hellenistic period was amazingly similar to that of our modern scientific industrial world. Then around 180 BCE, entering the Pisces Era of the Age of Aries, a change becomes discernable in the history of the ancient world. Reason, long the guiding light of Greek thought, no longer commanded the respect it once had been given. People began to long for a more emotional release and the orgiastic, emotional Oriental religions supplied the means. The Bacchic and Orphic cults spread along with the more sexual religious rites of the Great Mother Cybele, and the Goddess Ma from Cappadocia. Mithraism grew in popularity also, but the most popular religion by far was the Egyptian cult of Isis and Serapis. The rational Stoic philosophy of Zeno was transformed into an emotional but escapist philosophy. This reflected the more positive aspect of the new Pisces energy. On the negative side the need for a messiah affected the Roman people as their lives became more chaotic and violent. They sought that messiah in the form of various generals who lead Rome from being a republic into dictatorship.

Until about 180 BCE Roman foreign policy was essentially the same as our present American foreign policy. Nations defeated in war were allowed to rebuild and become friendly allies, retaining their sovereignty. By 150 BCE the emotional tone of Rome had changed quite drastically. Between 180 and 130 BCE Rome had become an imperial power, but her imperialistic policy was accidental, inspired more by fear than any desire for empire. The very idea of empire was abhorrent to her leaders as well as her citizenry. But the entire Hellenistic world, and an as yet unexplored Europe were entering into a period of intense political and social chaos. An increasing fear and paranoia was becoming quite palpable by 150 BCE. Foreign alliances could no longer be counted on to remain stable and peaceful. In 146 BCE the Achaean League in Greece rebelled, and Rome responded in a new and brutal fashion that shocked the entire Greek world. The Greek army was not merely defeated. It was destroyed. Corinth, her leading city, was totally destroyed, most of her men killed, and the women and children sold into slavery. Greece was then made a Roman province.

At the same time this "new brutalism" was applied in North Africa on an even larger scale in the Third Punic War between 149 and 146 BCE. Memories of the Second Punic War with Carthage, Rome's economic rival in the Mediterranean, began to resurface creating an irrational fear that Carthage would eventually destroy Rome unless she was destroyed first. Carthage was peacefully engaged in rebuilding her trading network in the western

Mediterranean when Roman conservatives, led by Cato, decided that Carthage had not only to be defeated but also utterly erased. Carthage must not be rebuilt and the Third Punic War stands as one of the most brutal in history. In 146 the walls of Carthage were breached, the city was burned to the ground, stone buildings were torn down and the plow was driven over it. Salt was then turned into her soil and a curse was pronounced on anyone who would try to restore the city. Fifty thousand survivors, mostly women and children, were sold into slavery.

The new brutalism spread. In 88 BCE Mithradates revolted against Roman rule not by fielding an army but by terrorism. He organized one of the largest and most comprehensive massacres prior to this present age. On a specified day every Roman and Italian, men, women, children, and slaves, were butchered with every kind of atrocity committed. The massacre even included Orientals to whom one owed money. One half the debt would be wiped clean by this act.

The new brutalism even entered Roman internal political affairs. By 133 BCE huge estates worked by gangs of slaves had pushed Rome's small citizen farmers off their land. Roman unemployment was just beginning to create the process of turning Rome into a welfare state. The Gracchi brothers, Tiberius and Gaius, Roman senators, both sought to institute land reform. For their efforts the Roman Senate, their fellow senators, had them murdered. The senate acted for the most part, with almost no regard for maintaining any kind of ethical principles. The morale of the army was very low, the poor were increasingly discontented, and there was seen a growing danger from the vastly increasing number of slaves brought into Rome.

After 133 BCE divisions within the state were deep and increasingly permanent. Party warfare was constant. Civil war became a vehicle for party politics, and the ultimate aim for each party was to annihilate opponents. In war a Roman victory was no longer enough. Democratic and republican armies intrigued against each other to be the victorious army in battle because the road to wealth and power lay exclusively through political channels. Generals were not merely military men. They were party champions, potential political saviors. As power concentrated in the hands of these political champions the brutality grew.

The six consulships of Marius began the process of changing Rome from a republic into a dictatorship. With him the precedent was set for the murder of political opponents. In 88 BCE the Roman general Sulla was called in to defeat Mithradates. Upon his successful return and installation as dictator he too began to murder his political opponents. He went even further murdering certain wealthy people who were not even involved in politics. He was after their wealth. When rebuked he began what has been called the "Terror of Sulla" with a cruelty and ferocity that shocked the Romans and served as a model for all future totalitarian attempts. He created his infamous proscription list published in the Forum, which listed the names of intended victims. People on this list were outlawed. They could be legally murdered by anyone whereupon their estates were confiscated and the proceeds split between the assassin and Sulla. Even their descendents were excluded from Roman citizenship. It has been estimated that some 40 senators and 1600 equites were proscribed. To further strengthen his position of power Sulla liberated 10,000 slaves from the many he had accumulated from the proscribed estates and created a private army of thugs answerable only to him. The dictator Pompey had even more personal and political power than Sulla, and Julius Caesar even more than Pompey.

Slavery had increased to such a large extent that out of a city of one million people in the first century BCE it is estimated that 1/5 to 1/3 of them were slaves. From the beginning of this era their presence on the huge estates began to create a reverse sort of slavery of Rome's citizens themselves. This was a Piscean self-imprisonment where slaves held most of the jobs. They were employed as free labor in a wide range of domestic, business, and industrial occupations. They were especially useful on the labor force of public contractors. Rome's citizens, on the other hand, were forced out of their jobs and out onto the growing ranks of a huge welfare mob that aimlessly roamed city streets.

Huge tenement slums were built on the outskirts of the city while the welfare mob became ever more uncontrollable. Violence and paranoia crept into the life of Roman citizens at all levels. Those in power sought salvation in the accumulation of more and more wealth. A new class of super rich people arose in Rome while the average citizen became poorer. A widening gap between rich and poor became evident. In response to the accumulation of wealth in the hands of fewer and fewer people a new breed of women entered Roman life, the courtesan. Rome became lavish and extravagant in the private sector. Parks and gardens were built. Yachts, paintings, and expensive mistresses were purchased. At this same time public architecture declined.

Entertainment took on a new and violent dimension. Theater with its basis in the intellectual problems of theme, execution, and moral point gave way to the mindless pleasures of the flesh. The excess of slaves in Rome supplied the raw material for the creation of bloody gladiatorial fights where slaves were taught fighting skills and then displayed those skills in enclosed arenas. These fights were to the death. Not only were they cheap forms of entertainment, they allowed, in a degenerate way, the release of frustration and anger in a time of social confusion and chaos.

These gladiators revolted three times in the first century BCE in a series of conflicts known as the Servile Wars. The slave Spartacus led one of these revolts.

Politically Rome was bereft of competent administrators by the first century BCE. Rome was now a nation of slaves and parasites. People entered politics solely for the purpose of gaining wealth. Nobody was concerned about political or social responsibility. Violence was an endemic part of Roman life. The century between 130 and 30 BCE stands as the most chaotic, troublesome, and violent period in all of Rome's one thousand year history.

In China the same processes were at work. The Han Dynasty is divided into two periods, the Early Han Dynasty from 202 BCE to 8 AD, and the Late Han Dynasty from 25 AD to 220. The Early Han Dynasty covered a period of social unrest and disruption similar to the Late Republic in Rome. There is evidence of a growing economic distress with Chinese peasants in increasing numbers fleeing the land for the economic promise of the cities. Prior to the Early Han in the Aquarius Era, the Chinese people were thrifty, hardworking, and responsible reflecting the Saturn qualities of self-discipline and reason. Saturn rules Aquarius. With the Early Han the mood changed towards one of greed, and affluence for the few. Extravagance became increasingly popular. Palaces and gardens were built for comfort and pleasure. Game was slaughtered in excessive numbers in order to put on huge feasts. Silk became the popular material for even common dress among the peasantry.

Outside the pleasure gardens of the royal family and the wealthy there was built up huge slum areas filled with peasant hovels. Violence increased from all directions. A strong increase in social injustice is evidenced in Chinese towns that seems to be rooted in the widening gap between the rich and the poor. Bands of disrespectful youths took to roaming the streets dressed in their own armor and carrying knives and other weapons. They were looking for money to steal. By 81 BCE evidence suggests that children no longer obeyed, or even loved or respected their parents.

There also seems to have been an increase in slavery, and many of the street gangs in Early Han times were slaves. Many government offices had large numbers of slaves, both male and female. Chinese workers became indolent, seeking ways to get around their duties. While the general population often remained very poor government slaves drew rations of food and clothing and some actually became fairly wealthy. While the peasantry were forced to work long hours slaves often sat around much of the time.

Government corruption was increasing at the same time that the government was trying to enact a welfare work system. They began to excessively proscript peasants into labor corps. Greedy officials increasingly overtaxed them. They were expected to fulfill the growing appetites of the wealthy houses for material goods. This and the need for military personnel all contrived to drive the peasants off their lands.

From about 120 BCE the government tried to control the work efforts of her citizenry in order to insure that manpower was being used effectively. She became increasingly anxious overseeing that enough man-hours were spent in the fields for her food while at the same time more hours were needed in the mines, the foundries, or in the trade and transport of goods. The government became more and more ineffective at administration, and there is seen at the same time a new policy of military expansion that may have been prompted by the same fears that fueled Rome's expansion. Prior to 120 BCE China may have felt a growing inability to deal with the increasingly irrational behavior of her neighbors. It was easier to conquer and control than to administrate and interact as allies.

Civil disorder, robbery, violence, and fear were the main themes of this era. In religion escapist religions based on occult powers entered Chinese life. These religions were popular, seen as a means of potentially affecting in a positive way the material fortunes of their practitioners. The rational philosophy of Confucius was heavily watered down with mystic otherworldliness.

Remarking on the Virgo opposite energy to Pisces during this Pisces Era, at the end of the Age of Aries, we can see that the division in Roman politics (and in China as well) was mirrored in every other country in the Near East and in Germanic Europe. The vast dependence on slavery throughout the Roman world, and in China, reflects Virgo's focus on servitude. More importantly Virgo, ruled by the planet Mercury, rules health and mental health (or the disintegration of mental health as Virgo rules disintegration). Playing on the schizophrenic fear of being split apart in the battle between good and evil that is common to Pisces, the mental capabilities of Rome's leaders continued to decline throughout this era. Reasonable solutions to her troubles, by rational standards, were no longer available. Her leaders at all levels of the administration were less and less capable. The main avenues of response to difficult situations were those of brutal and unthinking reaction. The normal level of consciousness in society had given way to a deeper, darker level where the mind split in two, good versus evil, creating a mental chaos that pervaded the entire Hellenistic world.

We very well might have the same scenario ahead of us today as we look into the near future of this present Pisces Era. Although we have already lived through 2000 years of Pisces, in the Age of Pisces, the near future will be a more intense version as we are now in a double Pisces bath, the Pisces Era of the Age of Pisces.

The Pisces Era runs from the year 1980 to 2160. The first phase of this era, the Aries Phase was from 1980 to 1995. Aries rules war and violence. Much of the violence of the previous phase, the internal terrorism and the rising crime rate that had afflicted most communities throughout the seventies, continued into this phase. Social violence rose to new levels. Inner city gangs like the Bloods and the Crips, rival gangs in Los Angeles, California, now armed themselves with automatic weapons and almost became what might be called criminal armies. Murder became rites of passage for initiation into these gangs. Drive-by shootings and other forms of senseless violence entered the American social landscape. Girl gangs soon began to become as violent as male gangs. Children also began to turn to violence at increasingly younger ages. In some shocking news reports from this time it was headlined that very young kids killed other, even younger children, often just to see what it felt like. By the middle of the 1990's there were some ten million violent crimes committed in America every year. This was a four to five fold per capita increase in violent crimes that were reported to police over the level of the early sixties. America had now become the most violent civilized nation ever recorded in the history of the world. This is quite an accomplishment for a nation that professes to be peaceful.

In other countries the general level of internal violence was even worse. In 1979 a coup in El Salvador lead to a period of intense internal violence. The government as well as civilian and semi-private groups each began creating death squads that were directed against their own people in order to quash any and all dissent, or the possibility of any kind of reform.

West Africa erupted in a devastating explosion of violence in the nation of Liberia. That country was relatively peaceful until Sergeant Samuel Doe led a coup and took over the government in 1980. Charles Taylor revolted in the late 1980's sending Liberia into a long civil war that overran the whole country. Soon the rebels splintered and began fighting among themselves as well as fighting both the Liberian army and West African Peacekeepers.

International terrorism expanded dramatically during this phase. Airline hijackings became a regular news event during this decade. Terrorism was becoming a major weapon of fanatic groups world-wide in their fight to promote their own agendas. Islamic groups lead the way in both numbers and frequency of terrorist attacks. Groups like Islamic Jihad, Hizballah, and the Palestinian Liberation Organization were in the forefront of this terrorism. The Irish Republican Army was also increasingly active in Ireland against the British. Terrorist groups were active in many South American and Central American countries. The North Korean government also engaged in terrorist bombing attacks. The spread of terrorism finally reached the shores of the US in 1993 when the World Trade Center was first damaged by terrorist bombs.

Wars erupt in all time periods. But in Aries periods there are usually more of them and the level of violence involved can be more intense. Aries in a Pisces Era, within the Age of Pisces, indicates that much of the violence comes from hidden sources, without any direction or control. Terrorism. The traditional rules of combat have been thrown out and replaced by the process of creating as much Piscean fear as possible. This was certainly the case in this phase. The violence prophesied in Revelations, either the Four Horsemen of the Apocalypse, or perhaps a buildup to Armageddon, intensified in this period in dramatic fashion. Humanity has been assailed by violence from within as well as from undisclosed forces without in true Pisces fashion.

The intensity of this violence softened somewhat after 1995 and our entrance into the Taurus Phase, 1995 to 2010. Taurus rules peace and stability. Beginning around 1993 there was seen the beginning of a noticeable drop in violent crimes. By 1995 that trend became more noticeable as the Taurean energy of peace took hold. The trend has continued nationwide. In addition the number and intensity of terrorist attacks around the world softened noticeably during this phase.

Taurus also rules money and banking. Since 1995 the major historical focus turned away from violence and towards the economy. In late 1994 Mexico devalued the peso. This move was an economically sound move designed to allow the peso to float and settle at the point of its real value. The value of the peso went down, and continued to go down. Mexico almost went bankrupt as a result. The US was forced to step in to prevent that from happening.

At around the same time the New York Stock Market took off like a rocket soaring from 2000 points to over 11,000 in just a couple of years. The stock market had never gone astronomical like this before. Although the market is still up, the stock market has become very volatile often changing by several hundred points in a single day. The outcome of this is that stocks are now considered to be highly over-valued, which is not a very stable position to be in. It is interesting that during this time economic analysts began to note that stocks were going too high and began cautioning investors of a potentially serious downturn. It never happened. What drove the stocks higher was the computer and the ability of individual investors to by-pass professional channels and do their own trading on-line.

Following the near bankruptcy of Mexico, wealthy Orange County in Southern California declared that they were on the verge of bankruptcy themselves. Then in 1997 the economic focus of this period hit home. A severe economic breakdown known as the Asian Flu struck Southeast Asia, spreading quickly to Japan, South America, South Africa and even Russia. It threatened to bankrupt every country it hit. It even threatened to send Japan, the world's second strongest economy, into bankruptcy. And many have not really recovered yet.

There has grown up a huge credit bubble that, if it goes, could bring down every economy in the world. Bankruptcies have increased dramatically since 1995 and have reached a serious enough level that credit card companies are backing legislation that would exempt credit card debt from bankruptcy protection.

Since the devaluation of the Mexican peso the world seems to have entered a period called, by economist Paul Krugman, a return to Depression Economics. This means that economic indicators that led up to the Great Crash of '29 have returned and are now controlling the economy. Traditional economic indicators no longer seem to dictate what happens to the economy. Fear and panic, emotional factors combined with greed, drove the Asian Flu far beyond reason to become a worldwide crisis when standard economic logic predicted that local economic practices would remain local while their economies sought to stabilize themselves. The dissolution of Pisces along with Piscean emotional irrationality, lack of direction, and illusion conspired to send the world economy to the brink of total collapse.

The economic focus has turned away from the serious economic problems that afflicted the US after the terrorist attack on the Twin Towers of the World Trade Center on September 11th, 2000. This was the symbolic economic center of the world at that time. Our subsequent mobilization and assault on terrorism is proving to be very costly, and because this is an economic period within the Pisces energy of dissolution, it might easily act as a trigger to push the US economy closer to the edge of collapse before the end of this phase in 2010. By September 2003, the cost of fighting in Iraq cost the US close to 180 billion dollars. It is interesting to note here that our war on terrorism answers easily to the Scorpio opposite to Taurus as well as to the general irrational fears of Pisces.

The third of the Four Horsemen, the rider on the black horse and who is traditionally associated with famine, carries in his hand a balance with which to measure the value or cost of goods. The image presented of "a measure of wheat for a penny" is an economic image. An economic revival came with the tremendous stock market ride after 1995. After 30 years of recession and economic trouble the West experienced the promise of a resurgent economy. But this resurgence was largely illusion, in true Pisces fashion. The new prosperity went to the top leaving the average worker still struggling with bills and mortgages and even less buying power than before. Much of the reason for this prosperity lay in the trend at that time of downsizing. Cut costs and make companies more cost efficient thus increasing the appearance of increased productivity and company health. Large numbers of people were laid off, most of them having to settle eventually for lower paying jobs elsewhere. In addition it is becoming apparent that more companies like Enron are "cooking" their books in order to create the illusion of greater health and attractiveness to potential investors. Most of the employees at Enron lost all of their retirement income from Enron stock while company leaders tried to steal money from the company when they realized that the company was going under.

Money is symbolic of what we value. It is only a medium of exchange that allows us the ability to purchase those things that support life on various levels. With money we can buy food, clothing and shelter. On another level it allows us the ability to buy tools that serve to enlarge our lives in some way, to bring beauty into our lives. It allows us to purchase enjoyment and adventure. It also leads to greed. Beneath all of these things that we value lay a substratum of spiritual values that supports and gives direction to our physical lives. This is especially important now that we are in the Pisces Era of the Pisces Age. Part of the process of end-time dissolution is rediscovering whatever it is that lays at the most basic and profound level of existence. To this end Pisces will tend to dissolve all of our surface structures in order to reveal the spiritual foundation that lies underneath. In this Taurus Phase that surface structure will tend to be the economic systems we have in place. The economy right now is being driven by emotional factors such as greed and fear. If we change that and consciously and in large numbers take up various spiritual practices such as prayer, meditation and other forms of compassionate and giving action that open us to the spiritual then the need to dissolve our economic systems will not be as necessary, and the dissolving process not as severe. The Pisces energy of this time will be enlivened in a positive manner and the Taurus energy preserved in a positive expression for us all. As silly as this sounds it fits a Piscean rational quite nicely, which is what may be required for creating economic stability in a Pisces time period.

Ahead of us in 2010 lies the Gemini Phase, running until 2025. Gemini rules movement, division, and education. This coming phase promises to be one of increased movements of people around the globe. Most of this might be from areas of conflict towards areas perceived to be more stable and prosperous. Gemini periods in the past have traditionally been periods of large mass migrations of people. One area where this is already a growing problem is along the border between the US and Mexico. The relative inability to stop the flow of illegal aliens will most likely dramatically intensify after 2010. That flow could easily become an overwhelming flood that cannot be stopped.

The prosperity of the West might be a target area of the potential coming mass migrations. People from depressed areas, from areas where the economy exists at the poverty level, or from areas of constant violence, will likely begin to move or be forced to move. These movements could conceivably put a lot of stress on countries that are the destinations of those movements. This could work to disrupt, and politically and socially fracture, many countries where stability is fragile at best. Even in more stable places the political and social questions that will arise concerning these movements of people will likely divide the political and social cohesiveness of those nations. Do we protect jobs and homes for our own? Do we open our arms to the needs of refugees? At what level does either action push resources and emotions to the breaking point? In the dissolving energy of Pisces these movements likely will further stress our environment, and social and political structures towards the point of outright division or even collapse.

Division, even without the Gemini tendency towards mass movements, might prove to be a major problem of this phase. Already politics in the US is becoming more partisan aligning strictly along party lines. Political division will become much more obvious and possibly even destructive. Argument and anger may increase as politicians tend to polarize into partisan camps. Each side will then see their own agenda as the only true way to proceed. Those agendas, hindered by opposing camps, will tend to incite fear, perhaps of doom, of leading the country to ruin. As fears increase so too will hatreds.

Religion is entering politics, in Pisces fashion, with the voting power of the Moral Majority. Religion, especially Christian fundamentalist religion, is notoriously dogmatic, fearful, judgmental and unmoving in its views of what is correct. This religious foray into politics could likely continue eventually creating a political division between a liberal secularist political view and a more fundamentalist Christian political vision. President George W. Bush has already expressed his desire to recreate America into a strictly Christian country.

This is a period that fundamentalists believe marks the apocalyptic climax of the prophetic war between God and Satan. Anyone that doesn't believe the fundamentalist line is suspect and therefore should be feared. This view will likely divide society as well as the world along religious lines. Gemini in Pisces.

Education might also find itself in serious trouble. There is the very real possibility that public education will approach the point of collapse during this phase. Already there are numerous signs that public education is in very serious trouble. Several programs have been proposed to deal with the increasing inability of public education to provide quality education to various segments of society. Home schooling is on the increase, and school vouchers allow many to use private schools while the public education system pays for their education.

In a Pisces Era the current attempt to promote a strictly secular education based solely on information essential for job and career may prove to be educations undoing. As silly as this may sound, especially when it comes to something like education, Pisces spirituality becomes extremely important in mitigating the potential disruption. The knowledge of Gemini in Pisces requires knowledge based on spirituality. This does not mean religious education. It means that education needs to look at the deeper spiritual layers of existence in addition to the type of knowledge that we teach today.

Success in job and career is based on emotional happiness, which is itself based on a deeper sense of spiritual belonging in this universe. Whether or not we may agree this spirituality embraces all religions, East and West, and all forms of spiritual seeking.

Modern education as we now understand it is very intellectual and was created in response to the mental energy of the Aquarius Era after 1800. This period we are now in, the Pisces Era since 1980, is becoming increasingly emotional and spiritual. More people, perhaps without even realizing it, are looking for something deeper in their lives. Drugs and drug abuse is a response to this deeper yearning. School and public education is not addressing these concerns and as a result will find itself increasingly marginalized as the learning curve, which follows the curve of the zodiac, turns farther away from the present shallow fact based educational system. Depression and suicide among school children of all ages is alarmingly high.

Spirituality, or the introduction into our public education system of universal and simple meditation techniques along with a wider range of courses designed to introduce and familiarize students with a broader understanding of the spiritual and emotional nature of life, can make a real difference. It can be the difference between the continued success or eventual failure of our educational system.

Gemini rules communication. As the world becomes more dependent on computer technology there could be an increased potential for the breakdown of global communications based on computers because of the electronic and changeable nature of the medium. This breakdown could disastrously affect all the services that support life today, and that are dependent upon computer technology. Dependence on computer technology rather than on the spiritual creates a somewhat prophetic split between what might be seen as devotion to the anti-Christ and the False Prophet against devotion to one's own inner connection with the divine. We honor our computers looking to them to improve our lives, to save us, in an environment where Pisces dictates the opposite. Simply by remembering the divine through techniques such as meditation we realign ourselves with positive Pisces energy thus healing the split of Gemini, changing Gemini divisiveness into Gemini inquisitiveness that will allow for greater understanding of different viewpoints.

Looking forward the Cancer Phase will be here between 2025 and 2040. Cancer rules home and food. In a Pisces era and age this period promises to promote the return of apocalyptic level famines and pestilence. Food sources will likely dissolve (Pisces) and disintegrate (Virgo). With weather patterns already dramatically changing creating more violent weather agriculture will become increasingly impacted. We are already depleting our available agricultural land at an alarming rate. Modern irrigation practices allow for an increased rate of evaporation that leaves behind a salty residue. By 2020 30% of the world's available farmlands will be too salty to grow anything in. By 2050 that will rise to 50%.

The scientific promise of genetically engineered food will likely prove illusory in true Pisces fashion. Pisces/Virgo also indicates that GE foods as they are called could even have dangerous side effects. There already is a growing body of evidence that genetically engineered foods can and do cause unforeseen severe side effects in many people.

Rainforests are cut indiscriminately at a dangerous pace and coral reefs are dying rapidly. Pollution affects a huge percentage of our drinking water, causing 80% of the world's health problems. Our oceans are in worse shape than we thought. They are severely polluted and over-fished. There are now 150 dead zones in the world's oceans where nothing can live. The agricultural runoff into the Mississippi River annually dumps these chemicals into the Caribbean creating a 5000 to 6000 square mile dead zone every summer.

The earth is at risk. And we, all of us, get our food from this earth. This means that when the Cancer Phase comes upon us we might very easily, too easily, experience devastating famines on a Biblical scale. They could easily affect the US as well as Third World countries. Famines led to the outbreak of various plagues that came with the Black Death in Europe and Asia in the 14th century. Researchers already warn that the world is on the brink of a new and devastating cycle of plagues in the 21st century that could easily include the West in spite of our medicines. The Four Horsemen of the Apocalypse could easily ravage the world during this phase.

Food and home represent the quality of nurturing that we all seek within our lives. As long as we maintain our separateness from others, Jew versus Gentile, Christian versus Pagan, True Believer versus Infidel, and secular versus religious or spiritual, we maintain an emotional environment of non-nurturing severity directed against those who do not believe as we do. This separation, intensified during the previous Gemini Phase, creates an environment in which Pisces energy will then dissolve that which we all need physically, our food and physical health, in order to reconnect with a feeling of being healthy and nurtured on a spiritual level. Pisces will serve up famine and pestilence in response to our prejudices and hatreds. In this sense we need to recognize the possibility that weather patterns and the workings of Mother Nature are somehow related to the collective emotional environment that human beings create around the surface of the globe.

Do unto others as you would have them do unto you. This Golden Rule is repeated in all religions. It is the Golden Rule because it is the most important rule of all. Nurture and accept all other religious views as you would have others nurture and accept your religious view. Honor and nurture the political and social views of all other peoples as we would like our political and social structure honored and nurtured by them. If astrology works, and history shows that it does, then there is a spiritual foundation that underlies the apparent physicality of the material world. This means that emotional energy, how we love and how we hate, and mental energy, our prejudices and our willingness to accept, accommodate and learn, directly affects our environment in ways that are not obvious to a material view of nature. The spiritual realm is our true source of nourishment.

Armageddon. We have translated this term to mean the final war between God and Satan fought between the warring armies of the earth. The Leo Phase coming between 2040 and 2055, rules the love of fighting and the ascendancy of the spirit. If there is to be a final battle, an Armageddon, then this phase answers the description of the time that it might likely be fought. Leo rules the ego and it is the ego that is seen as the imprisoning factor in humanity's struggle with the spiritual. The spirit gives the feeling of freedom and being in a state of unity with all of creation. The ego is that aspect of our consciousness that is concerned with the survival and comfort of the physical body. Because of this the ego is concerned with the relative physical world in terms of duality and opposition. It sees and judges everything that appears to be outside of us as either good for us, or evil. It is the ego that then spurs us on to action in terms of good and evil. In this respect then a case can be made that the ego works at the behest of the physical and oppositional process we call Satan, the Biblically acknowledged "Prince of this World".

The prejudicial stresses and judgmental dogmas of the Western Levantine religions, Judaism, Christianity, and Islam, could easily come to a head during this phase. Each might be pushed to a deeper belief that the other religions are Satanic in a very fundamental way. And in Leo they could too easily decide that the time to fight Satan would be at hand in an attempt to force the ascendancy of the spirit against the perceived forces of Satan. Arab Islamic Fundamentlist terrorists have already begun this war and the US has already responded. The level of fighting could very easily grow into a much larger conflict. It could also subside without any real resolution only to flare up later, perhaps during the Leo Phase.

Other forces might also be at work here. The US is actively trying to export its own quasi-religious secularist view of creation and society. We tend to see religion as fantasy, as opposed to the mathematically precise reality of science and scientific theory. We look to expand our economic base by working to increase markets for Western business based on the Western utopian ideal of material prosperity. Much of the conflict today between the West and Islamic nations in the Near East can be seen in these terms. The capitalistic West is involved in keeping the peace in the Islamic Near East. The fundamentalist terrorist activities of various Islamic groups against the West is, at a deep level, a conflict between a disruptive move to bring everybody into an all embracing Western world economy and a perceived need to maintain the spiritual purity and traditions of the Islamic religion.

In the West religion is compartmentalized and placed at the fringe of society. It is something that we say that we believe in but only on Sunday mornings. Religion is not to be brought into the workweek or into the work place. The two are separate and are kept that way by law. In Islam religion is a deep and pervasive aspect of all areas of society. It is an important part of the workweek and the work place. The faithful are called to prayer five times a day, everyday.

As this conflict has spread each side has taken to religious name-calling that reveals the fundamentalist religious nature of what is really happening. To many Moslems the West is now the Great Satan, interested only in non-spiritual materialistic concerns. To those of us in the West who have seen terrorist attacks firsthand or in the media, terrorist groups and Islamic countries that harbor terrorist groups have been labeled by the US as the Axis of Evil. From a spiritual perspective, and using spiritual definitions without judgment, both sides are correct in their assessment of what is Satanic.

The use of violence, in any form, goes against the universal directives of spirituality. It is not Piscean in nature. The planet Venus, ruling love and the heart, is exalted in Pisces. Thou shall not kill. Islam itself means surrender. It is a highly spiritual and peaceful religion that seeks surrender to the loving and compassionate will of Allah. The ideal of jihad has to be, in a truly spiritual sense, an internal struggle against the baser animal instincts we all carry within our hearts. This has to apply to what is called the lesser jihad as well. Islam is a religion of peace and gentleness. Killing is a violent strike in the spiritually defined Satanic "opposite" direction. This "evil" is intensified when civilian non-combatants are the primary targets.

In the West we have turned away from spirituality because of the overwhelming violence and blood thirst of our own religious history. As a result of the bitterness of the religious wars in Europe following the Protestant Reformation science and humanistic thought turned more and more towards a totally secular view of creation that saw religion as the opiate of the masses, or as a childish belief system that was created in order to assuage the fearful imagination of "primitive" peoples. The spiritual was discarded along with the religious. In this turning away from the spiritual message carried within religion the West merely transformed the satanic violence of our Christian history into an equally anti-spiritual and by definition "satanic" secular society. Antichrist. No matter how good or compassionate we think we are we have to remember that we are dealing with a double Pisces time period, in which the key words are I Believe, and which is the epitome of spirituality, not secularism. We also have to be aware that the definition of the Biblical term Antichrist is a term that indirectly equates Christ with God and with spirituality. Being Antichrist means literally being and living in a non-spiritual or secular manner. Both sides might easily answer to the definition of Antichrist with both sides pushing for battle during this phase.

The answer to this religious problem lies in the Piscean definition of spirituality. If we do not understand this and do not implement what we learn then this Leo Phase could easily explode into a phase of apocalyptic fighting.

The next phase, that of Virgo between 2055 and 2070, will build on what happens between now and then. Given our present state of awareness Virgo's rulership of disintegration and extinction could easily make of this phase a period of potentially devastating social and political fragmentation, as well as final extinction.

Fifteen years later, between 2085 and 2100, will come the Scorpio Phase, a period that will be ruled by death and suffering, and carries with it the popular image of Satan. If Armageddon hasn't happened before this time then the potential for an all encompassing war, or combination of smaller wars along with intense pandemic diseases and other disastrous releases of the collective unconscious stress, such as fear, hatred, and other deep emotions, is dramatically increased. This period astrologically fulfills the requirements for the manifestation of the final battle between good and evil predicted in the Bible. Yet even here astrology shows the way towards salvation and healing.

Scorpio rules transformation. If we learn to transform anger into creativity, hate into love, fear into compassion, then we abrogate much of the need to live through deadly, disastrous and violent historical events. The scorpion becomes the eagle flying above the muddy and fearful arena of attachment.

History as it unfolds in the next century may also take on additional forms of potential devastation for humanity. The earth's electromagnetic field is rapidly weakening. It has been calculated that this field will reach the point of magnetic pole reversal in about 2030. This will result in a reversal of the earth's magnetic field. These magnetic reversals have been associated with periods of mass extinctions of simpler life forms.

How is this going to affect humanity as large numbers of species already slip into extinction every day today? Are magnetic pole reversals connected with pole shifts? We must change the way we perceive our world and act according to the most life supporting and creative aspects of the astrological signs involved. This possibility we will look at in the next, and final, chapter.

PART 3

KEYS TO THE GOLDEN AGE
OF MANKIND

The Age of Aquarius holds the promise of truly being the much-prophesied Millennium of Christ, the Age of Enlightenment, the mythological return to the Golden Age. In Aquarius humanity is promised the potential, if we can live up to that potential, for immortality, for the ability to levitate or "walk on water", for the growth of incredible genius in every single human being. Utopian ideals common to all peoples will find fertile ground for tremendous success here. It will be a utopian age. Humanity will likely become unified into one family honoring many cultures and individual cultural diversity. Global communication will create support for the unheard of human ability for telepathic communication. All branches of knowledge, including spiritual, esoteric, and psychic knowledge will be explored and unified into a super-science where physics and meta-physics support each other. Brotherhood, equality, and the free pursuit of the hearts' desires, wishes, and dreams will be part of the pursuit of higher states of consciousness. The impossible will become possible.

This coming age will be one where our natural divinity as sons and daughters of God, or Goddess, will become apparent, filling every one of our lives with creativity and vitality. There will no longer be any differences in station or wealth. All people will experience their own nobility. We will all have intimate access to deep levels of omniscience and omnipotence. We will manifest Spirit directly in our lives for the good of all. These are all potential qualities of Aquarius, and the Leo opposite to Aquarius.

To gain this Golden Age of Enlightenment humanity must pass the barrier of a world dissolving in an apocalyptic end-time scenario. The old heaven and the old earth must pass away before a new heaven and new earth can be created, before a New Jerusalem can be built. In order to do this effectively it might be useful to redefine the nature of history and of humanity's place in history in relation to what we have discovered about astrology.

History is not the record of a series of accidental events. We are not isolated individuals in an accidental universe playing with the "laws of chance". There is a purpose to history, a purpose that is profound and astrologically ordered. It is a universe whose main purpose for existence is evolution and growth. The logic and beauty of the astrological construction of this universe attests to the existence of an overwhelmingly intelligent spirituality. How does this work?

Astrology itself, according to traditional Jewish rabbinical teaching, is the law that God, the lawgiver, creates the universe around. In this all-encompassing law no man is ever given the chance to escape the consequences of his or her actions. We are so immersed in astrological structure that whatever action we may take is intimately connected to our astrological natures and our innermost psychological processes, and is subject to the process of balance and debt. The circle of our individual life must be balanced before we graduate. We can never escape from ourselves. We must pay all of our debts before we will be allowed to move on to the next level. We are given the choice of free will within that structure to take what is called right action or to react against our challenges with karma-creating hurtful actions. Either way the actions we choose are recorded within each of us in our astrological memory and will be played back later, many times in subsequent lives, as retribution. If we choose right action and strive to love our neighbors all around the globe, and turn the other cheek when struck, then we come ever closer to our own graduation into a Golden Age. If we get angry and strike back then we activate the astrological balancing law of "an eye for an eye", also known perhaps as "what ye sow so shall ye reap". Even if we feel that we are in the right we react within the "Satanic" oppositional nature of this present astrological balance that we are trying to get out of. We create more karma for ourselves and mire ourselves deeper in this prison we call life.

Men and women were created in the image of God, male and female. The image that we are created in is the image of the zodiac, of God's animating circle. Time is the poetry of humanity's growth into its spiritual heritage. We are at present in the process of remaking that image into a much more angelic image than the one we now portray.

When looking at the astrological model of history just presented one very powerful image begins to emerge that illustrates how this works. Each time period is powered by the astrological sign that coincides with it. Time is also affected very powerfully by the opposite sign across the wheel from the primary sign. In the Age of Cancer, the Capricorn opposite sign also had a hand in the evolution of society and history during that age. These are the important points on the circle.

Time flows from the past into the future. If we step to the side of the zodiac circle and look at it from the side, it becomes a line. Viewing the circle from the side, we see two points opposite each other. As time moves out of the past and into the future, from left to right, that flow is not a straight line. The two points circle around each other as they spiral forward marking successive time periods. This image then is that of a double helix.

Given the conscious nature of astrology as it has affected history, it is not too outrageous to play with the idea that time itself is the genetic structure, within this universe, of God, or of the level of God that is this universe. Ancient cultures around the world worshiped time as a god, indicating the perceived conscious nature of time. The genetic nature of time may be the only truly logical conclusion available. The ancient maxim, "as above, so below", may have referred to this very phenomenon. The vast genetic nature of time reflects in perfect harmony the powerful individual genetic nature of all organic life here on earth. Genetic researchers insist that we are controlled by our genes. On the other hand astrologers insist that we are controlled by our stars. What if both camps are correct? If the double helix itself is an astrological structure, then astrology and genetics are two sides of a single discipline.

Only about ten percent of our genetic makeup codes for anything physical, ie. proteins or enzymes. Some researchers might put that percentage closer to about three or four percent. A small percentage of genes aids in this process of protein or enzyme creation. The rest is considered "garbage" in that scientists have little or no idea what they do. But what if some of these "garbage genes" code for astrological information essential for communication between humanity and astrological time? What if some genes astrologically connect us to the rest of the universe giving us that deep spiritual sense that we are somehow connected to all of life? These genes would be the same for all living creatures because they connect us all to the same time periods that we are presently living through.

But what about astrological individuality? Perhaps individual astrological genes are more closely connected to genes active in the creation of proteins. And maybe the astrological connection is deeper still. Perhaps the double helix structure itself is a powerful astrologically active part of the human genome. Is the orientation of the gene in an individual's cell important to an organism's growth and astrological individuality? Does the double helix structure itself transmit information to the genes that accumulate along that surface? Is the double helix structure connected in any way with the double helix structure of time? If astrology does work then what is it, within our bodies, that acts as agent for constantly changing astrological time periods?

We are supposedly affected by the movements of the planets in our solar system. They connect with each of us through some means of energy transfer. The question arises, why doesn't everybody change in the same way, and act as a single unit? If it was the gravitational pull of the planets, or their electro-magnetic emanations that affects us we would all be drawn to act in accord with everybody else on this planet. Yet we don't all act the same way. And astrology insists that we all have different horoscope charts.

As time periods change certain genes might conceivably turn off and on allowing us to respond at a cellular level to the change in astrological frequencies. Yet each individual still retains the individual astrological genetic makeup that they were born with for their uniquely individual horoscope charts. This would allow for maximum diversity within a tightly ordered evolutionary time sequence. Collectively we all respond in different ways to astrological time creating a cohesive astrological direction to history.

As astrologically infused sentient beings living within an astrologically ordered time-space world we might find that we have a certain power over what happens in this world. Time affects us through astrology and we respond. We see this in the astrological play of history. On the other hand we have within our subtle physiology the same astrological tools that time uses to influence us with. We can use that subtle energy in spiritually powerful ways to reverse that direction in order to positively influence the world around us.

Recent research in genetics reveals a genetic structure that is not hard wired and static. There is an amazing ability in DNA to communicate with the outside environment as well as with the entire body in general. In this communication a feedback loop allows information from the outside to be processed within the genome. Our genetic structure can then change in order to adjust to this new information. Perhaps this ability is a part of the possible connection between our DNA and the double helix structure of time. This means that by recognizing this potential avenue of communication we might have some ability to feed our own thoughts and desires back into this genetic loop in order to alter, for the better, the potential direction that time promises to take us in the near future. Our thoughts and emotions affect our DNA. The emotional and mental condition of our DNA "communicates" with the astrological genetic structure of time. Time then aligns itself with the collective "needs" of our world directing history towards what we require for evolution. In this case towards suffering or towards spiritual completion.

Pisces rules illusion, a quality that implies an ethereal image of reality that is not real in itself. Pisces is also a water sign that lends its watery nature to the process of dissolution. Whatever appears to be solid has a greater tendency to be washed away during this time period. Water itself is flowing and deep rather than solid and stable. And Pisces is a mutable sign meaning that it is a changeable sign. This is a very plastic time we are in, a time that is open to change either from the nature of this time itself or from our own collective spiritual/mental/emotional input into our world.

The end-times are a period of time where the real world begins to undergo the process of dissolution. At the surface level this dissolution manifests as social and political breakdown and increased levels of fear and violence. At deeper levels it manifests as changes in weather patterns, increased volcanic and earthquake activity, and a rapidly depleting magnetic field surrounding the earth. At a still more fundamental level we may be undergoing a change in the very nature of physical/spiritual reality.

God is Love, and Love is the answer according to all of the modern transcendental religions. The planet Venus, the planet of love and harmony, is exalted in Pisces. This means that the expression of Venus reaches its highest and most evolutionary expression during this time. Christianity, Islam, Hinduism, and Buddhism all teach the power of Love, of compassion and forgiveness, the path of devotion. But how do we express this spiritual Love in a practical way? The simple Piscean answer is meditation.

MEDITATION

We are in the Pisces Era of the Age of Pisces. We are also powerfully connected with the opposite energy of Virgo. We need to connect with these two energies in the most positive manner possible if we wish to succeed in this endeavor. Astrology being what it is will not support any other avenues of expression. We need to understand the signs of the times in order to use them to our benefit. In this we then have the free will to creatively flow with the signs of these times and succeed.

Pisces rules spirituality and contact with other worlds. In a spiritual context these other worlds are higher dimensions or heavenly worlds. The Virgo opposite to Pisces rules not only piety, humility, and chastity but also mental acuity, repetition, and technique. These are immensely important qualities. Meditation answers both of these requirements. Meditation is a technique (Virgo) utilizing the repetition of a powerful name of God (Pisces) silently within the deeper recesses of the heart (Pisces) and the mind (Virgo). This depth increases both emotional clarity and mental acuity. In fact meditation may be an expression of mental acuity that implies that we come to understand the Piscean illusory nature of the world around us and therefore turn within to the source of reality, of thought and wisdom itself. Meditation promotes piety, humility and purity of thinking. From this level of greater mental clarity we begin to enliven intuition, a Pisces type of non-rational thinking that accesses deeper levels of awareness. From this level we may find that we are able to come up with more successful answers to pressing problems.

Meditation also connects us with the energies of the coming Age of Aquarius and with its opposite sign Leo. This is important because meditation then becomes a powerful transition agent that not only helps us to survive the potential extinction of our species crisis we are now confronted with, but also guides us towards the incoming Aquarian energies. Meditation is therefore astrologically supported as an activity that is "blessed", so to speak, by both Pisces and Aquarius. Aquarius rules genius and the search for higher consciousness. The planet Mercury rules the sign Virgo but is exalted in the sign Aquarius. Mercury rules the mind and mental thought processes. Mental abilities, exalted in Aquarius, promise to dramatically improve as the energy of the Age of Aquarius gets stronger. Meditation connects us with deep, unused areas of mental potential bringing out the genius each of us possesses. It activates those unused areas of the brain that open the potential for greatly expanding our consciousness. The Leo opposite sign rules spirit, omniscience, and omnipotence. Meditation connects us with our inner spiritual powers promising the potential for each of us to quickly evolve into sons and daughters of God. That we would all becomes "sons" of God was a promise that Christ made to his disciples regarding this paradigm shift. Christ further tells us that we will all perform the miracles that he performed, and more.

All religions are built on a foundation of meditation. Our Christian religion seems to be the exception. Rather than promote meditation we seem focused on prayer but this may be due to a mistaken scriptural interpretation throughout our history. We have been absorbed in the fearful question of pagan influence in Christian life. One example cited to indicate what a pagan or heathen practice involves comes from the Sermon on the Mount episode where Christ tells his followers "when ye pray, use not vain repetitions, as the heathen do". This is the King James Version, a translation that is perhaps the most widespread version in use today. Because meditation is the repetition of a mantra this passage has been taken as a direct prohibition against meditation, being a pagan practice. But is this really the case?

Throughout the Old Testament we are repeatedly told that it is the name of God that will carry us to complete fulfillment. The same is true in the New Testament with the name Jesus Christ. We are blatantly told to do everything in the name of God or in the name of Jesus Christ. Although God and Christ are powerful embodiments of spiritual power it is through the use of the name of God and of Christ that we human beings can gain spiritual grace, peace of mind in a stressful world, and increased health. It is the name that is specifically mentioned as important to Judeo-Christian spirituality. In the Orient the name of God is considered to be a very sacred mantra, a word of power that is used on a daily basis in order to touch the ultimate transcendent mystery that is God in the process we call meditation.

A passage in Joel, chapter 2, verse 32 states this very directly. "And it shall come to pass that whoever calls on the name of the Lord shall be saved. For in Mount Zion and in Jerusalem there shall be deliverance, as the Lord has said, among the remnant whom the Lord calls." Calling on the name, repeating the name of the Lord, is the foundation of meditation in all cultures and all religions.

The Ten Commandments are seen as the cornerstone of Old Testament theology. Yet as a law code they are strangely incomplete, a fact noted by many scholars. As a law code the Ten Commandments don't seem to make much sense. The commandments against killing and stealing are self evident, yet they are at the end of the list, implying a lesser status than those at the beginning. Those at the beginning of the list, and hence the most important, are seemingly out of place as components of a code of laws. On the other hand the Ten Commandments do make sense as spiritual instruction in meditation.

The one commandment that catches the eye as important in this regard is the commandment against using the Lord's name in an empty, frivolous manner, or "in vain". This is the third commandment, following two that also have little ethical value but that focus directly on our meditative approach to God himself.

The first commandment sets the stage for proper meditation. Have no other gods before God. In this very practical sense gods are what we worship or whatever it is that we call upon in order to better our lives They are not necessarily gods of other religions. If God is transcendent and universal, if He is all that there is, then there can be no other gods to compete against him. They are all part of his totality, and thus sacred in their own right.

"Pagan gods", as we call them, might well be something else They are intimate to our lives and confront us every day in subtle ways. They are things like power, wealth, lust, revenge, worldly things or emotions that promise satisfaction or completion in some way that is dependent on the physical world and too often has little to do with God. Originally they were associated with the Goddess. Her area of influence included the physical world in a way that the masculine did not. Our word "material" comes from the Latin root "Mater", meaning Mother. Materialism, a minor aspect of Goddess worship, thus becomes a pagan religion in itself worshipping a pagan god of wealth. During the Age of Taurus, and the materialism and wealth that Taurus focused on matriarchal religions were seen as incomplete as time passed over into the Age of Aries and its masculine focus on overcoming obstacles. Attachment to wealth and power was an obstacle. These are the gods that are not to be elevated in our consciousness as equal to or before God himself, or even the Goddess herself. This means that it is very important, as a first step in meditating, to focus only on the spiritual aspect of life and of our meditation, to have no other desires, thoughts, stresses, or agendas when entering the meditation room.

The second commandment, have no "graven" or solid-carved images of God made, again doesn't necessarily mean not to create statues or other works of religious art. It is sometimes a necessary prerequisite for effective meditation. It gives us a focus away from the seemingly pressing concerns of everyday life. Based on the meaning of the first commandment about placing the material gods of ambition, power, wealth and other worldly concerns before God it can simply mean to not worship the physical world and the valued creations of the physical world. A graven image is a solid physical image, in antiquity an idol carved in wood or stone. Today in our secular technological world we should add metal, plastics, and other materials that we now use to build with.

In our modern highly technological world all the fun high tech toys we create become in reality graven images created in honor of the modern gods of technology and consumerism. This becomes especially evident with computers and computer technology. Artificial intelligence, another god that we place before God, has enlivened technology to the point that we worship these "idols" every day as saviors in our increasingly complex lives.

The third commandment begins to get to the technique involved.

This is the commandment that says do not use the Lords name in vain, or in an empty, worthless, or powerless manner. The name of God, in any religion, is considered to be powerful. YHWH, Jehovah, Allah, Shiva, Brahma, Buddha, Jesus Christ, Wakan Tanka, the Great Spirit, Inannna, Astarte, and many others from around the world are all names of God, whether masculine or feminine.

Throughout the Bible it is stressed that the name of God and the name of Jesus Christ, become a part of every persons daily life. The name of God is intended to be used as a power talisman, as the basis of meditation. That is why the name of God is pushed on us throughout the Bible as being important. This commandment becomes increasingly important as a reminder not to bandy these names about in meaningless daily conversation. Used in this manner these names lose their power and become just another word in our vocabulary. But used as a mantra, in meditation, they take on tremendous power to transform our lives, to bring us inner happiness and peace.

The next commandment that again has little ethical value as part of a legal code is the fourth commandment. Remember the Sabbath and keep it holy. This commandment simply states that regular meditation intensifies the effects of meditation. The Sabbath refers specifically to a particular day of the week that has astrological connections. The Sabbath is ruled by the astrological planet Saturn. The Sabbath is traditionally the seventh day of the week, Saturday in the Hebrew week, or Saturn's day, the day of rest, or of discipline, limitations and lessons, of doing nothing. Here doing nothing implies the cessation of external, everyday activity. It is a day for turning towards inward disciplines such as fasting, praying, and meditating.

Astrologically Saturn is said to rule the seventh chakra, or energy center, at the top of the head. It is here that we find release from the physical world. Without anywhere else to go consciousness rises upward into the heavenly realms, into spiritual release and connection. Ancient myths state that the Golden Age was ruled by Saturn. The ancient Hebrews decided that it would be wise to utilize the energy of Saturn for limiting one's attachments to the world around us. Saturday then becomes the most powerful day of the week for meditating and for connecting with God. This commandment might also imply, by extension, a daily practice of meditation on a smaller schedule, twice a day for maybe 15 to 20 minutes keeping one in practice for the long meditation on the Sabbath. Remember this, the commandment states, and keep this schedule holy.

The fifth commandment may be a transitional commandment. Honor your Father and Mother. It is important to carry the energy of peace gained from meditation back out into the world. When we come back into activity it is crucial to remain non-judgmental. In the mythic sense this means to honor both sides of creation. The world is created in a dualistic manner. Christians call this opposition the fight between good and evil. The Orient sees this as the cycle of yin and yang energies constantly circling and dancing with each other. Yin and yang are seen specifically as feminine and masculine energies and attributes. Here on this physical plane they represent the higher Mother and higher Father energy, of which our physical mothers and fathers are biological manifestations. By honoring this feminine and masculine balance in our own families we remain centered and powerful in our thinking and in our actions. By honoring our mothers and fathers we can see more clearly the balance of yin and yang in the world, so that our days will be long.

The next four commandments are specifically ethical commandments, giving these big Ten the appearance of a code of laws. They are commandments against murder, adulterous sexuality, stealing, and lying all presented in very brief single line sentences each. There is not a lot of explanation or additional information included, unlike the other commandments. It is as if these four are part of a separate ethical complex within the instruction. They may simply be the ethical actions required, after meditation, in order to further our spiritual evolution through right action, in activity.

The physical world we live in has four basic directions. The emotional universe we inhabit also may contain four basic directions, perhaps corresponding to the four physical directions. It may be that these four commandments refer to these directions, much like the four rivers of consciousness that lead out of the Garden of Eden. Following the previous commandment about remaining balanced between feminine and masculine principles, we are now told to remain centered in the heart, in that place of love and compassion between the four armed cross of fears and dangers of these four emotional directions.

These four elements arise from fear, not from the feeling of sublime connection found in meditation. There is a sense of separation that creates a sense of fear that one is alone in the world and therefore we strike out against the world in order to protect ourselves. We kill others because we are afraid for our lives or lifestyles. We feed our sexual lusts because we are afraid that we will not be able to find a deep heart centered union orl completion in the spirit. We steal because we are afraid that we do not have enough. And we lie because we are afraid we do not deserve anything. Fear interferes with living a spiritual and happy life.

The final commandment concerns the even more subtle dangers of desire in general. Thou shalt not covet thy neighbor's house, his wife, or anything else of his. This is a commandment that also does not easily fit into a code of law as they were understood in antiquity. But it does have strong correspondences to Eastern codes for meditation. Desire is a central consideration for deeper levels of meditation and the spiritual path. Desires keep us attached to worldly concerns, blocking our connection with the spiritual. Do not desire, either in meditation or in life. Do not desire your fellow man's house, or his wealth, or even his wife, etc. The question of desire is an important one in meditation circles. The focus on transcending desires completes the meditation cycle. It brings back to the fore the first two commandments about lesser gods being brought before the face of God, and of not solidifying those desires into powerful demiurges that tend to control one's life. Remain free of desires and these instructions in the spiritual necessity of meditation become complete.

In the New Testament the cornerstone of Christian prayer, the Lord's Prayer, also seems to work better as meditation instruction rather than as a prayer itself. At the beginning of this prayer Christ does not say to repeat this prayer verbatim for spiritual communication. He says to "pray, then, this way," implying more the manner of instruction. It can be restated like this: Pray in this manner. Pray using these steps or guidelines. Pray following these rules. It might go like this:

When meditating or praying, focus on our Father, which art in heaven. Have no other gods, graven images, or thoughts before

Him, entering a calm state of mental clarity.

When meditating repeat the name of the Lord, for hallowed, and powerful, be thy name. Do not use that name in a powerless fashion. Do not bandy that name about in a casual manner as if that name had little meaning. Do not pray for things and then as an after thought say "I beseech thee in the name of Jesus Christ." This is a rather powerless use of that name. Rather use that name powerfully, repeating it over and over again so that it grows in power. This is how you open the door of heaven, by knocking and knocking constantly on that door with the name of God, and that door shall be opened.

When this happens then Thy kingdom come(s) into our opened consciousness, where our busy minds have been calmed. From this mental and spiritual clarity thy will can then be done, on earth as it is in heaven. We take what we have gained from meditation back out into activity. We become beacons for God's will, his love and healing, to radiate that out into our immediate surroundings. We become part of the important process of creating heaven on earth.

Remaining centered and compassionate, we open ourselves even more to God's good graces. Through our meditation we relax, our consciousness bonding with God, and we learn to receive as God increasingly gives us this day our daily bread. From the center of love and kindness God then forgives us our karma, our debts and trespasses as we do God's work with love and forgiveness for all those who have created karma or have debts with and against us.

The last step in meditating and living a spiritual life comes back, as it does in so many systems of meditation, to the dangerous seductiveness of desires. Desires pull us off of that center where we have found God and Christ, within our own hearts. Remaining free from desire, and acting from that spiritual center of love and understanding, we are not led, anymore, into temptation, but are delivered from evil.

Finally we return to the first instruction by acknowledging the nature of God and the spiritual universe as the source of all power and glory throughout the universe and the dimension of time. Always keep this image in mind when meditating for it keeps the mind directed on the spiritual rather than on the lesser gods of power or greed. This passage ends with Amen, or Amun, supposedly meaning something like so mote it be, or so shall it be. Amun, the Christian Amen, is an old Egyptian mantra, a powerful name of God likely retained from the ancient Jewish stay in Egypt at a time when that mantra was extremely popular.

This is the Biblical end of the Lord's Prayer. It is the nominal end of the Lord's Instruction in Meditation. But it doesn't really end here. Christ continues with this sermon, this teaching on how to take our new understanding out into our work world. These spiritual lessons, or explanations pertaining to the Lord's Instruction in Meditation, include such jewels as the balance inherent in judging not, or else you will be judged in the same manner; about seeking first, through meditation, the kingdom of heaven and then all else will be added into one's life; to keep on asking, using the name of God as the vehicle of asking, and it will be given to you, to keep on knocking and it will be opened; and the Golden Rule, to do unto others as you would have them do unto you.

Meditation might seem strange to Christians at first, but it is not difficult. In this case it might be effective to create a very simple prayer built around the repetition of the name of Christ. It can be simple, without a lot of words, and it might goes like this:

> Jesus Christ, Fill Me With Love.
> Jesus Christ, Fill Me With Love.
> Jesus Christ, Fill Me With Love.

This meditation utilizes the Christian name of God, Jesus Christ. Any other name can be substituted from any other religion just as well. If one is more drawn to the feminine then use the name Mother Mary. Repeating this over and over again creates a spiritual power within that begins the process of spiritual healing. It also acts as a prayer in that we are asking for something. In this case we are not asking for personal things. We are asking for that which Christ himself came to give us, namely love and compassion. By asking for this, the love that comes is spiritual in nature. It cleanses the heart center. It creates an increased ability to forgive, both oneself and others. It gives the ability to express compassion for others, and all life in general. As love is the opposite of fear, this also gives more courage to live life in an ethical manner. The love of God not only includes love on a human scale, relationships and family, it is also a vibrational phenomenon. The love that is God vibrates so fast that it might be seen and felt as divine light and warmth. It is the emotional essence of enlightenment, of God's grace, and of heaven. It corresponds with the mental equivalent we call divine wisdom. It carries with it its own sermon, the light and warmth imparting a direct understanding of God's ways here on earth without the need for many words.

Jesus Christ, Fill me with Love
Jesus Christ, Fill me with Love
Jesus Christ, Fill me with Love.

Sunday service could be ordered around 10 to 20 minutes of this meditation, as a group, rather than around the often boring lectures we call sermons. Many might then be tempted to go back to church. This meditation could also be a big help to anyone during this critical time for the world if practiced on a twice daily basis, morning and evening when day and night, or Father and Mother, are at a balance.

Judaism has its own tradition of meditation using the Hebrew spelling of the name of God, YHWH, pronouncing each letter separately, Yod He Vau He. This meditation interestingly enough also relates directly to the fifth commandment in the Old Testament, to honor thy father and thy mother. Yod and Vau connect to the Father, while He connects with the Mother aspect of God.

There are several forms of Buddhist meditation popular in the West. Most are traditional systems including Tibetan as well as Japanese systems like Zen. These are all traditional Pisces spiritual monastic systems and they are all very effective systems of meditation. A more recent Buddhist teaching is known as Nichirin Daishonin Buddhism. This school as it is taught in the West is more open to a secular population and less monastic in its approach and is also very effective. The technique is simply chanting the repetition of the title of the Heart Sutra and the chanting of a prayer supportive of the sutra. It can be done by anyone without having to retreat to a monastery or to church, or to even become Buddhist in a religious sense.

There are several Indian or Hindu systems that have become popular in the West, and many Indian mantras have become familiar to Westerners over the last several decades. These are also very effective.

In a secular system such as ours in the West it would be valuable to incorporate a meditation for the public sector, such as schools, that can be applied without any overt religious connections. When the body feels frustration or fatigue it responds with a sigh. This is a natural physiological mantra. The sound of a sigh is a soft ahhh spoken almost silently in the release of breath. According to almost all religions the ahhh sound is considered to be a powerful spiritual sound connected with the process of creativity. It has been connected to almost all names of god from all religions. It is found in the end of Christian prayers, amen, and in the name of God, Yahweh. It is found in the names Allah, Brahma, Shiva, and Krishna, in the Plains Indians' Wakan Tanka, as well as in the older matriarchal Innana, and many others. Still, it is just a natural body sound/response to stress that fits perfectly in with a secular vision.

As a meditation for children in school, as an example, class might start with a five-minute period of long slow sighs. Breathe in slowly and deeply through the nose, and exhale slowly accentuating the ahhh sound bringing that sound into the vocal range, feeling it resonate in the chest. This breathing helps oxygenate the brain and the hidden mantra in this natural physiological reaction to fatigue and stress helps to calm the child and open his and her mind to greater levels of creative learning.

Perhaps the most effective system of meditation available to the world at large today is the Transcendental Meditation and TM-Sidhi programs of Maharishi Mahesh Yogi. Not all meditations are the same. Some systems utilize concentration such as focusing hard on the third eye located between the eyebrows, while others are founded on the process of contemplation in order to quiet the mind. According to scientific studies reported in the *Journal of Clinical Psychology* # 33 (1977) and # 45 (1989) TM, as Transcendental Meditation is called, was found to be over twice as effective at reducing stress than other stress reducing techniques, including meditations based on concentration and contemplation.

Studies measuring self-actualization, or realizing more of an individual's inner potential across a wide range of life activities such as personality stability and integration, self-esteem, emotional maturity, warm interpersonal relationships, and the ability to adapt to challenges, as reported in the *Journal of Social Behavior and Personality* #6 (1991), and the *Journal of Counseling Psychology* #19

(1972) and #20 (1973), show TM to be almost three times more effective than techniques involving concentration, contemplation, or other techniques. And TM's effectiveness covered a wider range of response in all areas of life.

Maharishi Mahesh Yogi, the founder of Transcendental Meditation, studied physics in India before he completed his spiritual education, and because of that he understands the importance of science in presenting any meditation system to the West. Aquarius rules science, technology, and empiricism as well as the search for higher consciousness. TM is presented in an Aquarian fashion towards an Aquarian goal. It is presented as a technique central to a technology designed specifically to expedite the search for higher consciousness. Its effectiveness can be empirically proven through repeated scientific experimentation. To this end the TM movement and others have conducted over 600 scientific studies covering physiology, mental potential, education, health and the reversal of the aging process, social behavior, work and business, crime prevention and rehabilitation, and even world peace.

TM produces a state of restful alertness called Transcendental Consciousness that has measurable physiological benefits for practitioners. TM produces a much deeper state of rest than control groups sitting restfully with eyes closed. The physiological indicators of deep rest were measured through greater decreases in basal skin conductance, respiration rate, and plasma lactate levels.

The brain also responded in very dramatic ways to TM. Through TM the brain's response to somatosensory stimulation were shown to be more widely distributed across the cortex of the brain. During the practice of TM a much wider area of brain function is activated indicating a broader mental perception of information with an accompanying greater level of understanding in that area, and an increase in interaction between the two cortical hemispheres.

During the practice of TM studies have found an increase in EEG coherence, an increase in blood flow to the brain, increased muscle relaxation and the decreased level of the stress hormone plasma cortisol. The effects of TM after we have meditated and have resumed our normal activity include increased EEG coherence, and the increased efficiency of information transfer in the brain, as well as lower baseline levels of heart rate, respiration rate, plasma lactate, and spontaneous skin resistance responses. Also found was an increased stability of the autonomic nervous system, faster recovery from stress, faster reaction times and faster reflex responses. These results essentially mean that the body becomes more efficient at dissolving accumulated stress and fatigue, thus becoming healthier and more integrated, and that brain functions become more orderly.

In studies conducted at Maharishi University of Management in Fairfield, Iowa students who have practiced TM and the TM-Sidhi programs for a minimum of two years showed a significant increase in intelligence, IQ, and an increase in the ability to make rapid choice decisions when compared to control groups from another Iowa university.

Education is profoundly affected by the regular practice of TM. Elementary students practicing TM showed, within one year of practice, significant gains on the Iowa Tests of Basic Skills. Another study showed similar gains in high school students on the Iowa Tests of Educational Development. And a third study found that, independent of IQ scores, the length of time students had been practicing TM correlated closely with academic achievement. There is also a marked decrease in dropout rates and increased self-actualization among economically deprived adolescents. These studies indicate that by practicing TM one's mind becomes more alert and comprehensive in function, and thought and action become more progressive and nourishing for oneself as well as for others. Society and the future of our world benefits to a greater extent.

TM affects health in a very positive way. During a five-year study of 2000 people who regularly practiced TM in the US researchers found an overall rate of hospitalization that was 56% lower than the norm. This included 87% less hospitalization for cardiovascular disease, 55% less for cancer, 87% less for diseases of the nervous system, and 73% less hospitalization for problems of the nose, throat, and lungs. Another study found that those who practiced TM actually showed a reduced thickening of the carotid artery (a reduction of arteriosclerosis) while a control group following a prescribed program of diet and exercise showed a continued thickening of the carotid artery.

TM, as seen through various studies, reverses the aging process in several categories. Harmonious social behavior is enhanced through the practice of TM. The regular practice of TM produced significantly larger reductions in the use of tobacco, alcohol and non-prescription drugs than standard substance abuse treatments and prevention programs. Standard treatment effectiveness rapidly falls off within three months. The effectiveness of TM, on the other hand, increases over time.

TM promotes increased capacity for warm interpersonal relationships. It effectively counters depression, increases tolerance, gives a more positive self-concept, stimulates positive values, increases sociability, and promotes a healthier family life.

Crime and criminal activity respond well to TM as well. In a study of 259 felon parolees of the California Department of Corrections who had learned TM in prison compared with a carefully matched control group who did not meditate, it was found that the TM group had fewer new prison terms and more favorable parole outcomes per year over a five year period after release. TM significantly reduced recidivism during a period from six months to six years after parole. Traditional methods that deal with recidivism such as prison education, vocational training, and psychotherapy did not consistently reduce criminal return to prison.

Other studies hold promise for whole metropolitan areas in dramatic new ways. During three different periods in three different cities, large numbers of people were brought together, their numbers exceeding the square root of one percent of the total population of these cities, to practice the TM and the TM-Sidhi programs. There was found to be a powerful correlation between the start dates of each of these meditation programs and a noticeable statistical drop in crime. When these programs were ended statistics show that crime again rose back to their normal pre-TM levels. These events took place in the Union Territory of Delhi in India in 1980-1981, Washington, DC between 1981 and 1983, and in Metropolitan Manila in the Philippines in 1984-1985. Time series analysis showed that these statistics were not produced by other trends or cycles of criminal activity, or to changes in law enforcement policy or procedure.

Finally TM and the TM-Sidhi programs may offer a certain level of potential salvation for a violent world. An analysis of independent data covering the years 1979 to 1986, when the Soviet Union was still a power in the world, found that large numbers of participants meditating in Fairfield, Iowa, in the US, totaling more than the square root of one percent of the total US population (approximately 1500 participants at that time), practicing the TM-Sidhi program corresponded to a significant increase in friendly positive US actions towards the Soviet Union. When larger numbers practiced the TM-Sidhi program in Fairfield, Iowa (averaging over 1700 participants) there was seen a significant and independent increase in reciprocal friendly positive actions by the Soviet Union towards the US.

Because spiritual energy lies at the base of all energies, physical, mental, and emotional, it is constantly seeking expression in life at all levels. We human beings are here on this earth as spiritual transmitters of this spiritual energy, especially now in the Age of Pisces. God created Man in his Own image, male and female, meaning that we are extensions of God, in his image, created so that he could continue to channel his energy into his creation.

Humanity was created as God's embodiment here on earth. And God saw that we were good; we are beautiful, and spiritually powerful. On the seventh day of creation God came to rest within the male and the female bodies he had created and it is through us that he continues to express his creation. It is now up to us to realign ourselves with our original purpose.

As we come together to meditate the spiritual energies intensify through our collective efforts, happy to have us back again as sons and daughters of God. These spiritual energies then begin to increase their expression in the physical environment, radiating out from anyplace where groups gather together to meditate collectively, to touch and heal the rest of the nation and even the world.

As stated earlier, the TM program may be the most effective program available today. Not only does the scientific research indicate the effectiveness of this program, but Maharishi also teaches other, advanced techniques, and is promoting other ways of enhancing the spiritual, healing energies of pure consciousness in our lives. The TM-Sidhi program is an advanced program designed to teach a sidhi, or meta-physical power, to practitioners. In this case the power is levitation. We might think that this power is suspect, the promise of a deluded mind. As we all know people cannot defy the pull of gravity. Yet one of the specific qualities, or promises, of the Age of Aquarius is the ability to levitate. Aquarius rules levitation. If we look at the last two hundred years, during the Aquarius Era of the Age of Pisces, from 1800 to 1980, human beings accomplished that impossible milestone with technologically assisted levitation. In 1903 the Wright Brothers proved the possibility of flight. By the latter half of the 20th Century human beings were flying all over the globe and beginning to fly out of the earth's local airspace and all the way to the moon. We figured out how to use various elements to levitate huge multi-ton vehicles upwards thousands of feet into the sky, and miles further.

In the coming Age of Aquarius astrology promises that we will figure out how to use our minds to achieve levitation without the aid of technology. In this coming age we will discover amazing new laws of nature that will allow not only levitation, but the attainment of the impossible, another quality of Aquarius.

Maharishi Mahesh Yogi is teaching just that mental technology today to advanced practitioners of the TM program. At present, sitting in a cross-legged position, these people only hop around as the law of gravitation competes in the collective awareness with the impulse to lift off. One of the things that come with this lifting off is a feeling of physical effortlessness. There is little sense of physical effort in this process, which differentiates this process from the attempts to hop from a purely physical standpoint. There is also a sense of spiritual uplifting that accompanies the lifting off process that is not present in a purely physical attempt. At the point of lift off the brain, as measured by the various categories of brain waves, becomes coherent. Usually our brains operate only in one state or another, and an alpha state, for example, is rarely vibrating in any kind of harmonious fashion with the other brain wave states. We are awake, or asleep, or in deep dream, but rarely do we experience any kind of aware coherence between states. This changes while practitioners practice the TM-Sidhi flying technique (Yogic Flying). All brain waves harmonize, somewhat like a score of beautiful music, so that there is an increased awareness between all states of activity at the same time. In this mental state we then open ourselves up to the very real possibility of discovering new and powerful laws of nature that appear to be hidden from normal mental processes.

At present no one has stabilized during the process of hopping into a true state of steady levitation. This world we live in is in an incredible state of transition. There is a lot of stress being released today, much of that in violent ways. And this is the first generation, outside of traditional spiritual enclosures, that is attempting this and there is usually a very long learning curve that pioneers generally have to go through before any new idea or activity becomes more easily accessible to the rest of the population. But the astrological nature of this technique, associated as it is with the sign Aquarius, promises to be a central technique to humanity's survival and graduation to the next level. When people do stabilize their levitating abilities, we will likely see a quantum leap in the coherent nature of thought expressing itself around the globe. All manner of scientific, political, and social programs will then become more Aquarian in nature, with pure Aquarian genius showing through all of civilized life.

THE RAPTURE?

The Age of Aquarius is scheduled to be here in 2160. In the meantime we still have a horrendous end-time challenge to deal with. But for many this end-time may be over soon. This promise comes from the Mayan long count calendar. One of 17 different Mayan calendars the Tzolk'in calendar ends on December 21, 2012, and because of this end date it has drawn global attention to it as indicating the end of the world according to some. Mayan elders tell us that this date is not the end of the world. It indicates a point when there will be a tremendous rise in consciousness around the world, and the entry into the Fifth World, the World of the Fifth Sun.

In the Pisces Era of the Age of Pisces this transition is indeed very possible, maybe even probable. Pisces rules contact with other worlds. It is extremely spiritual in its potential expression. But what of the potentially devastating earth changes that confront us today that support the more negative prophesies of destruction? Much of the Biblical prophecies concerning these end-times might have already come to pass. On the other hand as we continue deeper into this Pisces Era in this Age of Pisces those prophecies will likely repeat themselves on a more concentrated and destructive level. So then how do we view this beautiful Mayan prophecy in light of everything else that is going on around us?

According to Biblical prophecy there is projected to be a powerful precursor event that will "save" all those that are spiritual in their hearts before the full blast of end-time energy envelopes the earth. This event is called the Rapture. In this scenario all those spiritual people with pure hearts and refined spiritually functioning nervous systems will be taken off this earth somehow to a safe haven to wait out the end of days. This process may have already begun.

According to some the recent Venus eclipse of the Sun on June 8, 2004 marks the opening of a dimensional doorway to a higher Piscean spiritual world. Venus eclipses of the Sun come every 122 years and happen in pairs, eight years apart. Between each eclipse in such a pair the Venus energy of the heart is enlivened by the Sun creating periods of accelerated evolution. This eclipse supposedly has opened a doorway to a higher dimension, and this doorway will remain open until the second eclipse due on June 6, 2012. The definition of this eight-year period is said to be one of ascension to higher worlds.

Perhaps this period marks the prophesied Rapture where spiritual souls from all cultures and all religions will begin to feel this increasing spiritual energy as a real presence. If this scenario is true then with the coming of a dramatically increased spiritual consciousness, those with unrefined nervous systems, and with closed and judgmental hearts, will likely respond by un-stressing through increasingly violent activity. We all tend to exteriorize our defects, placing the cause of our problems on others. We then create individuals or groups to lash out against as our fears and stresses increase. We still look for scapegoats to take our sins on their shoulders. This then might allow the full explosion of end-time prophecy to unfold.

It is also said that out of this Rapture or dimensional doorway period human history will divide into two separate time-lines, one spiritual, peaceful, and filled with happiness and prosperity, while the other sinks to the level of increased fear, despair, and fighting. After 2010 we will enter the Gemini Phase of the Pisces Era. Gemini rules division, and in this double Pisces energy bath that division could conceivably divide this world into separate time-lines if we allow a Piscean type of reasoning.

Pisces is a water sign ruling a spiritual reality based on mysticism, dreams and other non-physical realities. It is a very plastic time where logic is a secondary form of knowledge behind spiritual intuition and direct mystical experience. Perhaps those who become spiritually refined enough to be raptured will do so through this potential splitting of time-lines. Pisces creates through the power of imagination, dreams, and mystical desire. Physicists today theorize that mature universes give birth to baby universes on a regular basis. They also theorize parallel universes. Will the splitting of time-lines accompany the splitting of earth into two separate parallel earths that exist side by side but on different energy levels or in separate dimensions?

Whether the Rapture will be a real event, or whether the Mayan date of 2012 really will signal a dramatic change of consciousness we must still deal with time. Time, as we have seen, has an astrological structure to it. Astrological ages are all too real and human history has been drawn along with the progression of astrological time periods through the zodiac. The Age of Pisces has already proven to be an end-time age, one that we are not yet done with. Ahead of us is Aquarius. The promise of Aquarius from this astrological perspective is truly tremendous. But history has also indicated that it won't come easily. We face disaster and extinction from many quarters. To survive, and to prepare the way for Aquarius, we need to take personal and collective action. We need to harmonize our lives with the highest ideals of Pisces, otherwise the lower energies of Pisces will take us towards the future forcibly by dissolving our worlds out from under us and feeding off of our fears. History seems to be heading towards Armageddon. To survive we need to tap into the most positive of Pisces energies. If the Mayan Rapture is a valid event we still need to become more spiritual. Pisces still requires that we harmonize our lives with the astrological nature of these times. Do we survive this end-time and lead humanity into the promise of a truly amazing Golden Age? Maybe. Do we continue our arguably insane secular, anti-Pisces course of action and draw down around us increasingly destructive end-time disasters? The receding Pisces imagery tells us that salvation resides in our worship of God, or Goddess, in all religions. Christ, the Islamic Mahdi, the Hindu Kalki Avatar, or the Maitreya Buddha will come to our rescue. In Aquarian fashion though, as we approach the Age of Aquarius, we will have to tap into the Aquarian energy of individual and collective humanistic genius as we on a human level become increasingly important to our own salvation. The Kalki Avatar, the Matreya Buddha, the Mahdi, and Christ will show themselves within each individual's heart making this return a New Age personal return. In Pisces we felt our separation from God, focusing all of our requirements for salvation on a savior. Aquarius requires that we become that savior, each and every one of us, so that our personal and collective efforts towards creating a deep spiritual connection becomes the primary path of salvation. It is therefore up to us to manifest this transition. The choice is ours to make.

Astrological Time

Contemporary Ages

Age of Pisces--------------------0 BCE to 2160 CE

Age of Aries--------------------------2160 to 0 BCE

Age of Taurus-------------------4320 to 2160 BCE

Age of Gemini------------------6480 to 4320 BCE

Age of Cancer------------------8640 to 6480 BCE

Pre-Agricultural Ages

Age of Leo--------------------10,800 to 8640 BCE

Age of Virgo----------------10,800 to 12,960 BCE

Age of Libra-----------------12,960 to 15,120 BCE

Age of Scorpio-------------15,120 to 17,280 BCE

Age of Sagittarius-----------17,280 to 19,440 BCE

Age of Capricorn-----------19,440 to 21,600 BCE

Age of Aquarius------------21,600 to 23,760 BCE

Age of Pisces----------------23,760 to 25,920 BCE

Astrological Eras

Age of Pisces	Age of Aries
Aries------------------0 to 180	Aries------2160 to 1980 BCE
Taurus------------180 to 360	Taurus----1980 to 1800 BCE
Gemini------------360 to 540	Gemini---1800 to 1620 BCE
Cancer------------540 to 720	Cancer---1620 to 1440 BCE
Leo----------------720 to 900	Leo-------1440 to 1260 BCE
Virgo------------900 to 1080	Virgo-----1260 to 1080 BCE
Libra-----------1080 to 1260	Libra-------1080 to 900 BCE
Scorpio---------1260 to 1440	Scorpio------900 to 720 BCE
Sagittarius------1440 to 1620	Sagittarius---720 to 540 BCE
Capricorn------1620 to 1800	Capricorn---540 to 360 BCE
Aquarius-------1800 to 1980	Aquarius----360 to 180 BCE
Pisces----------1980 to 2160	Pisces-----------180 to 0 BCE

Astrological Phases

Aquarius Era

Aries-----------------------------------1800 to 1815

Taurus---------------------------------1815 to 1830

Gemini---------------------------------1830 to 1845

Cancer---------------------------------1845 to 1860

Leo-------------------------------------1860 to 1875

Virgo-----------------------------------1875 to 1890

Libra-----------------------------------1890 to 1905

Scorpio---------------------------------1905 to 1920

Sagittarius-----------------------------1920 to 1935

Capricorn-------------------------------1935 to 1950

Aquarius--------------------------------1950 to 1965

Pisces----------------------------------1965 to 1980

BIBLIOGRAPHY

1. The Cambridge Encyclopedia of Archaeology. Crown Publishers. New York. 1980

2. Barnett, Lincoln. The Universe and Dr. Einstein. William Morrow & Co. New York. 1948

3. Beard, Charles A. The New Basic History of the United States. Doubleday Books. Garden City, New York. 1968

4. Becker, Robert and Selden, Gary. The Body Electric: Electromagnetism and the Foundation of Life. William Morrow. New York. 1985

5. Bennett, William J., Dilulio, John J. Jr., Walters, John P. Body Count. Simon & Schuster. New York 1996

6. Bills, Rex. The Rulership Book. Macoy Publishers. 1979

7. Boren, Henry C. The Ancient World: A Historical Perspective. Prentice Hall. New Jersey. 1976

8. Burns, Edward McNall. Western Civilizations. W.W. Norton & Co. Inc. New York. 1973

9. Bills, Rex. The Rulership Book. Macoy Publishers. 1979

10. Bennett, Evan. The Maya Epic. River Falls Press. Univ. of Wisconsin. 1974

11. Beard, Charles A. The New Basic History of the United States. Doubleday. Garden City, New York. 1968

12. Bentov, Itzhak. Stalking the Wild Pendulum: on the Mechanics

of Consciousness. Bantam Books. New York. 1977

13. Campbell, Joseph. The Hero With a Thousand Faces. Princeton University Press. Princeton, New Jersey. 1949

14. Campbell, Joseph. The Masks of God. 4 volumes. Penguin Books. New York. 1976

15. Clark, Grahame. Aspects of Prehistory. Univ. of California Press. Berkeley, CA. 1970

16. Clark, Grahame. World Prehistory in New Perspective. Cambridge Univ. Press, 3rd Ed. Cambridge, England. 1977

17. Craig, Gordon. Europe Since 1815. Holt, Rinehart & Winston. New York. 1964

18. Cottrell, Leonard. Egypt. Nicholas, Inc. London. 1966

19. Cremo, Michael A. & Thompson, Richard L. Forbidden Archaeology: the Hidden History of the Human Race. Govardhan Hill Publishing. Alachua, Florida. 1993

20. Cross/Lamb/Turk. The Search for Personal Freedom. William C. Brown Co. 5th Ed. vols. 1&2. 1977

21. Dobin, Rabbi Joel C. The Astrological Secrets of the Hebrew Sages. Inner Traditions International, LTD. Rochester, VT. 1977

22. Durant, Will & Ariel. The Lessons of History. Simon & Schuster. New York. 1968

23. Edey, Maitland. The Sea Traders. Time-Life Books. New York.1974

24. Eliade, Mircea. Cosmos and History: The Myth of the Eternal Return. Harper & Row. New York. 1959

25. Engel, Frederic Andre. An Ancient World Preserved: Records and Relics of Prehistory in the Andes. Crown Publishers. New York. 1976

26. Fagan, Brian. People of the Earth. Little Brown & Co. New York. 1977

27. Finkelstein, Israel and Silberman, Neil Asher. The Bible Unearthed. Free Press. New York. 2000

28. Frazer, Sir James. The New Golden Bough. MacMillan. New

York. 1922.

29. Gimbutas, Marija. <u>Goddesses and Gods of Old Europe: Myths and Cult Images</u>. Univ. of California Press. Berkeley, CA. 1982

30. Gleick, James. <u>Chaos: Making a New Science</u>. Penguin Books. New York. 1987

31. Goodman, Jeffrey. <u>Psychic Archaeology</u>. Berkley Publishing Group. New York. 1980

32. Graham, Lloyd M. <u>Deceptions and Myths of the Bible</u>. Carol Publishing Group. New York. 1989

33. Graves, Robert. <u>The Greek Myths</u>. Viking Penguin. New York. 1955

34. Green, Peter. <u>Ancient Greece</u>. Thames & Hudson. New York. 1973

35. Hamblin, Dora. <u>The First Cities</u>. Time-Life Books. New York. 1973

36. Hawkes, Jaquetta. <u>The First Great Civilizations: Life in Mesopotamia, the Indus Valley, and Egypt</u>. Knopf. New York. 1973

37. Heinberg, Richard. <u>Memories and Visions of Paradise</u>. Tarcher. New York. 1989

38. Johnson, Paul. <u>The Civilization of Ancient Egypt</u>. Atheneum. New York. 1978

39. Johnson, Paul. <u>A History of Christianity. Atheneum</u>. New York. 1977

40. Karlen, Arno. <u>Man and Microbes: Disease and Plagues in History and Modern Times</u>. Tarcher Putnam. New York. 1995

41. Kramer, Samuel Noah. <u>History Begins at Sumer</u>. Doubleday Anchor Books. New York. 1959

42. Krugman, Paul. <u>The Return of Depression Economics</u>. W.W. Norton & Co. New York. 1999

43. Lawlor, Robert. <u>Sacred Geometry</u>. Thames and Hudson. New York. 1982

44. Leakey, Richard and Lewin, Roger. <u>The Sixth Extinction:</u>

Patterns of Life and the Future of Humanity. Doubleday. New York. 1995

45. Manchester, William. A World Lit Only by Fire: The Medieval Mind and the Renaissance. Little Brown. Boston, MA. 1992

46. Meltzer, Milton. The Terrorists. Harper & Row. New York. 1983

47. Michell, John. City of Revelation. David McKay Co. Inc. New York. 1972

48. Michell, John and Rhine, Christine. Twelve Tribe Nations and the Science of Enchanting the Landscape. Phanes Press. 1991

49. Mumford, Lewis. The Condition of Man. Harcourt, Brace, Jovanovich Inc. New York. 1944

50. Mumford, Lewis. The Myth of the Machine. Harcourt, Brace, Jovanovich Inc. New York. 1964

51. Mumford, Lewis. The Transformations of Man. Harper & Row. New York. 1956

52. Oates, Robert Jr. Celebrating the Dawn: Maharishi Mahesh Yogi and the T.M. Technique. Putnam. New York. 1976

53. Oken, Alan. As Above So Below. Bantam Books. New York. 1973

54. Raup, David. Extinction. Norton. New York. 1991

55. Reinhardt, Kurt. Germany: 2000 Years. Vol. 1. Frederick Unger Publishing Co. New York. 1950

56. Renfrew, Colin. Before Civilization. Knopf. New York. 1973

57. Ridley, Matt. What Makes You Who You Are. Time magazine. June 2, 2003

58. Rudhyar, Dane. The Astrology of Personality. Doubleday. New York. 1970

59. Roberts, J. M. History of the World. Knopf. New York. 1976

60. Sabaloff, Jeremy and Lamberg-Karlovsky, C.C. Ancient Civilization and Trade. Univ. of New Mexico Press. Albuquerque, NM. 1975

61. Steindorff, George and Seele, Keith C. When Egypt Ruled the

East. Univ. of Chicago Press. Chicago, IL. 1957

62. Stephenson, Carl. Mediaeval History: Europe from the Second to the Sixteenth Century. Harper & Row. New York. 1951

63. Stone, Merlin. When God was a Woman. Harcourt Brace. New York. 1976

64. Teubal, Savina. Sarah the Priestess. Swallow Press. Athens, Ohio. 1984

65. This Fabulous Century. 8 vols. Time-Life Books. New York. 1970

66. Thorsten, Geraldine. God Herself: The Feminine Roots of Astrology. Avon Books. New York. 1980

67. Trager, James. The Peoples Chronology: A Year-by-Year Record of Human Events From Prehistory to the Present. Holt, Rinehart & Winston. New York. 1979

68. von-Franz, Marie-Louise. Time: Rhythm and Repose. Thames and Hudson. New York. 1978

69. Waters, Frank. Book of the Hopi. Penguin Books. New York. 1963

70. Wenke, Robert. Patterns in History. Oxford Univ. Press. New York. 1980

71. White, John. Pole Shift. A R E Press. Virginia Beach, Virginia. 1985

72. Yogananda, Paramahansa. Autobiography of a Yogi. Self Realization Fellowship. Los Angeles, CA. 1971

73. Zimmerman, J.E. Dictionary of Classical Mythology. Harper & Row. New York. 1964

CPSIA information can be obtained at www.ICGtesting.com
Printed in the USA
242350LV00001B/261/A

9 781595 409089